Nitobe Inazo

# Humanities Series, Graduate School of Letters, Hokkaido University

**Publishing Humanities Series**
Graduate School of Letters, Hokkaido University
March 2002
Graduate School of Letters, Hokkaido University, publishes a series of monographs, which are based on wide-ranging studies conducted in the faculty. We feel it is one of our duties to make the fruit of our research available to the public.

1. *A Study in Pindar: the poet and* $\tau\alpha\mu\iota\alpha\varsigma\ \kappa\omega\mu\omega\nu$
   Makoto Anzai
2. *Otomo-no-Yakamochi: the Manyoshu-Poet*
   Akiteru Hirokawa
3. *Hermeneutics of Art: Variations on a theme by Paul Ricœur*
   Kiyohiko Kitamura
4. *Kaion and Chikamatsu: their literary expressions and devices*
   Yasuyuki Tomita
5. *Le Paris ouvrier: travail, famille, culture*
   Michikazu Akashi
6. *Ancient Cultures on Coastal Areas of the Sea of Okhotsk*
   Toshihiko Kikuchi
7. *Hitomaro: poetics of time, space, and narrative*
   Hisashi Misaki
8. *Social Development and Cultural Change in Northeast Thailand*
   Yoshihide Sakurai
9. *Nitobe Inazo: from Bushido to the League of Nations*
   edited by Teruhiko Nagao

Nitobe's career, from the publication of *Bushido* in 1900 and through his long involvement with the League of Nations, was one of continuous development, informed by his attempt to reconcile the competing claims of nationalist and internationalist beliefs. This book adopts an international perspective by collecting together a number of essays by scholars from Japan, the UK and the USA, and tries to reassess Nitobe's achievement.

**Humanities Series**

**Graduate School of Letters, Hokkaido University**

# Nitobe Inazo
## From *Bushido* to the League of Nations

edited by
# Teruhiko Nagao

Hokkaido University Press

**Teruhiko Nagao** is Professor of English at Hokkaido University, Sapporo. Born in Nagano in 1944, he graduated from Tohoku University, Sendai, in 1968, and taught at Kochi University, Kochi, 1968-81. Since 1981 he has been teaching at Hokkaido University. His academic papers are on Shakespeare, Wordsworth, Coleridge, Byron, Keats and Tennyson. He is also the Chairperson of the Nitobe Studies Team in the Graduate School of Letters, Hokkaido University, since 1995.

©2006 by Hokkaido University Press
All rights reserved. No part of this book may be reproduced in any form without written permission of the Publisher.

Hokkaido University Press, Sapporo, Japan
ISBN 4-8329-6651-0
Printed in Japan

*The antithesis of patriotism is not internationalism or even cosmopolitanism, but Chauvinism. Internationalism is the extension of patriotism. If you love your country, you must needs love other countries without which your own country cannot exist and loses its raison d'être. If you love the world, you must, perforce, love best that part of it which is nearest to you.*
— Inazo Nitobe, Editorial Jottings, 7th June 1930.


*A good internationalist must be a good nationalist and vice versa. The very terms connote it. A man who is not faithful to his own country cannot be depended upon for faithfulness to a world principle. One can serve best the cause of internationalism by serving his country. On the other hand, a nationalist can best advance the interests and honour of his country by being internationally minded.*
— Inazo Nitobe, Editorial Jottings, 16th May, 1933.

Inazo Nitobe and the International Bureau Officials

James Eric Drummond (1876–1951)

Gilbert Murray (1866–1957)

# Contents

Preface                                                                xiii

## PART ONE (TEXT): NITOBE ON THE LEAGUE OF NATIONS

I. The Geneva Days: 1920–1926
   (1) What the League of Nations Has Done and Is Doing        4
   (2) The Organization and Activities of
       the League of Nations*                                  26
   (3) The League of Nations Movement in Japan                 57

II. Reminiscences after Retirement: 1927–1931
    (1) The Permanence of the League and its Achievement*      66
    (2) A Typical British Gentleman: Sir Eric Drummond*        71
    (3) A Savant Who Calls Himself a Primitive:
        Gilbert Murray*                                        81
    (4) Spiritual Phenomenon*                                  84
    (5) Ignorance is Power*                                    87

III. The Time of Japan's Withdrawal from
     the League of Nations: 1932–1933
     (1) Japan's Place in the Family of Nations                92
     (2) How Geneva Erred                                      99
     (3) Great Hopes for the League of Nations                 104

## PART TWO (COMMENTARY): BACKGROUNDS AND CRITICAL ESSAYS

I. Introduction. The Historical Context of Inazo Nitobe       107
   *Teruhiko Nagao*

| II. | Nitobe's *Bushido*: A Western Perspective<br>*Norman Page* | 125 |
| III. | *Bushido*: Romantic Nationalism in Japan<br>*Simon Edwards* | 131 |
| IV. | A Bridge Across the Pacific: Nitobe's Knowledge of English Literature<br>*Teruhiko Nagao* | 141 |
| V. | Chinda Sutemi, 1857–1929: Ambassador in War and Peace<br>*Ian Nish* | 153 |
| VI. | Nitobe and the Secretariat in London 1919<br>*Ian Nish* | 167 |
| VII. | Nitobe Inazo at the League of Nations: 1919–1926<br>*George Oshiro* | 185 |
| VIII. | Conclusion<br>*Teruhiko Nagao* | 213 |
| | A Nitobe Chronology | 221 |

\* indicates that the essay concerned is translated into English by the editor

# Contributors

**Ian Nish** is Emeritus Professor of International History, at London School of Economics and Political Science.

**Norman Page** is Emeritus Professor of English Literature, both at the University of Alberta and the University of Nottingham.

**George Oshiro** is Professor of Japanese History, at Obirin University, Tokyo.

**Simon Edwards** is Lecturer of English Literature, at Roehampton University, London.

# Preface

The aim of this book is, in the first part, to provide readers with the writings of Inazo Nitobe on the League of Nations for which he worked as the Under-Secretary-General from 1920 to 1926. *The Collected Works of Inazo Nitobe* published in 1969-70 and 1983-87 contains all those discourses, but they are scattered here and there among other work. Also while all his English writings have been translated into Japanese, the Japanese texts are not available in English translation. The editorial principle here is to arrange them into three chronological divisions: (1) 1920-26: when he worked at Geneva; (2) 1927-1931: when he wrote about the League in retrospect after his retirement, and (3) 1932-33: the period of Japan's crisis after the decision to withdraw from the League. Another editorial principle is to give a faithful translation of his Japanese writings, trying as far as possible to keep the original tone and meaning, thus making them accessible to English-speaking readers who will constitute an important majority in the international forum where Nitobe's achievement can most properly be reassessed.

We are apt to think of the League of Nations, in retrospect, to belong to a mere point of time in history, somewhat ephemeral, short-lived, and ineffective if not a failure. It was not strong enough to prevent the Second World War. But this is a misguided view. As the first attempt toward lasting world peace, the ideas, the aspirations, and the hopes that went to its advocacy were as noble, and as lofty as anything in history before or after. This movement attracted not only political leaders such as Woodrow Wilson, Jan Smuts, and Sir Robert Cecil but also many leading intellectual figures world-wide. Essentially, however, it was a product of its time with significant popular support, born out of the ashes and the tragic errors of the First World War.

In the case of Nitobe, the chance to contribute to this movement came rather like a windfall. But it was something more than mere luck. As a youth, he aspired to be 'a bridge across the Pacific.' Also, because of the wide range of his reading in Western thought and history, he had been perfectly prepared for understanding the meaning of the movement and becoming its promoter. We somehow feel that it had been part of his destiny.

Nitobe's writings show that he was fully conscious of the important role allotted to him. They remind us of the halcyon days in the immediate aftermath of the First World War. Nitobe's confident statement that nationalism and internationalism are two sides of the same coin tells us much about the optimistic atmosphere prevalent in 1920s. He proudly talks of how one imminent conflict was prevented by the League's interference (that is, the small-scale strife between Greece and Bulgaria in 1925. See below pp. 69–70). 'If one war could be stopped,' says Nitobe, 'why is it not possible for the League to stop all future wars?' He believed that it was possible. His concept of peace was of a dynamic nature. Peace is not a mere state devoid of wars; rather, peace is a thing to be built up by constant struggle against mankind's innate violence.

Of course, the brief peace was not so lasting as one might wish. The time was to come, too soon, when a harsh reality compelled people to choose between nationalism and internationalism; the time when the fine bridge would collapse among the tumult of war. But the memory of what had been, the memory of what was once realized, be it for ever so short a time, remains and points to a goal some day to be attained, all the more forcefully because of the tragic end.

The second part of the volume consists of seven essays written by five contributors from America, Britain and Japan. They focus on two of Nitobe's important achievements: first, the writing of *Bushido* and, secondly, his activities in the League of Nations. The text of *Bushido* (written in 1899 and published in 1900) is easily accessible nowadays in many editions, both in the original English and in Japanese translation, and can safely be dispensed with here. The writing of *Bushido* was an important event in Nitobe's life. It established the basis from which to promote his international activities. His life and work from *Bushido* to the League of Nations is one continuous development, based on the firm belief that nationalism and internationalism are one and the same thing; that neither nationalism minus internationalism nor internationalism minus nationalism is viable.

Teruhiko Nagao's "Introduction: The Historical Context of Inazo Nitobe" describes how Nitobe's nationalism and internationalism went together. Notwithstanding its nationalistic title, Nitobe's *Bushido* was an attempt to map the modernizing of Japan within the international context. The book's stance was at once nationalistic and internationalistic, and as such it was a prefigurement of Nitobe's greatest achievement, that is, his activities in the League of Nations. The two essays that follow represent contemporary Western views of Nitobe's *Bushido* by two literary critics, Norman Page and Simon Edwards. The second essay by Teruhiko Nagao, "A Bridge across the Pacific: Nitobe's Knowledge of English Literature," is an attempt to make up for the deficiency of literary studies in assessing the work and thought of Nitobe. It again emphasizes the fact that Nitobe's nationalism is one and the same thing as his internationalism and *vice versa*. Ian Nish's "Chinda Sutemi, 1857-1929: Ambassador in War and Peace" describes the exciting political situations at the end of the First World War, focusing on a Japanese diplomat Count Chinda, who was chiefly responsible for Nitobe's appointment to that important post in the League's Secretariat. "Nitobe and the Secretariat in London 1919" by the same author describes how energetically Nitobe worked for the League of Nations as its chief spokesman. It contains as appendix an important lecture given by Nitobe to the Japan Society in London 1919. Finally, by way of summing up, George Oshiro's "Nitobe at the League of Nations: 1920-26" provides us with an all-round account of Nitobe's activities as the Under-Secretary-General at Geneva.

Norman Page is Emeritus Professor of English Literature at both Alberta University and Nottingham University. He has published many books on a variety of English authors. Simon Edwards is Lecturer in English Literature at Roehampton University, London. He organized an international conference "Romantic Nationalisms 1750-1850" in 2001. Ian Nish is Emeritus Professor of Political History at the London School of Economics and Political Science. He has published many books on Japanese political history. George Oshiro is Professor of Japanese History at Obirin University, Tokyo. Born in Hawaii and educated in USA and Canada before coming to live in Japan, he can be seen as another bridge across the Pacific. Teruhiko Nagao is Professor of English Literature at Hokkaido University, a university founded on Nitobe's *Alma Mater*, Sapporo College of Agriculture, where Nitobe studied and later taught.

Finally I express my heartfelt gratitude to all the members of the

Nitobe Studies Team of the Faculty of Letters, Hokkaido University, who spurred me on to this task, and also to Ms Fatema Khondoker who checked my English with great patience.

    Summer 2005  Sapporo

*Teruhiko Nagao*

# PART ONE (TEXT)

# NITOBE ON THE LEAGUE OF NATIONS

*I. The Geneva Days: 1920–1926*

# (1) What the League of Nations Has Done and Is Doing

> Lecture delivered at International University, Brussels, 13th and 14th September 1920. Published in London, 1921. The Collected Works of Inazo Nitobe (Tokyo: Kyobunkan, 1969-70, 1983-87), vol. 15: 371-400.

A subject as broad in its scope, as high in its aspirations and as delicate in its operations as the League of Nations, must be discussed in its various aspects — historical, legal and political, economic and moral. New as the whole subject is, it is already possessed of an extensive literature which is constantly being enriched in every department. I shall, therefore, with your permission, devote my attention exclusively to one field of study of the League of Nations, namely, to its practical activity, confining my remarks to statement of a few concrete facts regarding some world problems that have been taken up by the League — by what organs they were handled and how they were treated.

Officially the League came into existence on the 10th of January, 1920. *What has it accomplished in these eight months of its infancy?* An adequate reply involves a further question. *Under what conditions did it come into operation?* For as in the study of living organisms Ecology furnishes indispensable data in explaining their character and activity, so a glimpse at the world conditions surrounding the birth of the League will throw light upon some phases of its work.

(1) The very fact that the Covenant forms a part of the Peace Treaty shows that the League was expected to come into operation under peaceful conditions. Its constitution takes peace for granted. It does not provide the power or machinery to stop a war once started. Its aim is to prevent war, to preserve peace. (2) Adapted to peaceful conditions and endowed with sufficient power to maintain them, it cannot cope with a state of warfare, neither can it work effectively side by side with another international organ or organs which have supreme authority to deal with war conditions. (3) It evidently did not occur to the framers of the Covenant that one of its greatest champions

*I. The Geneva Days: 1920–1926*

## (1) What the League of Nations Has Done and Is Doing

*Lecture delivered at International University, Brussels, 13th and 14th September 1920. Published in London, 1921. The Collected Works of Inazo Nitobe (Tokyo: Kyobunkan, 1969–70, 1983–87), vol. 15: 371–400.*

A subject as broad in its scope, as high in its aspirations and as delicate in its operations as the League of Nations, must be discussed in its various aspects — historical, legal and political, economic and moral. New as the whole subject is, it is already possessed of an extensive literature which is constantly being enriched in every department. I shall, therefore, with your permission, devote my attention exclusively to one field of study of the League of Nations, namely, to its practical activity, confining my remarks to statement of a few concrete facts regarding some world problems that have been taken up by the League — by what organs they were handled and how they were treated.

Officially the League came into existence on the 10th of January, 1920. *What has it accomplished in these eight months of its infancy?* An adequate reply involves a further question. *Under what conditions did it come into operation?* For as in the study of living organisms Ecology furnishes indispensable data in explaining their character and activity, so a glimpse at the world conditions surrounding the birth of the League will throw light upon some phases of its work.

(1) The very fact that the Covenant forms a part of the Peace Treaty shows that the League was expected to come into operation under peaceful conditions. Its constitution takes peace for granted. It does not provide the power or machinery to stop a war once started. Its aim is to prevent war, to preserve peace. (2) Adapted to peaceful conditions and endowed with sufficient power to maintain them, it cannot cope with a state of warfare, neither can it work effectively side by side with another international organ or organs which have supreme authority to deal with war conditions. (3) It evidently did not occur to the framers of the Covenant that one of its greatest champions

democratic nations, decided to join the League. Thus there are at present 41 States Members, and this number will, I believe, soon be increased to 53 by the accession of 12* more nations, largely consisting of newly created States and of some small Principalities which have formally applied for admission. Within the precincts of these 53 States are living 1,300,000,000 people — three-fourths of the population of the globe. In other words, there will be three times as many people under the ægis of the League as outside it. But numerical argument is not the main proof in favour of the League: rather — that the members given include most of the great Powers of the age.

As there are at present (counting the British Dominions as separate units) 78 independent States, the number of those outside the League amounts to 25: —

| | | |
|---|---|---|
| Albania | Morocco | Turkey |
| Arabia | Abyssinia | Montenegro |
| Armenia | Oman | |
| Azerbaijan | | |
| Bhutan | | Austria |
| Courland | San Domingo | Hungary |
| Lithuania | Honduras | Germany |
| | Nicaragua | Russia |
| Mesopotamia | Ecuador | |
| Afghanistan | Mexico | United States |
| Nepal | | |

One sees from the above list that a few of the important nations, such as the United States, Russia and Germany, still remain outside the League.

## The Assembly

Having enumerated the nations which constitute the League, let me proceed to explain the threefold organs through which the League

| | | | |
|---|---|---|---|
| *Esthonia | Iceland | Ukraine | Luxemburg |
| Finland | Latvia | Monaco | Costa Rica |
| Georgia | Lichtenstein | San Marino | Bulgaria |

would fail when it was actually put into operation. (4) Owing to unavoidable circumstances of political conditions in America and of the warlike state of Europe, the most important organ of the League, namely the Assembly, could not meet.

The first consideration impairs its activity in times of war and even throws the League into obscurity; the second deters it from exercising authority; the third deprives it of its universal character; and the fourth prevents its speedy inauguration.

Over and around these obstructions, barring the way of the new-born League, there hovered in many quarters ominous clouds of scepticism on the part of so-called practical minds which scorn the possibility of lasting peace, and on the part of idealists in whose opinion the League does not go far enough.

Born amid circumstances so adverse to its free development, what could the League do in the few months of its existence? What has it done? Or may not one more justly and certainly more charitably ask: "What has it not done that any reasonable person could expect of it?"

## States Members of the League

In recounting the story of its achievements, let me begin with its Membership. At the Peace Conference it was expected that the 32 Allied and Associated Powers, signatories to the Treaty of Versailles, would naturally and automatically become Members; but, as is well known, the United States refused to ratify it, and her example was followed by Nicaragua, Honduras, Ecuador and China; the last-named country, however, having ratified the Peace treaty with Austria, soon after became a Member. Consequently there were at the outset 28 Members. The League thus formed invited 13 States which had maintained neutrality during the war to join it. The well-wishers of the League of Nations were not without misgiving that the invitation might not be accepted by all.* It was therefore exceedingly gratifying that all the invited Powers, most of which are highly developed

| *Argentine | Venezuela | Denmark | Switzerland |
| Chile | Salvador | Norway | Netherlands |
| Colombia | Spain | Sweden | Persia |
| Paraguay | | | |

truth of this statement, I should like to demonstrate it by the work of the Council.

## The Council

The Council, the second organ of the League, should, according to the Covenant, consist of nine members; but on account of America's abstention it has at present only eight.

The Covenant provides (Art. IV. §2) for the admission, in due course, of great powers such as Germany and Russia, as well as for further representation of smaller Powers in the Council.

Though it is tempting to draw parallels from national institutions and to infer that the Assembly is a legislative and the Council an executive body — or even to compare the two with the usual bicameral system, it is premature to define the respective spheres of activity of these two bodies or their relations to each other. The question of the competence of either body is left for practical issues to solve, as these will be guided by the combined statesmanship of the nations concerned.

As the Assembly has not been called as first intended, the Council has been acting as the supreme organ of the League. As it now exists, the Council consists of the representatives of Great Britain, France, Italy, Japan — these four States being permanent members — and of Spain, Brazil, Belgium and Greece, temporary members. The persons representing these nations have been changed from time to time, according to convenience in attending the meetings. Usually, however, England has sent Mr. Balfour, France has sent Monsieur Bourgeois, and Belgium Monsieur Hymans. Countries situated a long distance from the place of conference — such as Japan and Brazil — have been represented by Ambassadors resident in or near the country.

Eight sessions* have been held, four in Paris, three in London, one in Rome and one in San Sebastian. The ninth will meet in a few days. The tenth session will be in Brussels on October 20th. The selection

---

*1, Paris, January 16th. 2, London, February 11th–13th. 3, Paris, March 12th–13th. 4, Paris, April 9th–11th. 5, Rome, May 14th–19th. 6, London, June 14th–16th. 7, London, July 9th–12th. 8, S. Sebastian, July 30th–August 5th. 9, Paris, September 16th–20th. 10, Brussels, October 20th.

acts; — the Assembly, the Council and the International Secretariat.

The Assembly is a conference of all States Members of the League, wherein each country will be represented by not more than three delegates. Each country has one vote; the number of delegates from each is not therefore of vital importance. How these delegates will be appointed or elected is a matter left to the discretion of each country. As is expressed in the term "The League of Nations," the desire of the framers must have been that the Assembly should voice as much as possible the will of the peoples therein represented. It is possible that many of the delegates may be appointed by governments, but approved by the popular representative bodies. It is also possible that some countries may send women delegates. The delegate or delegates will probably be accompanied by advisers, assistants and secretaries, experts, translators, etc. Delegates coming from distant countries will probably bring a large staff, since they cannot call in experts at short notice.

The first meeting of the Assembly was expected to take place in Washington last November; but various causes have prevented an earlier convocation than the fifteenth of this November when its first session will take place at 11 a.m. in Geneva. Here will come together about 100 delegates from perhaps 40 countries, to discuss methods "of promoting international co-operation and of achieving international peace and security." Great hopes are entertained of this new departure in human history — what William Penn would have called "a holy experiment" in world politics. Whether the Conference will turn out to be a Tower of Babel — a confusion of some twenty tongues — or a day of Pentecost with tongues of fire each understanding the other, is a question profoundly interesting; but I will not speak further of the Assembly, as two months must elapse before its work begins, and I promised to state only accomplished facts.

In passing, allow me to express faith in the outcome of this world parliament. Yet should the Assembly meet only for a few weeks and disperse without giving evidence of immediate, tangible results, let no one in his disappointment undervalue the moral gain accruing from the mere personal contact of national leaders coming from the ends of the earth. In the realm of ideas, to *come* and to *see* is to *conquer*, and it is on the broad field of humanitarian ideals that the League of Nations desires to outrival the conquests of Julius Cæsar. If anyone doubts the of the place has depended mainly on the convenience of the representatives. The cities I have named are in countries whose representatives are on the Council. Greece is a little too far, and as to Brazil and Japan, they are not exactly within walking distance!

The meetings last sometimes two or three days and sometimes a fortnight, depending upon the agenda. The sessions are in part public; but most of them are private, when the members sit round a common table and quite freely discuss the questions brought before them. Few things afford a more encouraging prospect for harmonious co operation, a more hopeful earnest of universal peace, than the sight of the leading statesmen of the foremost countries of the world coming together in close personal relations, holding different views and expressing them with utmost freedom, yet in the spirit of mutual understanding and concord. They come agreed to differ and differ to agree.

The official media of communication on such occasions as the above are the French and English languages, used interchangeably and without translation, unless this is specially asked for. A frank exchange of opinion is sometimes accompanied by heated argument: but where there is a will a way opens through discussion for an ultimate satisfactory conclusion.

When the items in the agenda have been thoroughly threshed out and conclusions unanimously reached, a public session is called, when admittance is free to all as far as space permits. Here each question is dealt with by a *Rapporteur*, who gives the pros and cons of the problem and makes a formal motion for the adoption of the resolution. There is no discussion in the public session. It is, as it were, reporting in public the result of the work accomplished in private.

Of the achievements of the Council, general publicity has been given through the Press and through the "Official Journal," the organ of the League. I can only outline the manifold phases of this work.

## The International Secretariat

In closest association with the Council is the Permanent International Secretariat, which is the third organ of the League (Art. 6 of the Covenant). It is here that all the secretarial work of the League — the preparation of the agenda, correspondence with States Members of the League, preservation of archives and other routine business — is performed. History gives instances of international leagues proposed and formed, which have, alas, failed. One reason for their failure is obviously the absence of an organisation to carry out the resolutions passed. The Secretariat is an institution to remedy this defect, hence it is more than a clerical agency. Its headquarters are at present in London: but they will be removed to Geneva within a few weeks. In its personnel the Secretariat is indeed international, composed of a larger number of nationalities than was contained in Anacharsis Clootz's representation of the human race. There are English, French, Italians, Americans, Spanish, Portuguese, Swiss, Danes, Belgians, Swedes, Norwegians, Dutch, Greeks, Japanese, etc.

The present staff appointments have been made by the Secretary-General and approved by the Council for a term of five years. The term of service was defined in order to bring about a change when desirable, and to avoid any possibility of stagnation and bureaucracy.

I wish to make it clear, however, that the staff of the Secretariat is not appointed as representing different countries. The appointees have, therefore, no direct connection with their own governments in their official capacity in the League. Some of them have held government positions in their own countries; but the instant they accept posts in the Secretariat their official connection with their own governments ceases, and they become members of the International Civil Service. Each appointment is based on the personal merit of the individual without regard to nationality or sex. Women are therefore amenable to any position in the Secretariat. The appointees enjoy all diplomatic privileges.

Under the Secretary-General, Sir Eric Drummond, there are three or four Under-Secretaries-General, and with them are associated Directors of some ten or more different sections, such as the Sections of Administrative Commissions and Minorities Questions, Economic Information, International Bureaux, Legal, Mandates, Political, Registration of Treaties, Social Questions, Transit and Communications. Besides these are departments for the internal administration of the Secretariat, such as Finance, Translation, the Library, etc. In each of these sections are members who may be considered experts in their respective spheres. Naturally a large staff of translators is required, besides various clerical assistants.

In addition to the staff mentioned, the Secretariat has in close connection with it specialist commissions of various kinds. The usual method pursued in dealing with any question is to utilise, as far as possible, an already existing body at work in the particular field, with the addition of one or more members of the Secretariat as liaison officials. The best expert knowledge is thus brought to bear upon the case in point. Should there be no appropriate body upon which to call, one is appointed to meet the need, as I shall explain later.

To an outsider this may seem an appalling conglomeration of nationalities, and doubts may arise as to their working together in harmony. From my personal experience of more than a year, I can testify that there is a fine *esprit de corps* prevailing in the Secretariat, due to the fact that the members are actuated by a spirit of idealism, and spurred on by a strong sense of responsibility in this new venture of world reconstruction. In my experience at home and abroad, I have noticed that in Civil Service there very often lurks a light-hearted vein of sarcasm sometimes amounting to positive cynicism, and a scarcely concealed jealousy, sometimes revealing itself in open criticism: but I confess that I have not once seen evidence of either in the International Secretariat.

One word more about the Secretariat. Its expenses are borne by the States Members of the League — for want of a more equitable basis of allotment — according to the apportionment of the expenses of the International Bureau of the Universal Postal Union. To arrive at the apportionment, all the nations are divided into seven classes.

The 1st class pays 25 units
The 2nd class pays 20 units
The 3rd class pays 15 units
The 4th class pays 10 units
The 5th class pays 5 units
The 6th class pays 3 units
The 7th class pays 1 units

This system is not altogether fortunate, and later on we hope a more equitable one may be found and adopted.

## General Remarks on the Work of the League

We have now briefly reviewed the three organs of the League. There is nothing autocratic, nothing bureaucratic in its organisation. One may even go so far as to claim that the League has no constitution. Indeed it has no constitution in the usual acceptance of that term. It is founded on the Covenant — a solemn compact between Sovereign States. The time may come when the scheme of a World State, as held by Mr. H. G. Wells, may be realised. The time may come when a new conception of sovereignty, such as hinted at by Sir Geoffrey Butler, may supersede the doctrines hitherto maintained. It is true that men, as individuals or nations, have, in their political activity, outgrown the machinery of national governments, and, in their intellectual conviction, the theory of state sovereignty. But the League, as it exists to-day, is neither a world-state nor a super-state. It is a great co-ordinating and co-operating scheme of war-weary peoples to make this world safe for democracy and for peace.

No one, not even the most ardent supporters of the League, will suggest that it is the most perfect instrument human ingenuity can conceive. To consider it incapable of improvement would be an insult to the highest instinct of man; but we must admit it to be the organisation most compatible with existing conditions. Indeed, its many imperfections are the best proof that it is intended for a practical purpose, and those who founded it, though inspired by a long vision, are not blind to the pitiless facts of human life. They can not, they will not sweep away old forms and institutions at once. These they will rather take over as they find them, and adapt them so as to give shape and substance to the long-dreamt dream of universal co-operation.

The caution with which the League has entered upon its work must be patent to any seeing eye. False hopes must not be entertained by exaggerating the powers of the League. For as the organist begins "doubtfully and far away" to let his fingers wander o'er the keys, so do all great enterprises have their slow beginning.

There have been difficulties, for the solution of which the general public looked to the League and was disappointed, but which, for technical or practical reasons, really lay outside its competence to decide. The League could not accept the mandate over Armenia,* because it has neither force nor money to exercise such authority. Another instance is that of the Hedjaz, which, while in a state of war, asked the League for help which it could not render, since it can act only in territories where peace has first been established.

For the better understanding of the character of the work accomplished by the League we should do well to consider its practical execution. We may divide it into two classes — (1) such duties as are explicitly imposed on the League by the Covenant: and (2) work of a more general character which, though not definitely prescribed in so many words, is implied by the Covenant. In each of these categories are urgent measures which demand immediate attention, and others which can well be dealt with at a later date. Such a classification, though useful to keep in mind, can scarcely be followed in disposing of problems as they come up for solution. Very urgent business may require time for solution, while a less urgent question can be despatched at once. I shall adhere to no categorical order, but will take up the subjects one after the other as they suggest themselves in the course of the lecture.

## 1. The Delimitation of the Saar Basin Frontier

The most urgent task imposed upon the League by the Treaty of Versailles was the appointment of three out of five members (the two others being French and German) of the Commission to trace on the spot the frontier line of the Saar Basin. (Art. 48 of the Treaty). This district contains many populous villages and towns. The work of delimitation, simple as it may seem in itself, was in fact extremely complicated. The authority of the League in this matter is exceedingly limited, consisting in the appointment of three members of the Delimitation Commission. This was done early in the year, within a week of the coming into force of the Treaty. The League appointed a British, a Belgian and a Japanese, and here its work ended, and it is not concerned in the actual execution of the terms of delimitation.

---

*The Republican Party in America estimates that it will require 60,000 "boys" to police Armenia and an expenditure of $276,000,000 in the first year, and of $756,000,000 in the five succeeding years.

## 2. The Government of the Saar Basin

The League is charged with the more important task of governing the territory of the Saar Basin for a term of fifteen years, at the end of which a plebiscite must settle its fate. (Art. 49 of the Treaty). For this purpose a Commission of five persons of different nationalities was appointed, and has been in office for several months.

The Saar Basin, under normal conditions, is an industrial region with an area of 220 square miles and a population of 700,000 inhabitants, offering no particular difficulties of administration other than those of ordinary mining districts. But when we are reminded that its mines were, according to the Treaty of Versailles (Arts. 45 and 48) renounced by Germany in order that they might be exploited by France, and that the labourers are German, we can easily see the perplexities confronting the Governing Body.

## 3. The Government of the Free City of Danzig

A somewhat similar task required of the League immediately after the war, was the establishment of Danzig as a Free City with a constitution and government. The Council of the League, in association with the Supreme Council, appointed in February Sir Reginald Tower as High Commissioner, and he convened the Constituent Assembly in the middle of June. So the delicate problem of dealing with all differences between Poland and Danzig, whose claims, ambitions and interests are so often at variance, falls upon the Administrator, who certainly is handling the situation with skill worthy of his past career.

## 4. The Repatriation of Prisoners of War

An urgent humanitarian call, rather unexpectedly made upon the League, is the repatriation of prisoners of war — particularly those who have been interned in Russia or Siberia. Of such there are perhaps over 200,000, a mere remnant of a much larger number of Yugo-Slavs, Poles, Germans and Austrians who have already perished there. Starvation, cold, ill-treatment and disease have carried away thousands before their own countries could send for them. As the Soviet Government deals with few other governments, it is not an easy task for the League to pursue this work; but let it be said to the credit of the International Committee of the Red Cross in Geneva, as well as that of the Y.M.C.A., that, in conjunction with their good offices, the League has been able to begin this urgent and arduous task. The Council wisely invited Dr. Nansen, the well-known Norwegian explorer, to undertake the necessary negotiations, and he is carrying out the work with his characteristic zeal and tact. To complete it, important financial negotiations are necessary; for many of the countries directly concerned can ill afford large out-lays and must be helped. The League will exert all its influence towards guaranteeing the necessary funds. The justification for the League's undertaking this task is "the mitigation of suffering throughout the world," laid down in Article 25 of the Covenant.

## 5. The International Health Bureau

Among other pressing demands which Peace and Humanity have made upon the League, have been some which were not definitely expressed by the Covenant or the Treaty, but which are clearly covered by their principles. Of such a character is the creation of an International Health Office (Cov. Arts. 23a and 25), which, in conjunction with the existing International Office of Public Hygiene and the Red Cross organisations, is intended to promote "the improvement of health, the prevention of disease and the mitigation of suffering throughout the world." A draft scheme for the organisation of such a body has been made by a small international Conference called by the Council. It will be submitted to the coming Assembly, so that, in a few months, we may see a decided step taken towards co-operation to improvement of health throughout the world.

## 6. The Anti-Typhus Campaign in Poland

But in the matter of health a case arose which could not wait for the action of an Assembly. Typhus has been raging in Poland and Galicia, and threatens to pass her borders, menacing the whole of Europe. Poland bravely did her utmost to stop the scourge. Not a town or a village has escaped, and half the doctors have died. Mr. Balfour, in his Appeals for help, says: "Prisoners returning to their homes, refugees flying for safety crowd the railways. Two millions of these unfortunate persons have passed the Polish disinfection stations since the Armistice, and doubtless many more have entered Poland without being subject to medical examination." But with all the dangers threatening her very existence, the resources of Poland alone are not adequate for the suppression of the epidemic. The Council has therefore taken up the task and drawn up plans for combating it. It authorised the Secretary-General to raise by contributions from different countries a sum of two million pounds sterling, of which £250,000 are urgently needed.

The League of Red Cross Societies, as well as a number of national Red Cross Societies, have nobly come to the rescue. This is a gigantic scheme of philanthropy: for utilitarian as any prophylactic measure is, when it requires a vast sum of money to be raised from countries far from the seat of danger, an appeal can be made only to their generosity. Participation in such a labour of love adds to the work of the League a "touch of nature that maketh the whole world kin."*

But philanthropy cannot wholly absorb the attention of the Council. Disputes among nations arise in unexpected quarters, and these must be instantly nipped in the bud.

## 7. The Aaland Islands Dispute

Pending the formal inauguration of an International Tribunal, when a question arises demanding technical knowledge, the League has to ask the opinion of specialists. Such is the case with the dispute between Sweden and Finland respecting the Aaland Islands, which belong geographically to the latter, but ethnologically to the former. Finland maintains that the desire of the Islanders to return to Sweden is not a case for the application of the principle of self-determination, but for the rights of minorities, and as such is a purely domestic concern. Sweden, on the other hand, claims that it is a case for the application of the principle of self-determination, and insists that it is a proper subject for the League to settle. When it was brought up before the Council this body referred the subject to a committee of three eminent jurists of France, Switzerland and Holland with a member of the Secretariat as liaison officer. Already a decision has been reached and the Council will act in a short time on their

---

*[Shakespeare, *Troilus and Cressida*, III. iii. 176–77: 'One touch of nature makes the whole world kin, / That all with one consent praise new-born gaudes.']

recommendation. The world has taken little note of this dispute, and consequently of the process of its solution. Certainly a calm discussion of jurists has nothing in it to appeal to the lovers of the spectacular, to whom a war between Finland and Sweden would have afforded something sensational. But if the League succeeds in settling this dispute, as it is to all appearance on a fair way to doing, it will establish a precedent for dealing in future with similar questions that may disturb the amicable relations of States, whether large or small.

## 8. The Permanent International Court of Justice

The case of the Aaland Islands demonstrates better than any arguments, how important is judiciary advice in the settling of international disputes. The world has long felt this need, as is evidenced in the attempts made by Emeric Lacroix (1623) and many others — more definitely by the Institute of International Law (1874-75) and by the Hague Conferences (1899 and 1907). Until now the world has not been willing to go further than Arbitration. The Permanent Court of Arbitration at the Hague was undoubtedly a great stride in the advancement of justice. All honour to the illustrious judges who sat in that Court! But even they looked forward to a better arrangement, and this better arrangement has come as a consequence of the worst times in human history. As Monsieur Bourgeois says: "From all parts of the devastated and tormented world rises a cry for justice. The military and moral unity which for five years held the free peoples together and concentrated their efforts in the defence of the right must survive with our victory: it can find no nobler expression nor a more splendid a symbol than the establishment of a Permanent Court of International Justice." The Council has been entrusted (Cov. Art. 14) with the adoption of plans for the establishment of such a Court, and as a preliminary step it invited ten eminent jurists from different countries "to prepare a scheme designed to satisfy absolute justice, to conciliate the legitimate interests of nations, to crown in the happiest manner possible the evolution of centuries." This learned commission held daily sessions for nearly six weeks (June 16 to July 24) in The Hague, and submitted to the Council a draft constitution of the Court, which will in turn be submitted to the Assembly at its first meeting. So in a few months, if all goes well, the world will see for the first time in history a permanent institution in a tangible form, to which may be brought cases of a legal nature concerning (a) the interpretation of a treaty: (b) any question of international law: (c) the existence of any fact which, if established, would constitute a breach of an international obligation: (d) the interpretation of a sentence passed by the Court. This great institution will be a Court of Justice and not merely a Court of Arbitration, and will hold a session each year at The Hague.

## 9. Treaty Registration

To usher in the reign of justice in the world, it is not enough to build a Palace of Justice, however magnificent, and to man it with jurists, however upright. Resource must be had to any means to avert attempted or even contemplated injustice. One of the most fruitful sources of trouble is the secrecy of international engagements. The League upholds open diplomacy. No less than four Articles in the Covenant (18–21) are devoted to the subject. Every Member of the League must register its treaties with the Secretariat. If not so registered they are not binding. Moreover, if a treaty should contain any obligation inconsistent with the terms of the Covenant, steps must be taken for its immediate abrogation. Already a number of treaties have been received in the Secretariat for registration.

While legal pressure is thus put upon Members of the League to prevent any secret engagements, Art. 8 of the Covenant commits them to a more positive step towards peace by pledging them to reduce "armaments to the lowest point consistent with national safety."

## 10. The Reduction of Armaments

It is a truism that tools in a man's hand become art of his body and incite him to use them. The presence of engines of destruction invites us to acts of violence. A reduction of armaments frees mankind from one powerful source of temptation. But nobody can be expected to be guileless enough to imitate the action of sheep in the midst of tigers. Disarmament or reduction of armament must be simultaneous. A beginning towards this end is made by the appointment of a Permanent Advisory Armaments Commission (Cov. Art. 9), composed of twenty-seven members selected from different countries. They have already begun their work by the study of the use of asphyxiating gases in warfare and the convention relating to traffic in arms in backward countries. The Commission is also collecting data from all the countries of the world, in regard to their armaments, and I believe that in a year or two visible results will be consequent upon their activity. It will also deal with

### 11. "The General Supervision of the Trade in Arms and Ammunition

with the countries in which the control of this traffic is necessary in the common interest." According to Art. 23 of the Covenant this is really putting into effect the Brussels Act of July 2nd, 1890, with further regulations applicable to the backward regions of Africa and Asia.

According to the same Article of the Covenant (c) the League is entrusted with the supervision over the traffic in women and children and the traffic in opium and other dangerous drugs.

### 12. The Control of White Slave Traffic

As regards the so-called "White Slave Traffic," between 1902 and 1910 two international conferences were held and agreements signed with the object of suppressing and making punishable any attempt at this trade. Voluntary societies, under various names, rendered no small aid in carrying out such legislation, and these have formed a central organ — the International Bureau for the Suppression of the White Slave Traffic. This Bureau now proposes to call a general conference, and the League will postpone any action until this conference, which one may call a congress of experts on the question, has met and made its recommendations. Meanwhile the Secretariat has appointed an official, specially charged with the duty of keeping herself informed on all questions relating thereto.

### 13. The Control of Opium Traffic

Together with the above question, another — the supervision of the execution of agreements with regard to the traffic in opium and other dangerous drugs — will most likely be brought up for discussion in the coming meeting of the Assembly. Conference after conference had been held before the war, in which a large number of governments took part, to devise some means of controlling the use of dangerous drugs. The last of these meetings took place at The Hague a few weeks before the outbreak of the war, when 44 out of the total 46 participating Powers signed the Opium Convention, 11 ratified it, 14 more were disposed to do so, while the remaining 19 did not express any intention of putting it into effect. So stands the famous Opium Convention of 1912. Now, however, the Members of the League, by the very act of signing the Covenant, have practically ratified the Opium Convention, so that, it is to be hoped, within a few months different governments will introduce in their respective territories suitable legislation to that effect, and the League is committed to seeing that this is done. England has taken the lead with her "Dangerous Drugs Act," passed last month, and other States, Members of the League which have not yet passed similar laws, are obliged to conform to the convention.

## 14. Mandates

Humanitarian principles, which transcend national interests, also find expression in the entirely new conception of the attitude advanced peoples have pledged themselves by the Covenant (Art. 22) to assume toward the backward races.

The Treaty of Versailles tolled the knell of Imperialism. Some may say Imperialism is by no means dead. I grieve to say that it still looks very alive. But though Imperialism is not yet buried, the Covenant has dealt it a fatal blow. Henceforth an Imperialist will not be tolerated in the polite Society of Nations.

Backward races will no longer be exploited as victims of Imperialism. They will be treated as weaker brethren in the family of nations. Their tutelage must be entrusted to more advanced nations, who should exercise it as Mandatories on behalf of the League until they attain the fullness of the measure of political stature. This new and noble principle of colonisation introduced, it is said, by General Smuts into the Covenant, opens a new era in the development of the human race.

It is to be noted that, according to the Treaty of Versailles, the right of allocating mandates belongs to the Principal Allied and Associated Powers, and not to the League of Nations. The legal title of the Mandatories is thus a double one conferred in part by the Principal Powers and in part by the League. The League is awaiting the appointment of the Mandatories by the Principal Powers. When this has been done the League will begin to act as administrator. In the meantime it is preparing the organisation of the Commission of

Control (Art. 22, 9).

## 15. The Permanent Labour Organisation

The spirit of justice which has prompted the framers of the Covenant to apply its principles to so-called inferior races, dictates that social justice be established in improving the existing conditions of labour throughout the world.

Part XIII of the Treaty of Versailles, covering some 40 long articles, is devoted to the world organisation of labour. It was by virtue of the formal provisions of these Articles that the International Labour Conference was called at Washington in October-November, 1919, some weeks before the ratification of the treaties. Thirty-one nations took part in the deliberations, and by their unanimous consent German and Austrian delegates were invited. Each country sent three classes of representatives, one of the Government, one of the employer, and one of labour. Quite a large number of women delegates also took part in it. After protracted, and often heated, discussions, six Draft Conventions and six Recommendations to the Governments were adopted, among the more important of which was the Convention of the Limitation of the Working Day, recommendations concerning unemployment, resolutions taken on welfare questions — such as the protection of women in childbirth. The International Labour Organisation held the second session of its conference in Genoa in June-July, 1920, when the protection of seamen was discussed, and when several conventions and recommendations were passed to the satisfaction of all concerned.

During the first Conference the Governing Body was elected, consisting of 24 persons, 8 of whom are nominated by the adherent states of the Organisation which are of greatest industrial importance. The rest are elected by the delegates at the conference, in such proportion as to represent the interests of lesser states, of employers and of workers.

This Labour Organisation forms a part of the League of Nations (Art. 392) — in a rather loose way, it is true, but still close and very friendly. The Secretary-General of the League is treasurer, recorder and registrar of the Organisation. He also nominates Commissions of Enquiry whenever one state is accused by another of failing to carry out a convention.

The International Labour Bureau, the office of the Permanent Labour Organisation, was inaugurated in London last spring and soon after moved to Geneva, where it is engaged in active work. It would be superfluous for me to dwell on the significance of this world organisation of labour. He who runs may read.

### 16. The Commission of Enquiry on Freedom of Communications and Transit

Any scheme of universal organisation, whether of labour or of health, can scarcely hope for realisation unless the nations can be brought together within speaking distance. Distance not only lends enchantment to the view, as a poet says,* but also enchantment of souls to their narrow habitats. The Covenant has contemplated better methods of securing and maintaining, "freedom of communications and of transit and equitable treatment for the commerce of all members of the League." (Cov. Art. 23e). In fact throughout Part XII of the Treaty of Versailles one meets repeated reference to this question. (Art. 336, 338, 342, 376-379, 386). You will remember that the Treaty of Versailles has internationalised a number of European rivers. To carry into effect the provisions referred to, the Commission of Enquiry on Freedom of Communications and Transit was established. The Council is inviting, subject to its further approval by the Assembly, the States Members of the League to send special representatives to a general conference on Communications and Transit to meet in Barcelona as soon as possible after the meeting of the Assembly. The conference is expected to draw up the measures for the execution of Article XXIII (c) of the Covenant, as well as general conventions on the international régime of transit, ports, waterways and railways referred to in Articles 338 and 379 of the Treaty of Versailles. The Conference will be asked to formulate plans for the creation of a permanent organisation to be in close touch with the League. Already a report has been submitted by the President of the Commission, and before long we may see an international conference dealing with this all-important theme.

---

*[Thomas Campbell (1777-1844), *Pleasures of Hope*, I. 7 (1799): 'distance lends enchantment to the view.']

## 17. The Financial Conference

The Covenant and the Treaty clearly indicate that transit, communications, health and labour should be made more international; but they were not explicit about the most serious issues involving the fate of mankind. As Mr. Vanderlip answered to the query "What happened in Europe?" the glaring facts now threatening the very foundations of peace and social order are the economic and financial situation of Europe, indeed of the world. The framers of the Covenant were not unaware of their magnitude; but perhaps they did not anticipate that the situation would become as bad as it has since turned out to be.

The Treaty has provided for a Reparation Commission in which only five countries are represented. In determining the amount of German debt, which is its chief duty, a wide survey must be taken of her economic resources. But so intricate and interlocked are economic relations among nations, that an organisation aiming at a broader co-operation is deemed necessary for the solution of questions so complicated as currency, prices, exchange, etc. That such broader co-operation is feasible was illustrated by the temporary post-war organisation of the Supreme Economic Council, consisting of delegations from the four powers specially interested, and the Council of the League, after careful deliberation, decided to take the initiative in convening an International Conference, in order "to study the financial crisis and to look for a means of remedying it and of mitigating the dangerous consequences arising from it." As many as 34 States will take part in it. The date of meeting was postponed from time to time, but has now been fixed for 24th September, in Brussels.

It is a commonplace to remark that nothing binds nations more closely and more firmly than economic relations, and we hope that the coming Financial Conference will prove more strongly than ever that commerce is a most loyal handmaid to peace. The Conference may well grow into a more permanent institution for more efficient and effectual service in the reconstruction of the world.

## The Real Test of the League

We have brought under brief review the earliest achievements of the League. From the routine standpoint of the Secretariat we have divided these into explicit and implicit measures, and then explained how they have been undertaken according to the degree of urgency. A more logical classification may be as follows: —

(1) Judicial. — Constitution of Permanent Court of Justice. Treaty Registration, Aaland Islands question:
(2) Political. — Saar Delimitation and Administration, Disarmament, Government of Dantzig, Mandates Traffic in Arms:
(3) Economic. — Financial Conference, Labour Office, Transit Commission.
(4) Moral or Humanitarian. — Anti-typhus campaign, Control of White Slave and Opium Traffic, Repatriation of War Prisoners, Creation of Health Office.

Thus one can see what a wide field has been covered by the League. At the same time I know that present results are disappointing alike to sanguine spirits, over-zealous for the cause of the League and eager to forward it, and to hypercritical minds to whom nothing is ever right.

An old Oriental proverb says "He who takes no part is an easy judge, but he who acts hesitates." Indeed, if those in responsible posts should act as boldly as the onlookers advise, what would the world be like! As well may you expect a dancer to keep step to a hundred tunes played on every side! This does not mean that all music should cease. Far from it! Let not the reproof uttered twenty centuries ago be repeated to the League: "We have piped unto you and ye have not danced!" The world's best opinions — be they expressed by private individuals or by organised bodies — will find careful response in the actions of the League, and in these actions the world's thoughts will find not only their fulfilment, but also stepping stones to higher conceptions, for thought without action is dead. The noblest document can be turned into a mere scrap of paper. On the contrary, a few words, by themselves apparently insignificant, can be so interpreted and so applied in practice that they may become unerring maxims for further action.

The League is started as a working organ for world democracy and peace. The Covenant is its Bible, and, like many passages in the

Bible, the Articles in the Covenant are open to vulgar and higher criticism, and we hear much of both kinds. But the surest evidence of religion is the life of its votaries; so the test of the value of the League will lie in the practical application it makes of the Covenant. A tree shall be judged by its fruit. No argument will convince a sceptic of the efficacy of the League better than "a deed done in the body." A wise man of the nineteenth century has said that "doubt of any kind cannot be removed except by action."* Not rashly, nor falteringly, but cautiously and firmly then, let the League fulfil its mission. Guided by high principles as laid down in the Covenant, advised by expert knowledge and fortified by enlightened public opinion, I trust the League will so act as to justify its creation and existence, until a higher form of world organisation, foreshadowed by poets and philosophers, shall have taken its place for the perpetual reign of justice and peace on earth.

---

*[Goethe, *Wilhelm Meister* 1: 386: 'Doubt of any kind can be removed by nothing but activity,' quoted by Carlyle in *Sartor Resartus*, IX: 'Most true is it, as a wise man teaches us, that "Doubt of any sort cannot be removed except by Action." ']

## (2) The Organization and Activities of the League of Nations [Trans. by Editor]

*The Shorthand notes of the lecture delivered at Waseda University 16th-18th December 1924 — one of his League propaganda lectures in Japan he refers to in his report, "The League of Nations Movement in Japan," which will follow this. Translated from The Collected Works of Inazo Nitobe, vol. 4: 401-444.*

### First Lecture

I came to a university campus after 6 years' absence, though I still retains the title of professor and have a university connection as an emeritus professor. My connection, however, is not merely superficial, as I hope. While abroad, I always think of Japanese universities and try my best to do whatever contributions I can do for Japanese universities. When asked to talk to you, therefore, I immediately accepted the invitation with great pleasure. Of course, I am not so presumptuous as to think that I can give you a totally new information. Most of your professors, especially in the fields of economics and law, may have had observed the activities of the League of Nations with their own eyes. And as for the organization of the League itself, they have a far deeper jurisprudent knowledge than I have. What I am going to do here is only to talk about the things I saw with my eyes, a little short-sighted eyes as they are. I have no intention to dwell on the theoretical sides of the organization, for, if I do it, I will never be free from mistakes. I may in some points refer to the so-called fundamental principles, but my reference will never be a profound one, for profundity is not in my character. I saw such and such facts and deduced that they came from such and such principles — in other words, secondary principles as it were, not primary, will be my topics.

I will begin with the name. We have our own nomenclature in our language. It is "The League of Nations" in English, and "La Société des Nations" in French. German people call it "Völkerbund." Each country may have its own nomenclature, but only the English and

French names are regarded as official.

The official language used in international conferences had usually been French. So, at the time of the Versailles Treaty, it was a hot debate to decide whether English or French should be the language. Woodrow Wilson was a prominent figure in that conference and due to his influence it was decided that both French and English should be used. This episode shows that the Anglo-Saxon people have rapidly gained their predominance in the world — a fact becoming apparent from only four or five years ago. The name of the League of Nations is only an example of it. We can see similar signs in many things. Thus it was agreed that the League should be called both in French and English names; that both names should be regarded as equally valid.

They didn't say that French and English should be the only "official languages" of the League; they wanted to avoid offending other countries. To limit the use of languages to French and English is convenient, they said, and more practical, for, if Spanish and Portuguese, for example, are to be used, too, even though it may much facilitate transactions related to their countries, publishing the League's reports in various languages will cost much; the printing expenses will be five times or even ten times as costly, which will then rebound to each country's charges — which no one can say don't matter much. This monetary argument was strong enough to make most countries to withdraw their insistence on the use of their own language. The League didn't prohibit the use of other languages. Each member was free to speak in his own language, but they were asked to pay for the interpreters. Thus no one will protest against us if we decide to speak in Japanese, provided that we are ready to pay for the interpreters. Which way to take is all up to us. Probably it will be much cheaper for us to use French or English instead of sticking to our own language.

Next question is for what purpose this body called the League of Nations was established. One of the aims is to stop wars and prevent future wars. And, secondly, in order to prevent wars, to remove various disputes and causes of war by other means than arms and weapons. The idea is not new. It is an age-old idea preached from ancient time by many religious people and statesmen. In our country, as early as the beginning of the 7th century, Prince Shoutoku said, in his Constitution of 17 Articles (A.D. 604), "Peace is the most prized thing." I think I can say, at the risk of being scolded by constitutionalists, that peace was regarded as the basis and the main purpose of every society of every country; and that we don't need any explanation for the fact. On the other hand, I am not unconscious of the existence of a quite contrary opinion: that peace is not attainable. A recent example is Treischke. In Britain, too, not a few people assert similar opinions. Even such a person as Ruskin, who loved to talk about literature and art, once said that war is inherent in human nature; that war can't be stopped unless we can change the mind of people. Also some people emphasize how the progress of human society has been made by wars. Perhaps, it is not necessary for me here to repeat various opinions of various people which you might already know. The other day I met an American and asked him why his country doesn't join the League. His answer was quite simple, like this: Human history shows that war will never cease, and every progress has been made by wars: that we should not speak of stopping wars, because it is impossible.

In my opinion, while it is the League's aim to try to stop wars, the League doesn't aim to change the mind of people. Some people say, our masculinity manifests itself in disputes, and disputes lead to wars. Hence, to stop wars, we must take away masculinity from our mind, which is the same thing as to castrate ourselves. But such an opinion is extreme. The League of Nations never professes to turn men into women, nor to change all the people into saints and angels. It only proposes to change the way of war, to improve the method of dispute. Everybody is endowed with an instinct which psychologists and sociologists will call "pugnacity" — I don't know any Japanese word for it — or shall we say, a fighting spirit, an instinct to dispute, an instinct to make war. Just as the hair of our head is curved to some extent and no one's hair is straight, so an anomaly of war is rather our normal condition, a thing taken for granted. But, if it comes to that, we are similarly endowed with an instinct of possession, a desire to get something, and also a sexual desire. The advance of civilization will not aim at taking away this sexual desire from the mind of people and castrating them by means of social rules and institutions. Society will try to protect private property by means of law, but it will never try to remove that instinct of possession deep-rooted in human mind. Only, it will be a dangerous thing to let these instincts go their way without any regulations, as when a person wants to have something in somebody else's possession and straightway tries to snatch it from him by twisting up his arms, or when a person feels a sexual desire for a woman and straightway tries to pin her on the street. Therefore, regulations of some kind or other are needed in any society. The same is true with our fighting spirit. If it is let loose without regulations, we will have people who quite freely fire a pistol, brandish a sword and so on. To fight is not a bad thing, but if we fight, let it be a fight of gentlemen. And the fight of gentlemen is nothing other than a fight armed with speech and debate. The League of Nations aims to settle disputes by debate. Therefore, people define its conference room figuratively as an advanced form of arena or battlefield. As you have probably read in newspapers, when the Peace Pact was discussed, Mr. Ishii took a command and Mr. Adachi stood on the battlefield, fighting sometimes against 10 people, sometimes 20, and sometimes 30, in the general Assembly of the League of Nations. It was a glorious fighting. An argument was fired from this party and the other party fought back with an argument of law. Another argument went from this side and the other side returned the fire with an argument of politics. This side responded again with still another argument. That was indeed a fight of speech and debate. For this reason some people, like the above-mentioned American, argue that it is impossible to extinguish a fighting instinct in us. But such an opinion is beside the mark. The League of Nations aims to regulate the manner of war, though a strange way of saying, or the method of strife. To prevent wars and to change the way of disputes — this we can safely conclude to be the League's aspiration and goal.

There are various causes of war. The League should try to eliminate them. The most common is an economical cause. Also a sense of honour can cause war. In the present-day world, religion may not cause war, but it is possible that people fight for honour of their own country. However, the most frequent cause of war is economical interests. In order to prevent this kind of war, the League decided to promote the economical cooperation among nations. Also cooperation in education or learning should be aimed at, though we have no special article for it in the Covenant. The League thinks cooperation among nations to be desirable also for such moral problems as prohibition of the trade of white slaves and opium. These problems have an emotional element, too. Although they are not specified in the Covenant, the League tries to promote discussion of these social problems as part of international cooperation, which will eventually help prevent wars, nipping their cause in the bud, and conduce to the primary purpose of the League, which is to remove all possible causes of war in order to realize a world without war.

Then, what is the means to realize this purpose? I think there must have been many attempts from old to hold meetings for this purpose. For example, the concept of the international law court which arbitrates between nations in time of dispute and judge the right or wrong of the nations involved — such a concept must be age-old in any part of the world. I am not a connoisseur enough to say, but if we look a little minutely into Plato, it will not be difficult to find out such a concept in him. We will be able to find a similar concept in Buddhist scriptures, too. I think every country has its literature and thought giving expression to such an idea. If we take up a time when learning began to take a little advance, we can pick up as an example a 14th-century French Dubois [?] who proposed to establish an international law court and set down minute provisions for it. Coming a little downward in history, we find, some 300 years ago, William Penn, one of the founders of the Quakers' Society, dreamed of a peaceful society, not only in his own colony of Pennsylvania but also in the whole world, and planned something like our League of Nations. His plan was very minute covering all the details. For example, he said each member-state should be treated as equal without any distinction between first-class and second-class powers. The conference table, too, should be arranged in such a way as to avoid making a difference of upper and lower seats. A round table was proposed for that purpose, with equal seats placed around it. Not only the table but also the room itself should be round, for the distance from the entrance may make a difference. Doors should be placed all around the room lest different distances from the door should create inequality. He sent this minute plan to monarchs and kings of various countries and to influential politicians.

Thus there must have already existed some twenty or thirty people who considered how to maintain peace in the world, that is to say, attempted at something like the present League of Nations. Lange wrote a book on this subject. His first volume was already published and the following two volumes are to be published before long. Indeed, if we include the Eastern countries like China and Japan, I think we can conclude that this ideal of the united nations has been repeatedly discussed among scholars from several hundred years ago. You may have read in the English-class textbook Tennyson's phrases such as "Parliament of Man," and "Federation of the World."* Did he anticipate by these words the present movement of the League?

The idea of the League of Nations was never limited to the world of thought. There did exist numerous actual conferences which aimed at the same goal as the League of Nations. The most famous example is the Holy Alliance. There monarchs and emperors of great powers met and pledged themselves to everlasting peace. You will be surprised if you look into the original text of their agreement, for it is not so much a political agreement as a religious oath addressed to God. They referred to Holy Providence, Holy Saviour of Mankind, love of Christianity, and suchlike pomposity of words. The same is true with the quite recent Peace Conference at The Hague. The problem with them, however, was that such a lofty ideal expressed in such a high-flown language was not acted up to for long. Meetings and conferences were held, but, after that, the agreements were simply forgotten. People met and stirred up each other. Some went so far as to bring with them their holy priests and let them pray there. They talked big, using such expressions as "in the cause of humanity," "in the name of religion," and so on. After going back to their own country, however, they forgot all that were said, and there was no way of carrying out the agreements. The reason is that they didn't think of continuation of efforts. Those meetings and conferences were temporal in nature. They were lacking in a permanent character, and that was their weakest point.

And the League of Nations founded five years ago — what difference does it have from those foregoing enterprises? People very often say that the League, too, may follow its predecessors' path; that, since preceding attempts all ended up in failures, the same may be true with the League. To such an objection, I have replied — I didn't argue, but pointed out one plain fact. It is this: whereas all the

---

*[Tennyson, "Locksley Hall," l. 128.]

former attempts were destitute of an organ to continue the movement, the League has its own new invention — an organ called the Secretariat. The League has another organ called the Council. But this is not open all the time. While its meeting is held about once every three months, the Secretariat is working all the time of the year except Sundays, from early morning till late in the evening. We don't stop our work even on New Year's days. Constant work enables us to arrange various resolutions of the general Assembly or the Council meeting, check whether each agreement is being carried out in the members-states, and, if not, to give warnings to those countries. This is the work of the Secretariat. We say to those countries, "Your country signed such and such a treaty, and yet we haven't yet received your ratification. When will it come? Please let us know by telegram." We sometimes repeat the request three or four times. This is indeed a new addition which has no antecedent in history. We are rather glad to have an organ which will make sure the continuance of the League. So, this is a difference of the League of Nations from other foregoing similar attempts.

The other organs of the League are not much different from those already attempted. The first organ is the general meeting, "the Assembly" in English, and "L'Assemblée" in French. This may be compared to the Parliament of each country. Its general meeting is held once a year. The first Monday of every September is the date set for it.

Each member-state sends one to three delegates to the general meeting. They are supposed to be the representatives of each country. Anything signed by delegates who are opposed to their own country's government will be invalid. Also if a delegate, when back in his country, reports to the government that he made such and such an argument and the government is opposed to it, that delegate's speech, however good it may be, will be of no practical use. Thus it is essential that delegates should truly represent the government of each country. Therefore, the delegates are sent by their governments, and the number of the delegates is from one to three for each country.

When voting, one country has one vote no matter how many delegates it has sent. And the actual number of delegates varies from country to country. The Assembly has Six Committees, as I will explain tomorrow or the day after tomorrow, in order to execute its work. Each country attends all these six committees. Even three delegates will not be enough to cover all these. So, many countries send at least six representatives instead of three. Some small, poor country cannot afford to send so many. In that case, one person must play more than two persons' role. He sits for the First Committee for about thirty minutes, then goes out to another Committee and votes. Some make an inquiry about the time of voting beforehand and run from this committee to that very busily. But most countries send at least six persons. Three among them are delegates, and the others are called substitute-delegates, who are empowered to take place of the delegates in case of emergency. Thus delegates and substitute-delegates will make up a party of at least six members. And they are usually accompanied by many more people such as advisers, secretaries, and specialist engineers. Japan sent a party of one hundred and fifty or sixty people at the time of the first meeting of the Assembly. If this were England or France, when some specialists' help is needed, a telegram would be enough to summon them within a night. But such a thing is not possible for Japan. Japan must prepare in advance various specialists who might be consulted, and then send them away in a gorgeous pageant of people, some with their lances, some holding up parasols, and some unfurling ensigns.

Speaking of the Assembly, I have something to say to you for your good, and that is Japanese people's poor linguistic ability, a regrettable fact as it is. Observing Japanese people's way of communicating with people of other countries, I cannot but marvel at their badness. I need not go so far for an example, for I myself, who ought to have got a better ability considering my career, still feel difficulty and inadequacy, I confess, after so many decades of practice and at this age of maturity. If it is difficult for me, it will be more so for young inexperienced people like you. Probably this belongs to our national character, but this becomes a grievous disadvantage in a conference where only French or English is used. Not only does it make it difficult to express opinions, but also it can arouse a groundless suspicion. Japanese people don't have a good reputation abroad, and one of the main allegations is that Japanese are underhand or treacherous people. They say Japanese people are uncanny because they don't speak much. If it were that Japanese people are foolish and don't have anything to say, that would be harmless and people would feel much more comfortable, but actually they are as clever as other people and have got as perfect an understanding of the situation; therefore, they are uncanny, to foreigners' eyes. I think this is a serious matter. I want to advise you. If you are going to work abroad, language will be essential, trivial though it may seem. People endowed with a good linguistic skill will come off very successful. Recently our university professors are very good at foreign languages. One such person came to Geneva, and it went very well. His linguistic skill was exceptionally good, and accordingly his success was exceptionally good. Here is a possibility of great gain as well as loss. Among students of Japan, if somebody shows his ability in foreign languages, there is a tendency to regard him as a mere talker. But they are wrong. Mr. Adachi did fight so effectively over that Peace Pact on behalf of our country. Of course, his success owed much to his profound knowledge and wisdom as a jurist, but at the same time, without his linguistic ability, he would not have been able to fight in such a superb way. He did it, not merely at the psychological moment, but throughout all the morning. I would like you to reconsider this. Language is no trivial matter.

Delegates are sent by each member-state. The number of members-states is at present 55. The number has increased year by year. New members join every year. A recent case is Santo Domingo which joined two months ago. Generally speaking, non-members-states are a minority; Russia, Germany, Turkey, Ecuador, Afghanistan and the United States. They are only six or seven, if my memory is correct. Moreover, Russia, while declaring that the League of Nations is nothing but an institution of Capitalism, still cannot ignore it and sends inspectors to catch up with its proceedings.

As for the United States, although the League was realized according to Wilson's proposal, as is well known, that is the very reason the United States refused to join. People there objected to the idea of the League just because it was advocated by Wilson whose personality became so unpopular there. Also people there have got various misunderstandings, some of which are grievously distorted interpretations, concerning the ideal of the League. To mention some of them, people say that the League of Nations is a kind of super-state, a state placed above states, and therefore the United States will not join it. Also there is an objection to the Articles 10 and 16, about which I may explain later. Perhaps, the last mentioned reason is the only rational argument made there about the League. However, American people, far from being indifferent to it, are studying the League of Nations with a surprising diligence. They are rich people, you may say, and at every Assembly meeting, they come to hear the conference in a great number, old and young, in a caravan of automobiles. Everyday during the session, they listen to the League's lectures from 8 to 10 in the morning, learn there the day's subjects with all detailed explanations, and then attend each meeting for the rest of the day. It is difficult to find people so studious of examining the League's activities.

Going back to the former topic, I mentioned that the members-states are now 55. Also I named the countries which are not members. There are some more non-members-states. They are small countries, such as Iceland, Monaco, San Marino, and Liechtenstein. I don't know how much you are good at geography, but each of them lays claim to an independent country. These countries once or twice expressed their wish to join the League. But they are too small. Smallness as such is no problem, for in matter of fact such small countries as Luxemburgh, Switzerland, Holland and Panama are members. But Monaco and San Marino, for example, are too small — so small that, even if they join, they will not be profited by it enough to counterbalance their membership fees. Once admitted, the League should charge the fees, but the fees are not worth paying because it does not bring any profit. Any application for membership should be taken up by the Assembly for resolutions, but we deal with such applications before they go to the Assembly, persuading them that the membership may not worth while for them; that they had better withdraw the application. As for the United States, it is not a member-state, but practically is as good as a member. The League has various commissions, such as Commission of Enquiry on Transit, and Commission of enquiry on Custom Formality. Also there are commissions for the control of opium traffic and of white slave traffic. Such commissions have American members. There are some twenty of such commissions in all, and there are American members in some eleven or twelve of them. Not a few of them are official representatives sent by the U.S. Government. Also there are many unofficial representatives.

Each of the 55 members-states sends six persons to the general meeting, so that some 300 to 400 people meet in the conference room.

It is a rented house even now. Thus some 400 people meet in the general meeting, and the chairman is elected at each conference. There are no regulations or rules for the election of chairman. In practice, there is an effort to elect chairman from small countries as much as possible — a fact which could be reported only by persons who actually attended the conference. At the time of the first conference, a Belgian, Hymans, who had been and was the Foreign Minister of that country, was elected chairman. Belgium suffered much in the last Great War. She suffered more than France. People had some sentimental feeling for her heroism, and it was first proposed that the first conference of the League be held in Brussels. However, Wilson's opinion, upon inquiry, was for Geneva, and that proposal was not realized. That is why a Belgian was elected chairman in the first conference. The second conference was chaired by a Dutch, the former Foreign Minister of that country. The third was chaired by a Chilean, a certain A. Edwards, who is the Chilean Minister to France. He showed a perfect command of both English and French, and is also a great expert in conference proceedings. The fourth conference was chaired by a Cuban. The fifth by a Swiss, and his name is Motta, once Prime Minister of Switzerland, who as a young man experienced Foreign Secretary or Head of Political Department. He is a lawyer, a man of character, and a learned man with power of eloquence. Once at the election of chairman, a certain Japanese was nominated as a good candidate for his excellent ability in chairmanship. We Japanese were rather flattered by this, of course, but at the same time we were worried. The chairman was usually elected from smaller countries. It would be no problem if people interpret it as some change in policy of election, but some people might still think that Japan is among smaller, uninfluential countries. Some other reasons added to it, that person wasn't elected after all.

Next, I will talk about the proceeding of the Assembly. It is no different from that of the parliament; it is just as you would see if you attended our Imperial Diet. The only difference is that you see different colours in the faces of the people. Another difference is that there is no such thing as booing and jeering. It is very quiet — quite naturally because those people attending are former Prime Ministers, Foreign Ministers, or have an experience of Foreign Ministers many times or of important posts in the Cabinets each in their country.

Such eminent persons constitute about one third of the members. Another third are diplomats. The Japanese representatives are all diplomats, though for the first conference Japan sent Mr. Mekada and others. The remaining one third are professors. You can't underrate the professors I am speaking of here. Especially in new countries such as Latvia, Estonia and Finland, there are no persons that have a career of Prime Minister or some other Ministers. Those countries have no other way than to elect representatives judging them chiefly by their personal characters, and the result is that professors are sent as representatives. Such being its members, there can be no jeering or booing during the meeting. Of course, some may steal out of the room to smoke or whisper to the person sitting nearby, especially when the speech is made in a language foreign to them. But they never do booing or jeering. Apart from such differences, the proceeding of the Assembly is almost the same as that of ordinary parliamentary meetings. What will become of the proceedings and the resolutions of the Assembly must be explained by making reference to the second organ of the League, namely the Council, and this will constitute my tomorrow's talk.

## Second Lecture

Yesterday I talked about the biggest organ of the League, namely the Assembly. The Assembly's works are done by various commissions, which report their conclusions to the Assembly, and the Assembly discusses them and, if passed, they become the Assembly's resolutions and are committed to the Council. Today's talk is about the Council, but before that I think it necessary to say something about Commissions or Committees which are the agents of the Assembly.

The subjects for discussion in the Assembly are prepared by the Secretariat on the basis of applications from members-states. The preparation doesn't include such minute details as the day's schedule, but the topics to be discussed are decided in advance, and notified to each country two months earlier. Therefore, when delegates meet, they come each accompanied by their specialists in the fields related to the topics. However, unexpected subjects can very often be proposed. An extreme case is when a new motion is brought forward during the conference. There is a special committee to deal with such new proposals made during the session, and the committee discusses whether to adopt them or not, and adjusts them into the agenda. Most of those unexpectedly proposed subjects are usually not so serious matters, and will easily find approval.

In the beginning, as I said yesterday, the chairman will be elected. The chairman makes an opening speech. Then the annual report is read. The report itself is submitted by the Secretariat, and reported as by the Council. Last year's conference took up such and such subjects, its resolutions were treated since then in such and such ways, and the things stand in such and such conditions today — all this is reported by the Secretary-General on behalf of the Council.

Individual influence plays a big role on such occasions. You may be able to read various articles of the League's Agreement in a book form even here at a great distance from Geneva, and you will be rewarded by it. But many unexpected things happen in the course of actual proceeding. Therefore, you may be also interested in my report of what actually happens, and I say personal influences, which are not set down anywhere in the Articles, have a great weight there. Men of great influence or personality often decide the course of discussion regardless of the Articles of the Covenant. Their influence is quite different from that of others even if they make a similar argument.

If such people stand up and say something, it will have a great weight which can't be explained by the Articles or any other established rules. Bourgeois, from France, is such a personage. Bourgeois and Balfour are called the parents of the League.

Some people may say that these people are influential because their countries are powerful. But such influential persons can come from smaller countries, too. Even if they are from smaller countries, men of character will be influential and persuasive. It should be borne in mind that such personal elements, such influences, though mentioned nowhere in the Covenant, have place in the actual proceeding of the League.

Thus a lot of people, some influential and some not, are met in the Assembly, and various subjects are submitted to it for discussion. Those subjects are sorted out and allotted each to the relevant Commission. There are six Commissions. The first Commission is for constitutional questions, the second for technical organization, the third for reduction of armaments, the fourth for budget and financial questions, the fifth for social and general questions, and the sixth for political problems. The number of the members states is 55, and each country sends one representative to each Commission. As I said yesterday, some countries send only three representatives to the Assembly in all. When, as is very often the case, the first three Commissions are held simultaneously in separate rooms, and then the remaining three held next day, those three representatives can manage to cover all the Commissions. But sometimes when five or six Commissions are held simultaneously, they will be very busy going to and fro between different rooms, playing Yoichibei here and Kansuke there [both characters in *Forty-seven Men of Rectitude*, a well-known Japanese revenge play]. Care is taken as much as possible to avoid more than three Commissions being held at the same time, by shifting the hours. Still it can't be avoided sometimes. The best way is that each country send six representatives.

Before formally submitted to the main conference, each subject is allotted to the relevant Commission to be discussed there. The results of the discussion is reported to the Assembly by a member of the Commission who is most learned in the subject or by the representative of the country which has a direct concern in the problem. This reporter is called Rapporteur, and appointment to it is regarded as a great distinction. Each Commission has its chairman, but, depending upon the topic, if it is a problem relating to opium, for example, the Commission appoints the Chinese delegate, or if the Chinese delegate happens to be linguistically poor, somebody who is most keen on the problem and has studied it deeply is appointed. Then the rapporteur reports the results of the Commission to the Assembly. Usually he reads from his manuscript, not much long, some three or four pages, and sometimes only half a page. He need not be minute in his report, for people know the details, having heard the results beforehand each from their delegate. They know who attended the Commission as their delegate and what he objected to or agreed to. They know the results before being reported of them. It is a kind of formality. The report is read, that the Commission's resolution is such and such. Then a formal discussion of it is made in the Assembly, and if the Assembly accepts the resolution, it becomes the Assembly's resolution.

The Assembly's resolutions are then sent to the Council: "Council" in English and "Conseil" in French. It consists of members from ten countries. Four among them are from Britain, France, Italy and Japan, and they are permanent members. The remaining six members are chosen in the Assembly from other countries on a yearly basis.

In choosing the members of the Council, the Assembly doesn't nominate individuals but countries which should send the members. However, it is difficult here again not to be influenced by personal elements. Sometimes it happens, especially when they set their eye on some great persons, that they choose countries just because of the persons they wish to have as members. Branting is such a person. He did many things for the League. People wanted to have him in the Council, even if his country Sweden is not specially in their favour. The same is true with Hymans from Belgium. He knows everything about the League, and, unlike Branting, is a man of talent with a brain as sharp as needle. Therefore they chose Belgium. The members are chosen annually, but can be reelected. Thus Belgium has been chosen from the beginning to the present. The same is true with Spain and Brazil.

Thus the Council consists of ten countries. The Council meeting was held frequently in the early years, almost every month, ten times a year in my memory. But recently as people have got used to the work, and as there are not so many urgent subjects, it is agreed that the meeting be held four times a year, that is, once three months. The actual text of the Covenant has set it down that the Council be opened once a year. Actually it is held four times a year.

At first they met in the cities of the Council members' countries, as, for example, the first meeting was held in Paris, the second in London, the fifth was held in Rome, the eighth in Spain. It was held in the countries from which the members were sent. But now it is held exclusively in Geneva. It is held in other places only in some exceptional cases. The reasons why it must be in Geneva are twofold, though this, too, is not set down anywhere in the Covenant. Firstly, if the meeting is held in some country, it will inevitably be held in that country's capital. It will be Paris if in France. A countryside town will not be chosen. London if it is in Britain, and Milan or Rome if it is in Italy. In such places, the members will have an audience of the King, or will be invited by the Prime Minister. They will meet them and also the newspaper-men of the country. Such things are unavoidable. The members will become susceptible to the influence or atmosphere of the country, and, without knowing it, they will find themselves agreeing to any proposal made by that country. Therefore, the best place is in a neutral country, where people are free from all such influences. Geneva is an ideal place. There can't be no political influence. The second is a financial reason. It costs much if the Council is held in other places. But here in Geneva are secretaries, interpreters, and typists all ready for work, and that will cut the expenses considerably.

As for the meeting room, the largest room in the Secretariat is offered for it. Inside the room is a long and narrow table. There are ten Council members. They elect the chairman from among them, and the chairman's term of office is until next Council meeting, that is, three months in normal cases. The chairman takes the central seat, of course. (Here, Nitobe illustrated on the blackboard.) Beside the chairman sits the Secretary-General, and then France and Spain etc. on this side. On the other side, British and Japanese delegates, and Belgium etc. You may think it strange that the Secretary-General should sit beside the chairman. Nevertheless, he assumes a haughty attitude there. Thus it will appear that the Secretariat's function is not limited to clerical works. Its head thus sits between the chairman and the British delegate in the Council meeting. Here, if anyone speaks in English, it is immediately translated in France. If some other person speaks in French next, it, too, is translated into English immediately. Very competent people do it. They do it very quickly. Depending on the subjects, each representative may need the help of his own secretaries and advisers to deal with the problems in question. The Japanese delegate is usually accompanied by three secretaries or councillors. The British delegate and other delegates, too, never come by themselves but are always accompanied by two or three, and in some cases five or six depending upon the subjects. Those assistants cannot sit at the table. They sit behind their own delegate. The whole room being full of such people, it is sometimes difficult to distinguish delegates from non-delegates. Delegates are generally older people, and young persons are secretaries. Some of them are very handsome, but that doesn't have any effect here, no matter how effective in some other places. The Secretariat people such as directors of various sections and secretaries arrange themselves behind the

Council members, and are ready to answer any questions which might be put during the proceeding, as, if it is the subject of public hygiene, the director of the relevant section and other specialists in that line will stand up and explain the matter in question.

The table faces the seats for the public, and anybody can hear the discussion. The meeting is perfectly open. Diplomatic negotiations made in secret will arouse suspicion. Therefore, every discussion should be open.

The date of the Council meeting is not fixed, but generally starts on Monday. This is not a rule but a custom (which enables people to travel to Geneva on the preceding Sundays and prepare for the meeting). The meeting lasts for a week at the longest; in most cases it is over in five days. Why is it, you may wonder, that such an important international discussion can be dealt with only in five or six days and only four times a year?

The reason is this. If some topic is taken up — let us be specific and say, the problem of opium, and the Assembly agrees to a large resolution that, opium being a harmful thing, its traffic should be banned; that it should be prohibited, then this resolution is committed to the Council. The Council discusses it. Granting it desirable to prohibit opium, the Council has no power to set down an international law, nor does it have a right to demand that each country should incorporate its prohibition in its penal code. Therefore, the Council reaches an agreement that the whole problem should be submitted to a thorough scrutiny and examination. Is it so harmful a thing, all over the world? Is it right to prohibit it totally when it is sometimes used as medicine? These questions should be assessed. The Council also discusses how to assess these details. Thus, taking it for granted that opium should be somehow restrained, the Council proposes to study the problem further, and ends up in asking the Secretariat to make a proposal on how to examine this problem, and to prepare it by next Council meeting.

Therefore, we can say that the function of the Secretariat is an extension or continuation of the Assembly's and the Council's work. The Secretariat has the sections of public hygiene and of opium traffic. On the Council's request to make a further inquiry, they set about it, as, for example, the section of public hygiene after discussing who is the best authority in the world, sends a telegram to that person and consults him. People know who is to take charge of the opium problem at the next Council meeting. If it is a Swedish delegate that is to report to the Council, the Secretariat people will visit him at his place to give him information they have collected, or they will ask him to arrive one day before the meeting. Then the Director of the section shows him documents they prepared by consulting the specialist, with their opinions that this far might be done by the League but that this much might not be dealt with. Since that person is not a specialist and rather new to the problem, he agrees to it. When his turn comes to report in the Council meeting, he reads the Director's manuscript, and the Council, too, with no specialists among them, agrees to it. The Director sits beside that reporter all the time, ready to whisper to his ear in case some question is put to him. I hesitate to say because the newspapers may report it in a misleading way, but all the minute works are done by the Secretariat. As for the larger subjects, each country has its own policy and can't compromise. But other minor subjects having little to do with politics are dealt with almost entirely according to the Secretariat's plans. That is, the Secretariat has many small things to do. You may guess how busy it is from the mere fact that I had no time to come back during the first five years. Sometimes when an urgent matter comes to us, we must work day and night to inquire into the matter and prepare our proposals. We must also answer to many questions put to our report. If, for example, the establishment of the International University is proposed, many questions come to us, such as what kind of institute it might be, from where the professors are to be recruited, and so forth. We give a detailed explanation — more detailed than is written down in our documents. Now, after the explanation made by the reporter, the Council goes to voting. In this way many important problems are dealt with one after another very quickly. The reports submitted to the Council are some five pages at the longest, some of them half a page. The Council responds to each of them by Yes or No.

It is agreed that the Council's resolution should be unanimous. This is very important from the legal point of view. It is sometimes alleged that the League is under the sway of the great powers. But the fact is that, since the Council's resolution requires unanimity, any small country can raise an objection and stop it. Contrary to the general supposition, some people even say *sotto voce* that smaller countries are holding sway over the League. The two arguments put together, we must conclude that neither holds dominance. Some people say that the League is Britain's agency. British people, on the other hand, complain that French influence is too strong. The fact lies somewhere in the middle.

Thus I explained how the Council carries the resolutions of the Assembly one step further and commit them to the hand of the Secretariat to make them more practical. The Council requests the Secretariat to prepare plans and proposals to such and such an effect. The rest remains in the responsibility of the Secretary-General, and about this I will explain later.

Here I must mention one thing which is very important but remains unsettled as yet, that is, the relationship between the Assembly and the Council. You may think that there must exist some customary or broad understanding, but, as a matter of fact, no law has set down their respective powers. Nor can we resort to custom when the organization is as young as five years old. This is an unsettled problem. Some people explain it by analogy, saying that the Assembly corresponds to the Parliament and the Council to the Cabinet. Indeed, some people tried to define the two institutions on the basis of that analogy. And yet this problem is as old as the League itself. I well remember Lord Balfour, before the start of the Assembly, worrying much, as unusual in him, about this problem of the Assembly-Council relationship. He expressed an apprehension that these two bodies may collide with each other some day. If such a conflict arises, it is as if we had a revolution at the start. However, said Lord Balfour, this should not be settled theoretically. We must remember that this is an organization which has no precedent in the world. Rather than settled beforehand by analogy and parallels, this problem should be left unsettled and open, to be committed to our common sense from case to case in actual contexts. This was his argument, which I felt typically British. The situation now is not much different. The relative powers of both are left undefined. Broadly speaking, however, we can say that the Council corresponds to the Cabinet and the Assembly to the Parliament. Though the Assembly can take up and discuss important policies, it must concede the execution of them to the Council. In this respect the Council may be regarded as occupying the supreme position. Therefore, those countries which have seats in the Council, especially those countries which have permanent seats, bear a heavy responsibility. We are lucky to have such a person as Mr. Ishii as our delegate, an old stager comparable to that snake which lived in the seas a thousand years, in the mountains another thousand years and finally became a dragon. But the present-day Japan is not a good soil to produce such international-minded people. The Council seat is very important as I said just now. Japan is in need of producing many such people. That is why I came here to talk to you, yesterday and today.

## Third Lecture

As there may be some here who didn't attend my yesterday's and the day before yesterday's lectures, let me repeat my words that my talk is not concerned with the legal and theoretical aspect of the League of Nations nor its fundamental principles, but merely with its practical aspect how it operates in its actual context. In order to explain its operation, my talk is focused mainly on its organs. One might include as the organs of the League the permanent International Court of Justice and International Labour Office. However, historically speaking, the International Labour Office, for example, preceded the League of Nations. Though advocated in the same Covenant, it was established some three months earlier than the League. However closely related, they are actually based on different foundations. When I speak of the League's organs, I mean other organs which properly belong to the League in a narrower sense, and their functions and operations are my subject. The first of its organs is the Assembly about which I talked the day before yesterday, the second the Council my yesterday's topic, and today's talk is the Secretariat and various committees associated with it. I talked about the Commissions of the Assembly the day before yesterday, but what I mean by committees here are not those Commissions but the Advisory Committees set up to help the Council. There are many of them, some twenty committees, and I am going to refer to them, too, in my explanation of the Secretariat.

And here is an important fact. It is needless to say that the resolutions of the Assembly are authoritative, but the actual execution of them must be committed to the Council. And the Council, too, doesn't have power to enforce the resolutions on each country. The resolutions are written down in Agreements and become duty for those countries which ratified them. But for those countries which have not ratified them, the power of resolutions is that of moral authority at most. The resolutions are just as if each country came to the Assembly and agreed that for such and such problems such and such measures would be desirable. Only that. That is to say, they can't be put into practice until each country ratifies them and makes laws of its own. The resolutions of the League as such have no compulsory power. Therefore, one can't accuse the League of being a super-state, for it has no such power nor authority.

Thus, after a resolution is passed by the Assembly and by the Council, the rest of the work — for example, notify the resolution to each country, make inquiries such as "Is your country going to make your own law to put into practice that resolution to which you agreed in the Assembly?" "To what extent are you going to carry it out, or have you already set about it?" or "We are investigating into this problem and would like to know what the state of affairs is like in your country," and gather as much information as possible — all this becomes the work of the Secretariat — called "Secretariat" both in English and in French.

As I told you before, the Secretariat's function is the continuation of the work started by the Assembly and the Council. Many attempts were made in the past to reach an international agreement, but most of them failed; after an agreement reached, people very often forgot it and didn't carry it out. The cause was the lack of any chance or organization to urge each country to make it into practice. The Secretariat was established to make up for that flaw or deficiency for the first time in the world history, though, strictly speaking, this is not true. In fact, there are several international organizations such as the Universal Postal Union and others which have their secretariats.

And I am rather well acquainted with these matters because my chief role in the Secretariat is in the International Bureaux Section whose function is to correspond with the secretariats of other international meetings and organizations. As such I am always in touch with them, inquiring what became of their officials or what are their main occupations now. Let me add in this connection, since this may be a topic of some interest to Japanese people, that I took responsibility for publishing *Handbook of International Organizations*. The third edition of this is to be issued next year.

Thus there had already existed several lasting secretariats of international organizations at the time of the League's establishment. But they are all small secretariats with thirty or forty officials working for their respective narrow scopes of activity. Unlike most of these, the Secretariat of the League can be properly said to be the first trial to cope with larger purposes — including not only politics and economy but also laws, social problems and education — in contact with the governments of various countries, and to draw as many countries as possible into its activity.

Its origin was the Peace Conference at Versailles. That the League should have its Secretariat is set down in the Covenant. The Covenant has also prescribed that the first Secretary-General should be such and such a person. Other officials were to be appointed by the Secretary-General. But he was not entitled to appoint them entirely on his own. The appointment of the officials required the Council's agreement. Even after the agreement, their positions are provisional within first three or six months. Only after those months does their appointment become valid and formal, not from the first. It was just like that when I was appointed. And the person who was appointed Secretary-General — it is a post of a considerable importance and people there are worrying what will become of the Secretariat when this person ever resigned — the person now in this post is Sir Eric Drummond from Britain. He was elected Secretary-General because President Wilson set his eye on this person during the Peace Conference and insisted that when the Secretariat has been established this is the man devoutly to be wished for its head. It was not because Britain insisted upon its head being a British. Thus the Secretary-General was elected in the Conference, but to establish the Secretariat was beyond one man's power however able he is. So, the Organization Committee was established in order to start the Secretariat.

If my memory is correct, Count Chinda from Japan was its member. Lord Robert Cecil was the member from Britain. They met and discussed how to establish the Secretariat, what people they should recruit, and where it should be located.

As for the location, after much discussion, Brussels and Geneva came off the two alternatives. And then, at Wilson's strong insistence, Geneva was chosen.

As for the structure of the Secretariat, it is divided into more than ten Sections, as I said before, and certain committees in some Sections are at the same time working as standing committees for the Council I talked about yesterday. Also it was thought desirable to distribute equally important posts to England, France, Italy and Japan. Since the Secretary-General was elected from Britain, the newly-created posts of Under-Secretaries-General were for balance's sake assigned to France, Italy and Japan. Their role is that when the Secretary-General is absent one of the Under-Secretaries-General should take his place as Deputy-Sec'ry-Gen. The Secretariat began its work on the tenth of January 1920, and the hour was fifteen past four in the afternoon. At the time that the Peace Treaty came into effect, America's attitude was not certain as to its membership. Since there was still some prospect of its becoming a member state, a certain American Raymond Fosdick had been appointed Under-Secretary-General, making four Under-Secretaries-General in all.

Thus there are at present three Under-Secretaries-General next to the Secretary-General. And next to the Under-Secretaries-General are Directors, each responsible for a Section, which some people call "Department." It is always called "Section" by the Secretariat people, either in English or French pronunciation. Omitting other sections of a different nature which can't properly be called Sections, the best way, in my opinion, is to say there are twelve Sections in all. In this matter as in others, there are no clear-cut rules or descriptions. The same is true with office regulations; we don't have any. They say this is the British method. When I was appointed to my post, they told me that my role is such and such. Upon my inquiry in what manner I should carry it out, they answered, "Do it as you like." We started almost without any rules. At the beginning, the payment of travelling allowances was very generous. "I have some business in Paris." "Do you? Then, please go there." "How much will you pay me for it?" "Any amount you wish to be paid — all for the trains, hotels, taxies and other things." But that was at the beginning. Now there are minute rules, and the situation there is not so different from here in Japan.

Now I will describe each Section one by one. First, the Political Section. Of course, this is an important section, but, fortunately, its work is not much. If it were busy, the future of Europe would be dangerous. It is concerned with politics, that is, political conflicts among nations. The Director is Mantoux a French. This is a very scholarly person, and actually was once a university professor. He is well read in economics and the author of *The Industrial Revolution*. This section has a lot of people — members as they are called. There are some seven or eight members, including a British and an Italian. They are keeping guard all the time, as if from a watchtower, lest some strife should be brewing up somewhere. They are always doing such things as reading newspapers or sending telegrams, for in case some disquieting events are happening among European nations, third-party countries, according to an article in the Agreement, can appeal to the Council and demand that the Council meeting should be held in order to mediate between those countries and prevent a possible war. It would be an embarrassment if the Secretariat were found blind to those happenings when such an appeal came to the Council. Therefore, they are keeping a lookout, not anxiously for a war, but hoping there will be none. Fortunately, very little is happening at present, but still they are busily looking out, taking up magazines, reading newspapers, and corresponding with responsible persons of various countries in order to get information about each country. They say they need members who are acquainted with the affairs in the East, too, but, to tell the truth, they cannot yet afford to pay any attention to the East. How to reorganize the Europe after the great fire is enough to occupy their mind. And, as a result, the affairs of the East are left out at present, but as the League widens its scope, those affairs, too, will begin to come into their concerns.

The second is the Economic and Financial Section, which deals with economic and financial affairs, as obvious from its name. This is a large section. As I told you yesterday, future wars, if any, will be caused mainly by economic conflicts. In order to attain economic cooperation, a constant investigation into economic problems is essential. Some fifty or even hundred members from the Secretariat are working for this section. To study the world economy is a painstaking labour. Here I should mention something about what may be called the League's Technical Organizations. I mean, each Section of the Secretariat is working at the same time virtually as an advisory body for the Assembly or the Council, and for each country's delegates it serves as a counsellor in technical matters. The Economic and Financial Section, for instance, is also a body or committee of specialists, meeting many times in some cases, from year to year, to investigate economic problems. It gives advices and suggestions to the Council as their counsellor. Thus we can say that the League has in it an advisory group of specialists. At present the Director of this most important Section is a British, Sir James A. Salter. He is a true gentleman — such a type as will immediately be recognized as a British — very reticent and very clear-headed. While he was working as a government official in the Exchequer, his name was many times mentioned in newspapers in a praiseful tone as the mirror of the officials not merely of the Exchequer but of the whole government. People talked of him as the right person for the Secretariat. They said his presence would enhance the prestige of the League itself. He is the author of *Allied Shipping Control*, a book which was written on his own experience and published recently.

The third is the Health Section. Here, too, people are looking out as from the watch-tower over the world's sanitary condition. If they detect a specific epidemic raging in some country, they will ring an alarm bell to the neighbouring countries. Its branch office for the East is to start in Singapore next year. Since epidemics are so common in Indo-China, the Health Section has a special lookout for that region, and it is already agreed that Japan will send officials to that branch from their department of public health. Also in Russia, devastated so much by recent Revolution with many sanitary facilities destroyed, epidemics such as cholera, typhus and many other diseases have spread to the whole country. A hygienic line was once drawn along the Western border of Russia to prevent the contagion into Europe. That work was done by this section. The Director is L. Rajchman, well-known for his study of bacteria. He is a Jew, as will be obvious to any eye at first sight, and very clear-headed, competent and as keen as razors in business management. His achievement is great. So talented a person, it is said of him that he will become a Prime Minister of Poland some future day. However, he is a scholar as has ever been from the first. I keep friendly terms with him. He is a man of character, too, and full of interesting topics. This section has a great number of people, with many Americans among them. The reason is that this section deals with many problems, such as the hygienic condition of the Near Eastern countries, the standardization of a blood test, the variety of epidemic diseases all over the world and how to prevent them. The work of this section is so well appreciated that the Rockefeller Foundation makes a donation of several hundred thousand every year to this section. The work is very good, they say, covering the whole world's hygienic condition, and since they have no equivalent research institution in their own country, they will give this section such and such an amount of fund to enable it to carry on a research on such and such a problem. This is the purport of their donation. As the scope of this section's work widens, the number of officials is increasing. Several Japanese are among them. Apart from this section, there is a body called the Health Committee, which meets several times a year and discusses all the physiological subjects such as hygiene, bacteria, opium and others.

The fourth is the Section of Social Questions. It doesn't deal with labour problems. That is the work of the International Labour Organization. The subjects here are opium, traffic in women and children, relief work for Armenians under Turkish persecution, and suchlike humanitarian problems. The protection of children, too, is its work. The Director is a British lady, Dame Rachel Crowdy, still very young, some thirty-three years old, rather delicate in health, but, during the Great War, she worked in the battlefield as chief nurse, superintending four thousand girls. After the war she was given a title of Dame which corresponds to men's Sir. There are many ladies working as officials in this section. Annexed to the section are various committees consisting of specialist members. Most important among them is the Opium Committee, as probably well known to you, too, for such zoologists as Miyajima and Kaku and other people, and also Yotaro Sugimura from the Foreign Ministry attended the committee meeting recently. To that meeting came an American Congressman, Porter, accompanied by four or five people. That is to say, America is member to this committee. Another is the Advisory Committee on Traffic in Women. The members are those people who are most engaged in it — not that they are trafficking women, but that they are the people who made best efforts to stop such traffic. The most eminent among them is the world-famous Miss Baker, nearly eighty years old. She has been engaged wholly in this campaign since the age of eighteen. She is regarded as the highest authority in this matter and a very energetic lady. Fifteen or sixteen of such people from various countries constitute this committee. Among other committees is one for the protection of children. All these committees help the work of the Section.

The fifth is the Mandates Section. Mandates are those parts of Africa and Asia which were once Germany's and Turk's territories and entrusted after the war to the Allied powers for them to govern. For example, Japan takes charge of the Caroline Islands and Marshall Islands and is expected to govern them in such a way as to promote their own cultures, not as its colonies. The proprietary rights of the mandates come under the League, and those countries which govern them are doing it on commission. They are to be returned to the League when a certain development has been achieved. The governing countries must be true to this purpose, and they have responsibility to report to the League from time to time concerning the population, education and hygienic condition of the mandates. If, for example, syphilis is prevalent in some mandate, a question may be raised as to whether or not Japan is responsible for it. Then this section sets about an investigation into whether or not the disease had already been there, coming from Europe, before Japanese people came in. Such investigation is the work of this section. Related to this section is the Mandates Commission. It is an important committee with many brilliant specialists from various countries as its members. Among its members, for example, is a former governor of some African colony. They meet and discuss the merits and demerits of each other country's colonial policy. It is an influential committee, anyway. While this committee pursues its work, the Mandates Section deals with every business matter concerning mandates. The Director is W. E. Rappard, a university professor of Switzerland. This section is always threatened by heated debates and quarrels, and the director's important work is to pacify the members lest the debates should develop into violent ones. Mr. Rappard was elected director of this section because of his affable character.

The sixth is the Section of Administrative Commissions and Minorities Questions. Let us begin with the Administrative Commissions part. The League has certain lands under its direct control or jurisdiction. Perhaps, legally speaking, the lands cannot properly be called territories, but in effect the lands are as good as territories. The

Saar Basin is one such case, as you may already know. The land is situated on the borders between France and Germany. It was Germany's territory before the War. The land is rich in mines, and we may compare it to Japan's Kyushu. The Peace Treaty gave France the right to mine coal there. The reason is that the German army destroyed the mines in Northern France. In compensation for that, it has been agreed that France can mine in the Saar Basin for fifteen years. But the landownership for that area was retained by Germany. It would be difficult for France to mine in other country's land. Thus it has been agreed that the land should be under the control of the League. The Saar Governing Commission was established for that purpose and it is endowed with the power and rights of a landowner. It is in this sense that I said the League has its own territories. The League is to retain the Saar Basin for ten more years. When the fifteen years has expired, the inhabitants of the land, according to the Treaty, are to decide by their popular vote on one of the three choices: to have part or all of it merged into France, or to have it returned to Germany, or to maintain the *status quo*. Another case is Danzig. Poland was quite eager to possess it, for the town is essential for Poland to have an access to the seas. As a result, it was agreed at the time of the Treaty that Danzig should remain a free city and be controlled and protected by the League. Thus the governor of Danzig, called High Commissioner at Danzig, is in office there appointed by the League. To administer these affairs falls into the function of this Administrative Section, and it entails many office works.

Closely related to this is the problem of the minorities. Some independent countries, such as Poland, Romania, and Serbia, while they have no need of the League's government, have racial minorities living within their territories. Such are the Jewish people in Poland and the German people in the same country. The German people in Poland are exposed to a threat of persecution by the Polish in revenge for the German persecution during the wartime. Also there is a general tendency in that country to discriminate Jewish people. To protect the rights of those minority people is the League's obligation and mission. Minority people are minorities mainly in terms of race. But other kinds of minorities exist in the world, such as religious minorities. In a Catholic country, for example, Protestants may be persecuted as a religious minority. Minorities are very often deprived of their freedom of religion. To protect their religious rights falls into the League's work. Another kind is linguistic, minorities in terms of languages. For example, if in Poland — this I mention as a supposition, not as an actual fact — some people are to be suppressed because of their language — for example, if the German people living in that country who use German as their everyday language may propose to teach German in their village and their proposal is not permitted — then the League will interfere and protect the German minority from the country's suppression. This is the case of linguistic minorities. This happens very frequently, and a special committee has been instituted to deal with this kind of troubles. Complaints of various kinds, some very cruel and dreadful, reach this committee. The Director is a Norwegian, Mr. Colban. All the members of this section should be strictly neutral. That is why a person from Norway, reputedly the most neutral country, was appointed to its head. He was a consul general in some South American country for a long time, and was once talked of as possibly coming to Japan as a consul.

Next is the Legal Section. We may compare it to our Cabinet's Legislative Bureau. It deals with everything connected with law. This section has many members, a lot of jurists and bachelors of laws, even doctors of laws among them. They are engaged in debating and theorizing all day early and late.

Next is the Financial Administrative Section. Their work has nothing to do with the world economy. It is the accounts section of the League. The League's activities are supported by the contributions by members-states. Japan's contribution is some eight hundred thousand yen per year. Collecting those contributions, paying salaries to the Secretariat officials, and reckoning travelling expenses — all these works fall into this section. A very important section it is. The section has two or three committees of its own, somewhat corresponding to a board of auditors and superintendents, and some two or three committees for budgeting.

The ninth is the Transit Section. The Director is a French, Haas. He is a person who did a major service to Japan, too, and was medalled for that by Japan. Sailing on international rivers, such as some parts of the Danube and the Rhine, traffic on international roads, scheduling the trains running from one country to another, and all other concerns related to transit are dealt with in this section. The section has a committee of a considerable influence which meets every year to discuss these matters.

The tenth is the International Bureaux Section, and it is this section that I am put in charge of. Various office works related to each country's international affairs and the Postal Union fall into this section. But I am rather busier with other matters, for problems which do not properly belong in any of other sections, a rubbish heap as it were, all come to me. The reason why they come to me is this: the Secretary-General and all the other Under-Secretaries-General are very busy communicating with their own countries, going and coming back frequently between Geneva and their countries, Geneva and London or Geneva and Paris. On the other hand, my case is contrary. I came back this time for the first time after five years' absence from Japan. Japan is too distant from Geneva for me to go and return so frequently. The result is that I am the most easily found out person within the Secretariat. And it very often happens that the Secretariat is consulted about some problems for which it has no relevant section, educational problems, for example. People don't know where to pass on the documents of those questions and proposals sent to them. Thus those papers will come to me. This is why I am so busily occupied there.

There is one more, very important section and that is the Disarmament Section. The Director is a Spanish, Madariaga, a very clever person. A man of literary taste, he set up a debating circle and I was once elected chairman of it. He very often joins this circle and displays his loquacity. Annexed to this section is a very important committee with eminent persons — we should say great masters in their professions — as its members, that is, Robert Cecil from Britain, Attolico from Italy, with a glorious career as Foreign Minister and Finance Minister for a long time in the Italian government, and that famous scholar Lange from Norway. Some forty of influential people make up this committee and constantly carry on negotiations with countries of the world. Committees like this have power to express their opinions to the Council.

Thus far I have described various institutions working for the League, that is, the Secretariat, its various sections and the technical organizations annexed or related to each section. The other day I talked with the Minister of Education and heard that the number of the people sent by Japan to the League, including those attending various committees, amounts to eighty. Even if problems closer to Japanese interests are not being dealt with there, Japan, as one of the five great powers of the world, has an obligation to join in and cooperate with this world-wide organization.

I feel, to my regret, that Japanese people are a little deficient in the so-called international mind. I have talked to you about the League because I believe that it is now an urgent necessity for Japan to nurture the international mind, the understanding of international affairs. Japan experienced a sudden internationalization without being fully prepared for it. Therefore, we must make a great effort to cast off our past segregation or seclusion without delay. You may wish to have a good wife and a good salary. Such are indeed important matters for your life. But I hope you will set your eyes also to a loftier aim and make efforts to enlighten yourselves. It is solely for this wish that I talked here to you. Finally, I thank you for your patient attention.

## (3) The League of Nations Movement in Japan

*A Report on the trip to Japan: submitted to the Geneva office, April 9th 1925. The Collected Works of Inazo Nitobe, vol. 23: 121-133.*

A theoretical idea of the League of Nations and the interest in its ideal is surprisingly wide-spread in Japan. It is evidenced by the avidity with which lectures on the League are attended and in the space allotted to it in newspapers, and — may I in all humility add? — in the welcome accorded to me as one connected with it.

Unlike other movements which, when they have strong advocates, are sure to invite hostility, the cause of the League has been but little criticised in Japan. The Minister of Foreign Affairs told me that neither he — nor his predecessor — has ever had any difficulty in obtaining in Parliament what he asked for the expenses of the League. On the other hand, the fact that the League has no enemies has been taken as an argument that it has no zealots; and the fact that the budget is so easily voted, as a proof of indifference or at least of lukewarmness.

These cynical views contain a grain of truth, but only a grain. The zeal for the League is largely confined to the educated youth, and this is a hopeful pledge for its future. The more so, as this zeal is not a blind sentiment on their part, but is combined with earnest study. The older generation as represented in the higher governmental service, the parliament, the larger business circles and the professions, is lacking in enthusiasm except in a few instances. This exception includes the leading spirits of the League of Nations Union. They all admit that the League is a good thing and that Japan must stick to it as other great nations are in it. As to its costliness — let it be remembered that, besides the allocation, the Japanese Government spends nearly 1,000,000 yen yearly in salaries, travelling expenses, telegrams, etc. Parliament does not begrudge this large sum on the ground that, having once committed itself, it must pay. Utilitarian motives play no part in the mute readiness to bear the cost. A sense of honour is the sole reason for this.

It is not inconsistent, however, with the general approval of the League idea that there seems to be lurking some doubts as to its practical utility for Japan. Everybody has heard of the League. He knows it exists. All the papers had long telegraphic communications about the debate on the Protocol and later on the Opium question; but the distance between Japan and Geneva deadened the sound of the disputants' voices. The League looked so far off, and its work touched the country so lightly. The nearest contact between Geneva and Tokyo took place when Dr. Norman White went on his mission, but his work was of a special and circumscribed nature. Many studied the League, but few knew it. In talking with the representatives of all classes of the profession — officials, members of Privy Council, of Parliament, professors and business men, I find that the reasons for their doubts or for their comparative lack of enthusiasm (I can scarcely call it objection) may be reduced to the following points:

1. Is not the League a super-State — "a house on a roof", as we say? Does it not intrude into the sovereign rights of an independent State?
2. Can war really be avoided, when the history of every nation has shown it to be so frequent and apparently so inevitable?
3. Can man ever be so tamed as to outlive his instinct of pugnacity?
4. For the maintenance of world peace, is the League radical enough in its conception and democratic enough in its constitution, and universal enough in its composition?
5. Is it true that the League is secretly manned by the Jews, whose ultimate purpose is the disruption of all organised society?
6. Are the nations of the world, including the Members of the League, really inclined to resort to peaceful means, or is not so-called "Peace" a pretence for a veiled preparation for war? What is the meaning of the Singapore Base?
7. Is not the League an instrument of the Great Powers for the prosecution of their own selfish ends?
8. Is it not an organisation convenient and profitable only to Europe? What benefit does it confer upon Asia and upon

Japan in particular?
9. Is the League worth the money our country pays for its support?
10. As long as America stays outside its pale, can the League be of much use to Japan?

These summarise the questions that lurk in many a mind, in a way often too vague for definite expression or for want of proof. Nevertheless they deter people from taking a more hearty stand for the cause of the League. As yet they are mostly doubts casting clouds over and around the League, and making it a hazy institution. Only in a very few minds have these doubts developed into suspicion, and in still fewer do they amount to opposition. May I briefly repeat the statements I made on these subjects?

Regarding the first point, whatever difficulty there may be in the jural explanation of it, it has been empirically proved by the five years history of the League that any fear of danger to a State on this score is perfectly unfounded, especially as all the authorities of the League have time and again declared that the League is not a super-state.

The second and third questions are of such an academic and at the same time a popular nature as can be met with equally academic and popular antitheses.

The issues involved in the fourth question are by no means as acutely discussed as in Europe, largely due to the fact that the principle of democracy (whatever that may mean) is not as strongly established in the Far East. Here and there in the extreme Left we notice the Russian hand working, and its strongly red colour is of course incompatible with the blue of peace. It is so occupied with general propaganda as to afford little time to make assault on the League in particular.

The fifth point can easily be disposed of, since it is entirely without foundation. It is very unexpected that such a rumour should even find entrance into Japan, where anti-Semitism is scarcely known and absolutely uncalled for; but it is said that a small military clique makes use of this imported movement simply because it must imagine some object of attack, even if it be only a windmill, and the League is dragged in incidentally as if it were a part of the sails!

The sixth question is assuredly the hardest to answer satisfactorily. The utmost that could be said on this point is that, as the League is neither an absolutely pacifist nor a universal nor a compulsory organisation, each member is left free to prepare itself for an emergency. I ventured a suggestion that this British enterprise — the Singapore Base may be a political manoeuvre on the part of the Conservative Government to pander to the demands of the Pacific dominions. In the meantime it is up to Japan herself to do everything in her power to allay inordinate, albeit ungrounded fears, and nowhere can she do this better than in the halls of the League.

Regarding the seventh question, it is idle to deny that the Great Powers exercise a dominant influence, or else they would not be Great Powers. If domination means menace, or the exercise of power in any objectionable sense, is there any proof that they do so through the instrumentality of the League? If Great Powers are self-seeking, have they become more so since the establishment of the League?

The eighth and ninth points, respecting the direct benefit conferred on Japan by the League, touch a rather sensitive spot. It certainly satisfies morally disposed individuals to feel that by being in the League the country is fulfilling its promise, and that in so doing lies its reward. But this is too elevated a view to be shared by the man in the street. He must be told that his country gets back an adequate return for its sacrifices in some shape or other. My contention is that such a return is in the position occupied by Japan in the Council as a permanent member. The ordinary man must be told that this position is not only highly honourable, but very valuable in ordinary times and priceless in extraordinary times. As far as the yearly allocation is concerned, it must be considered as an insurance policy against War, and as such it must not be expected to yield immediate profit. Moreover, Japan will find in a few years that the wisest course for her to pursue in her diplomacy is to bring it in line with the world's public opinion as mirrored in the League. Such a course, far from being a passive obedience to a super-national body, as some ultra-nationalists fear, can rightly be viewed as an active utilisation of the League on the part of Japan.

The tenth point, viz. America's attitude to the League, is of vital interest to Japan. This was the first question put me by the Prince Regent when I lectured before him. I could only express the hope that the United States may come in, and the belief that she will. I could however point out some indications in the hopeful direction —

the formation of the Non-Partisan Association; her desire to join the International Court of Justice; her participation in different committees of the League; the serious study made of the League by a large number of her citizens, etc. Whether America is in or out of the League, Japan's membership must not be affected by her. Japan is in, and in she must stay. If she leaves, that will not improve her relations with America. On the contrary, it is more likely they will worsen. It seems the noblest, and in the long run the wisest thing for Japan to do is so to conduct herself within the League as to prove herself above suspicion, and thus even pave the way for America's entry.

It is far from my purpose to go into the details of the various questions which are troubling the public mind whenever the League is mentioned. Questions like these are constantly tackled by the League of Nations Union in its various organs. As yet this body has a membership of only 2,300, consisting mainly of individuals from the middle and upper classes of society and hence sometimes criticised as being too aristocratic. It counts among its directors and councillors some of our best public men — statesmen, lawyers and others. It publishes a monthly magazine, gives frequent lectures and round table talks by prominent people, holds summer and winter schools, issues pamphlets, etc. There are at present, in different parts and institutions of the country, nineteen branches. Of these, ten were inaugurated while I was in the country.

Thanks to the activity of this body, information about the League has spread far and wide among the intelligent classes. As was hinted in the early part of this report, its work encountered but little opposition. However, one could not help feeling the presence of two obstacles in its way; — these are the glum silent look of disavowal on the part of two great forces, namely the military and educational. By the former, because of the general unpopularity of the military organisations at present, no open or direct opposition is made. As to the latter, the educational system being so thoroughly grounded in the theory of the absolute sovereignty of the State and in the exalted position allotted to the Throne, the educational authorities are exceedingly jealous of any doctrine or opinion that may possibly infringe upon their sacred dogmas. It will seem inconsistent to state in the same breath that all school books (text books being under strict State control) contain some account — be it historical, geographical or ethical — of the League of Nations. This inconsistency does not disquiet the pedagogical conscience as long as the League is represented as an ideal institution, which the government has joined of its own accord for the maintenance of the peace and welfare of the whole world. Indeed, presented in this way, the consideration of any direct benefit to be derived from membership dwindles into a mean dimension. The teachers would be proud to explain what an important role their country is playing in the quasi-philanthropic "Parliament of man". What the official mind is afraid of is that the interest and dignity of the nation may be compromised by affiliation with a super-national organisation. "The World" versus "The Country" — here lies the ticklish point, and the authorities are wary of people who habitually or professionally uphold the claims of "the world" as possibly antagonising the State. For this reason the League of Nations Union could not at first obtain access to some of the most influential educational institutions, and hence it has been a matter of deep gratification, if only from the point of view of propaganda, that they have recently opened their doors to the idea of the League. The ultimate success of the League depends anywhere on the participation of youth in its ideals and work, but nowhere more emphatically so than in Japan.

In closing this report, allow me to jot down a few personal notes. I left Marseilles on 2nd November 1924, arrived in Kobe on December 8th and in Tokyo the following day. I left Kobe for the return trip on February 15th. I had thus altogether 78 days or 11 weeks in the country. Out of these 11 weeks, 6 were to be considered to be *en mission*. Of the 78 days, 46 were taken up by the lecturing tour and 25 by interviews which I gave to the Press or which were given me by people of importance. The rest — only a week — I had left for my own personal affairs. Thus nearly the whole of my sojourn was taken up with League propaganda. As this was entirely in accordance with my intention when I left Geneva, I was only thankful that the way opened so readily for my task. Altogether, during the trip I spoke 85 times and the audiences totaled, at the lowest estimate, more than 50,000. In the annex I have set down further details about my lectures. It is a trying custom in Japan that a lecture is expected to last at least an hour and usually 1 ½ to 2, and in the countryside as many as 2–3 hours. I have marked the ten branches of the League of Nations Union at whose inauguration I had the pleasure of being present.

In making addresses, I was particularly careful (1) to clear the doubts to which reference was made in the early part of the present report; (2) to describe the construction and the practical working of the different organs of the League; (3) to narrate what it has already accomplished; (4) to stress the general spirit of world cooperation — what may be called the international mind, and (5) to make clear Japan's position and responsibility in the League. I emphasised these points first because even those who studied the League were not *au courant* with the routine process of its activity, and secondly because very soon after my arrival I found that nothing impressed my countrymen more convincingly of the reality of the League than a realistic description of its actual working. The points 4 and 5 were chiefly intended for the edification of the younger generation. I attach a syllabus of my lecture given before the Prince Regent. For other audiences I followed much the same plan, of course changing details according to the character of the people I was addressing. The most important people I had to speak to were the Prince Regent, a company of royal personages, the members of the Privy Council, a group of members of the Lower House, a large gathering of representative bankers and of industrials. I was told that when it was made known in the newspapers that I was expected to return home, some 150 requests for lectures reached the Foreign Office, the League of Nations Union, and my house. I could not comply with all of them on account of my short sojourn. As the lectures were repeatedly rather elaborately reported in the Press, sometimes in a series of half a dozen articles, they found a wide publicity.

I regret to say that I was forced to suspect that the so-called League news from Geneva is freely tampered with in Japan — sometimes viciously twisted or even fabricated. During my short stay I came across at least two instances of this distortion. One, a rumour that the League is sending a mission to Japan to study whether the geisha is entitled to the status of an artiste or to be treated as an object of "traffic in women and children"; the other, about an ugly split in the League and national rivalries within the Secretariat to such an extent as to demoralise and disorganise it entirely.

Whether such misleading statements are the usual stuff on which our public is fed, I did not ascertain. Anyhow, better communication is desirable. The great advantage I enjoyed in setting to right some gross misconceptions about the League, was my residence in Geneva, for which reason I could speak with some show of authority. I saw more clearly than ever that it is highly important for my compatriot members in the Secretariat to write more frequently from headquarters here to our vernacular press, with a view to correcting misinformation, to arouse new interest and to build up a deeper and sounder public opinion about the League.

Of far greater importance will be the despatch of some League functionaries to the Far East. They will not only demonstrate the reality of the League existence but will carry with them the atmosphere of Geneva. Of still greater importance for propaganda purposes, would it be to hold an international conference of some kind in Tokyo under the direct auspices of the League. Such a meeting might well be of a regional character, say perhaps in connection with the production of or traffic in, opium; or it may be of so universal a nature as to transcend all national boundaries, as, for example, a strictly scientific problem. The increasing knowledge about the League is sure to be accompanied by a popular demand for a more tangible sign of its usefulness to the Far East. It is only reasonable to meet this demand in some way or other.

*II. Reminiscences after Retirement: 1927–1931*

## (1) The Permanence of the League and its Achievement [Trans. by Editor]

*from* East and West in Contact, *published in 1928. Translated from* The Collected Works of Inazo Nitobe, *vol. 1: 332-337.*

The other day I was asked by a friend of mine, "How long will the League last?" I didn't understand his question and asked what he meant. He said, "If we look at the history of the world, we will find that many such attempts were made before but all failed. From this we can deduce that it, too, will die away before long. It is almost a law of history that, while nations may be enduring, international organizations are fated to be short-lived." I replied to him a little jeeringly, "You are a true historian. Historical knowledge is all that you can boast of. I fully admit that you have a great knowledge of the things past, that you are an admirable historian. But you are immature as a man." My general idea of historian is that of a man with his eyes on the back of his head, looking back to the past only, and in some cases not at any moment looking around him. In a word, he is a cripple of some sort. I myself love to read history, but I don't want to be a historian. To revisit the old is rewarding, indeed, but we must also be willing to know the new. That is the only true way of learning a lesson from the past. We have eyes on our front, and that means our most important task is to look forward with hope, faith and creativity. Speaking of the League, it's true that similar attempts in the past all failed. But if we infer from this that this attempt, too, will fail, we are ignoring man's hope, faith and creativity.

I can point out two new facts which didn't exist before, in support of my hope and belief that the League will last long into the future. The first is the changed nature of war in our time. The war of the past was fought by a particular class. Even if people spoke of the whole country going to war, people actually involved in it were not the whole nation. Monarchs and kings, nobility and other ruling class people did it. One warrior's success brings about many people's death, they said. But what did common people do in the ancient civil wars between the two houses of the Genji and the Heike? Probably they were forced to work for some toilsome labours or the supply of provisions. But they were quite indifferent to which side would win. This must have been the same in other countries. Even when a universal conscription system was proposed, people actually engaged in war were soldiers, and ordinary commoners were not involved. In the late war, on the other hand, a blockade method was adopted, and as a result, people of both sides suffered from shortage of food. Probably, soldiers suffered less than those people left behind in the country — older people, women and children who suffered greatly from shortage of food. Also recent invention and use of poison gas made all the people, soldiers and civilians alike, equally potential victims to it (unless some ingenious gas be invented which will pass over people above a certain age, and women and children). A system of universal conscription was realized in its literal sense. The result is that people are now raising a loud cry against war. The cry is universal, from both sexes, and from both upper and lower classes. Japan joined the Allies, but its land was safe. Many people were even profited. Japanese people didn't experience the cruelty of war. The situation was different in Britain and France, to say nothing of Belgium. Exposed all time to the threat of enemy planes' attack, it is said that during all those four years women didn't have security enough to change their clothes when going to bed. Moreover, with husbands and sons taken away as soldiers, women of all classes had to work in munitions and other factories, compelled to it by shortage of labour. Even children, who had no means of expression for the pains of labour or the horror of enemy planes, no less keenly felt the cruelty of war through the shortage of food. Here I cannot help adding some words of apprehensions for our country. Although we had many civil wars at the time of the Meiji Restoration and felt the cruelty of war to a great extent, yet, those days past, it is as if we are now regarding war as a means to get wealth or distinction. I am afraid that very few people in this country know how strong the wish for peace is in the West.

Another factor that makes me hopeful for the League is that the League has established institutions to secure its permanence. Past attempts were nothing more than a promise-making; great personages were met, with even emperors among them in some cases, and made a promise. However, the promise was short-lived, expiring as soon as it was made. No instrument or means existed to reproach them for not keeping their words. No one blamed them for not carrying out their promise, nor asked them, when found not to have done anything yet, whether they had will to carry it out or not, or if they had, from what time they were going to start on it. Now, the present League is different. It has established several institutions which are working all time. It has a contrivance by which to force its members-states to carry out what they agreed to do. These two factors I have described make the League a quite different thing from any similar attempt made in the past. And that is why I say the present League will last long.

Another important question is, "Can the League of Nations stop wars?" Some people argue that the cause of war is inherent in human nature. Instinct to fight, or pugnacity, as psychologists call it, is to be found even in girls. Boys are particularly prone to mischief; they can scarcely suppress their fighting instinct, and pull their mother's hair or bite at her ears when they don't find any good target for their instinct. Human nature being such, there is no stopping wars in human world. This is all too simple-minded an argument, but prevalent in the world. And some people of considerable influence make an objection to the League on this argument. Two or three years ago when I met a certain General of the U.S. army and asked him why his country doesn't join the League, he brought forth that argument. The supporters of the League, too, admits the pugnacity latent in human nature; that fighting instinct is particularly strong in male persons. But just for this reason do they argue that it must be controlled. They do not mean to eradicate this instinct. "You want to fight?" they say, "Then you may do it, but don't do it in a cowardly manner, taking your enemy by surprise. Do it as fair play in a gentlemanly way, and preferably without resorting to weapons." To admit the fighting instinct as innate in human nature is one thing. To let it loose is quite another. It will be too dangerous to let loose our instincts without any control. Here is a child. So young and so tender, yet it is already endowed with an instinct to possess. If it is a flower, it reaches its tiny hand to grapple it. To prevent it from being snatched by others, the child crams it into its mouth. This is an instinct. But human society has means to control it. We have laws and systems of possession and property. Those who go against them will be punished by penal laws. Also we have a moral code which appeals to our conscience. Indeed, we have various means to control instincts. Or, to take up another example, the sexual instinct is probably the strongest among all instincts. Supposing we say, "Oh, this is our instinct. There is no stopping it. Don't interfere. Let it be," what will become of our society? Just because it is an ineffaceable instinct in us, the great sages of old built up the marital system and provided means of controlling it. The ideal of the League is the same. We admit the existence of the fighting instinct, and therefore we try to control it.

So much for the argumentative side of this problem. Now I turn to the question of whether or not the League of Nations ever stopped or prevented wars. The world is very peaceful these three years. But before that, during the five years after the great war, the situation in Europe was very precarious and threatening — to such a degree that no one would be surprised if any war broke out in any place. It was not once or twice that in some countries the people had already been mobilized and an actual war was about to start between the countries. Indeed, three or four real wars broke out. And every time it happened, the League interfered and stopped them.

Let me take up a rather dramatic case. In 1925, a strife broke out between Greece and Bulgaria. A skirmish among the guards of both countries strolling with guns along the borders was its cause. Then Greek soldiers marched as deep as four miles into Bulgaria's territory. The situation was now no longer a mere quarrel of guards. The Bulgarian government sent a telegram hastily to the League. That was an early Monday morning of a fine weather in October. We received the telegram at six o'clock on Monday morning, and by eleven o'clock of the same morning, the Secretariat made a phone call to the French Foreign Minister Boullian who happened to be the chairman of the Council at that time, and consulted with him about an immediate convocation of the Council meeting. The members of the Council are now fourteen, but at that time they were nine. The nine Council members were immediately called. It was a good luck that most of them lived in places relatively near to Geneva. For example, the Japanese representative Viscount Ishii was the Ambassador resident in Paris at that time, and it was very easy for him to come to Geneva immediately. The most distant case was Sweden. Its representative came by plane. Thus the meeting was held on Thursday. The representatives from Greece and Bulgaria, too, joined the meeting. And on Saturday the same week we saw the treaty of peace agreed on and the whole thing thus settled within a week. Many people say that it was made possible because the countries involved were such smaller countries as Greece and Bulgaria; that it would not be so easy if Britain and France, for example, were the countries at strife. Obviously we can't hope that the method applied to smaller countries will be as effectively applied to greater countries. But I believe, if it is proved that an international strife can thus be settled without resorting to weapons, the way will be opened to develop a more universally applicable method of settling disputes among nations, small or great alike.

History indicates this goal to us. Or even without resort to History, we know that our eyes are set on our front, guiding us to Hope, Faith and Creativity, and that maxim of peace preached by the ancient sage* as the most prized thing will surely be realized in the end.

---

*[Prince Regent Shoutoku Taishi (574-622).]

## (2) A Typical British Gentleman: Sir Eric Drummond [Trans. by Editor]

>from *East and West in Contact*, published in 1928. Translated from *The Collected Works of Inazo Nitobe*, vol. 1: 338-349.

When speaking of a campaign or an enterprise, it is a common fallacy to think that it will be carried on automatically or mechanically, overlooking the fact that it is mainly pushed on by the efforts of individual persons. Of course, there are some cases in which not individuals but an organization itself plays a larger part. In many enterprises, their importance may come from the name of the body transcending individuals. But everybody will admit that any cooperative enterprise has its basis in individuals, as in the case of the government whose cabinet, while working in a mutual responsibility, relies upon one or two individuals, or as in Christianity which, though a world-wide movement, came originally from Jesus Christ. The same is true with a temperance movement or a labour movement; we can specify some or other individuals deeply involved in it in its history.

The League of Nations is now nine years since its establishment. Similar attempts were made several times in some three thousand years of human history. All of them, however, disappeared; some in a few decades and some longest in so short time as three years. It is remarkable, therefore, that this organization should have lasted for nine years, without showing any sign of fading, in this rapid-changing century. And this world-wide activity, too, was the work of a very few individuals in its origin. Needless to say, if those few people acted according to a too advanced ideal or to an outdated principle, without regarding the true need of the time, they would not be able to hope any success. They can be successful only when their ideas are not too much removed from the time, that is to say, when they keep to an ideal which is practical enough to be carried out, and devote their energy to its realization. They will be successful because in that case we can say that the time itself supports their efforts. Therefore, in some respect, we can even say that those individuals are mere spokesmen or representatives of the time. Whatever the conclusion to this interesting question, anybody with insight will agree that there are always the works of individuals behind any large-scale organization or enterprise.

The Assembly and the Council of the League of Nations are bodies of a council system, and as such the scope of the activity of each member is limited even though they are motivated by a few members. The Secretariat, on the other hand, can easily be coloured by the character of the main person. The Secretariat is a huge organization, unprecedented in the history of the world, comprising people of over 40 nationalities. The total number of the officials amounts to more than 600. The head of the organization has naturally a heavy responsibility, and the atmosphere or morale of the people working under him is strongly influenced by his attitude.

The person occupying this important position is Eric Drummond. He was born in Scotland, and descended from a family boasting of ancestors who were great feudal lords of Scotland. His family has a hereditary title of Earl of Perth. His elder brother has inherited the title, but since that brother doesn't have any heir, he will inherit the title some day. When young, he entered Eton, and, after graduation, instead of going to university, entered the Foreign ministry, working as an ordinary official and then as a private secretary to the Foreign Secretary and the Prime Minister. He was attached to the British delegation throughout the peace conference at Versailles. His character and skill impressed Woodrow Wilson, who strongly recommended him to the post of the Secretary-General of the Secretariat. Wilson's motion adopted, his post was set down in the Treaty. Born in 1876, he was 43 at that time, and is now at his prime of life, aged 52.

I was travelling in Europe when Count Chinda recommended me to a post of the Secretariat of the League. I had no idea of what work it would be like. It would be a quite new office work, experienced by none yet. I had no way to judge whether or not I was a right person. I put various questions to him as to the nature of the work. Of course, the Viscount, too, could not but answer me on his own imagination. There were no office regulations set down. Only he expressed his belief in the trustworthiness of Drummond, and told me all that he had heard from Drummond. According to him, Drummond wished to have in a high position of the Secretariat a person recommended by the Japanese delegation of the peace conference. And the qualities required of that person were threefold: (1) he should understand both English and French, (2) he should have "tact," that is to say, skill or judgement in dealing with men, and (3) he should have a good character. Business ability was not mentioned. Nor was learning. Still I was not sure whether I could meet the three requirements. Since I felt myself utterly deficient in business ability, I declined the offer twice. Also I asked advice from several friends who were travelling with me at that time, such as Viscount Gotou, Tsurumi, Tajima, and Iwanaga. They all insisted on the advisability of my accepting the post. Some of them hinted that my reluctance would be nothing less than a treason to my country. Another imposed on me a duty to recommend a suitable person in my place in case I declined the offer. In fact, I recommended two or three persons who all surpassed me both in career and talent. However, the result was that those people were found not to fit in with the post in some way or other and I finally accepted the offer.

Once determined, I visited Count Chinda and asked him more about the nature of the post I was going to assume. He said that, since he, too, had no idea, the best way was to visit Eric Drummond and ask him directly. He encouraged me, saying, "Probably Drummond, too, will not be able to describe exactly what the work of the Secretariat would be like. What I can say for certain is that, among many British people I met during my long stay in Britain, Drummond is one of the most friendly persons, a man of character, kind, sincere, and trustworthy. To work with him will be as easy and as desirable a thing as one could wish."

Before long I visited Drummond, accompanying Count Chinda, at the Secretariat of the League, which was placed provisionally in London at that time. My first impression of him was just as I had heard from Count Chinda, that is, I felt I was in the presence of a typical British gentleman as I had met in novels. After I joined the Secretariat, I had many occasions to be with him. What characterized him were (1) an extraordinary talent in business; (2) a strong memory; (3) whole-heartedness in everything, allowing nothing to be left half-done, not only in business matters where it is especially prized, but also in other spheres apart from business; (4) kindness; (5) frankness, that is to say, he always expresses his opinions without reserve and also has enough capacity to listen attentively to others' opinions. Another characteristics which will complete the description of his character is that he hates making a public speech.

His dislike of public speeches and public places looks contradictory to his present position and inconceivable when we think of his high birth. Serving as a private secretary to a Foreign Minister and a Prime Minister for a long time and also as an official of the Foreign Ministry, a post which entails everyday contact with a Foreign and Prime Minister, he must have had days of dealing with many people. And yet he sometimes shows shyness, almost a maidenlike shyness, characteristic of British people. It is different from timidity. He becomes quite outspoken when he is going to disagree, even if the opponent is Earl Balfour or Mr. Chamberlain. His is not timidity but simply shyness. I still remember a comical happening. It was within two or three months after the establishment of the Secretariat when his private secretary came to my room and said, "The Secretary-General wants you to come immediately. Seven or eight delegates of women's organization are coming and he wishes your company." I went immediately and found him arranging seats for those delegates, a seat for himself, and beside it a bigger seat. Pointing to the last-mentioned seat, he said, "Would you please sit down here?" Saying so he dragged that big seat nearer to his own seat. It didn't look like a preparation to receive female guests, but rather it looked as if he were going to guard himself from some gang. I could scarcely suppress my laughter.

When they came in at last, he behaved very well. He was a born gentleman after all, and there was no lack of manner in him. But still his attitude was a little awkward in an innocent or childish way as if he were nervous in the presence of those ladies. I had several similar experiences after this. Also, especially when he had to make a speech, his embarrassment was great. He used to say to me, "When I have made a promise of a speech at a dinner table, even if it is a simple short talk, I feel sick and become unable to do anything in the whole afternoon." On another occasion he was invited by a group of students, not a big group but a group of some 40 or 50 students, and asked to make a speech. Early that morning he called me and wished my company, and I said, "Of course, with pleasure." He said, "Could you make a short speech, too?" "No, your word will be enough. My speech is not necessary." He said, "I want to be as brief as possible. To tell the truth, I have at my hand a manuscript of a speech which I prepared long ago for such an occasion. Do you think this will do?" He took out two sheets or so from the drawer of his desk. He looked so worried that I even felt some pity, but at the same time he was so childish that I couldn't help loving him. He wanted to go to that meeting with me, and said he will have a car sent to my house. But when I said I had another appointment just before the time of the meeting, he proposed his going to the place of that appointment to fetch me and go to the meeting together. He came to the place and we went to the meeting by his car. On this occasion, too, he blushed for shyness and read the manuscript as a speech for 5 or 6 minutes. But in conversations, he never shows this shyness or awkwardness. He talks very freely with Ministers and Ambassadors of various countries. Also with women, he looks a little shy at first but soon becomes animated and talks with smile. He not only talks but, when he is with students, he even entertains them by performance and trick. He doesn't assume a pedantic attitude nor puts on airs; he is free from affectation. In the Secretariat where hundreds of officers from various countries are working, he meets many people. Meeting them in the corridor or by the gate, he seldom talks to them, which may be mistaken for some proud attitude, but actually it is his shyness, as people find after some acquaintance with him.

He likes playing golf and fishing. Whenever he has time, he is engaged in either of the two. I thought he is not a reader and he himself confessed it. But he once told me that he makes it a rule to read King Arthur's story twice a year, and I think this suggests his character. King Arthur is a prototype of British ruling-class gentleman. Reading Arthurian story twice a year speaks strongly for his character. Two years ago (1926) some American scholar published a book in which he parodied the Arthurian story and won a considerable popularity. Opening this book, Drummond got very angry, and throwing down the book on the floor, accused it of being harmful to humanity and an outrage to morality. However, it seems that he has no interest in books. He says he studied philosophy in his youth, but now the story of King Arthur and probably some other books which will give nutrition or solace to his mind are all that he reads; he doesn't show much interest in scholarly matters. He himself says he has not any ability in scholarship, but this is not unique to him, for most British people share this tendency. British people seem to be proud of being not so intellectual. Once in a meeting people discussed the desirability of postal stamps to be issued by the League of Nations. A man from some country stood up and asserted that such stamps will do much to propagate the ideals of the League, saying, "In my youth I collected postal stamps. My parents encouraged me and advised me, too, to learn about the population, area, manners and customs of each country while collecting them, and I have got much knowledge by this means." Then Drummond cracked a joke, saying "If such a thing had been imposed on me, I would not have collected stamps at all." I don't know whether it is a fact, but at least on surface British people pretend not to be interested in learning.

Or it may be a fact. Lord Drummond has a clear and sharp mind, and we may ascribe this to the fact that his head is not hampered by too many pieces of irrelevant knowledge. His excellence lies in his clear judgement which enables him to deal with things smoothly without any impediment. As a result, I never found papers and files left piled on his desk. He replies to every mail, however trivial its purport, immediately, just as a sound comes when a Bell is struck. Of course, in order to make a correct and speedy judgement, one must have detailed knowledge of facts. He is possessed of an extraordinary memory in matters he takes in charge. I heard his strong memory was a legend inside the British Foreign Ministry. I myself experienced something of it. When some news comes, he very often surprised his men and colleagues by enumerating various precedents which were forgotten even by an officer directly concerned with them. In connection with this, I had a small episode with him, which, since it is a rather trivial one, I think I can report here without any sense of shame. I once asked his opinion about some problem. He advised me to settle it after consulting with the representative of such and such a country. I thought it rather a strange way to do. There had been no such precedents. However, since it was a problem deeply involving British interest, I inferred that his intention was that it had better be committed to a hand of a representative of a different country rather than decided by his own hand, in which case his decision might be taken as a partiality. I followed his advice, but was surprised to find him much displeased with my dealing, accusing my conduct rather severely. This was quite unexpected to me, so I pleaded my own cause, referring to the corrections he made on my papers. I wrote, "This problem was a little complicated at first, so I asked your advice and dealt with it following your advice. Since you are dealing with so many problems everyday, it is natural that you should forget it. You seldom forget, but if it comes to that matter, I pride myself on my power of oblivion, in which I will never come below you. That is why I never accuse other people's oblivion. However, I have a memo in my hand recording all the details of this matter. I hope you will remember the details of our first discussion by the help of this memo." After this foreword I showed him all the details recorded in my memo. Then he sent me a letter of apology. The incident was not grave enough to speak of apology or pardon. But this incident bespeaks his frankness.

Nearly seven hundred people are working in the Secretariat, and they are men and women of various nationalities. Disputes can happen. More often than not some member complains to him of some other's conduct. On such occasions, he shows relevant documents to both parties, lets them plead their own causes, and after that he expresses his own opinion and judgement. If this were done by a Japanese, facing a difficulty, an effort would be made to settle it peacefully by hiding the documents from the accused party. Drummond was quite detached from such trivialities of emotion and behaved in quite an open and frank way of a British gentleman. His manner was pleasing and won my respect.

In opening the Secretariat, Drummond didn't prescribe any rules. He let it start without any office regulations set down. The surprise I felt at that time still remains in my memory. If this were taken up by a Japanese, or a German or a French, he would begin by laying down all kinds of rules and regulations supposing every possible situation. Around the time when the Secretariat was started in London, the number of the officers was not so many. I went to the general affairs section and asked about the office hours. The officer answered that it is up to me. To my question what is the meaning of it, the officer explained that, depending upon the amount of the work, I may have to come early or sometimes I can come late. Also he told me to find a private secretary according to my need. But I had no means of finding out a secretary in London. I was appointed to the Secretariat post suddenly while I was still in the midst of my travel. I had no acquaintance in London. So I relied upon Drummond for the selection of my private secretary.

Soon after the appointment I travelled abroad on an official business. I asked about my travel expenses and the answer was that I should write down all the expenses needed for my travel and then all the expenses will be paid to me. And if any unexpected expense was incurred while travelling, that, too, would be paid after my return. There was no provision about travel expense and we were treated quite as gentlemen. Because I had been accustomed too well to the Japanese official way, I almost felt something wanting. As the number of the officials increased and more and more people from various countries joined us, such a generous treatment went away, and various restrictive regulations came in, not only about travel expenses but also about the limit of the entertainment of guests and the limit of the number of the people who can attend the parties. Somebody said that it would have been better if Drummond set down rules and prescriptions at the time of the Secretariat's establishment. But to start with no rules prescribed and introduce rules afterwards when needed is the way of the British people and the way of Drummond.

Laying perfect trust in him, I often asked his advice on matters other than official. I asked him to recommend a good secretary, for I had not been well adjusted to official life even in Japan and still less to the official matters of the West. I wanted a person who would help me, especially in making documents in languages other than my mother tongue. His answer was that he himself made many mistakes in matters of language though in his own language; that I need not worry because all such things would be done by a secretary quite competently. In fact, however, he was famous for his competency in drawing up plans and documents when he was working in the Foreign Ministry. Working as a private secretary under several Foreign Ministers and afterwards as a vice-minister as well, he had got a reputation as a master of plan-making, and it was said of him that no addition nor any revision was needed to the documents prepared by him. I myself was taught by him how to make up plans and documents just as a pupil learns from his teacher. He found for me a very good secretary, a British lady who once worked in the Foreign Ministry. She helped me faithfully and very competently throughout those seven years I was in duty, and I still retains a deep gratitude to her.

Drummond has a noble character naturally from his high birth. Also he has a career of entering into the Foreign Ministry at an early age, always in touch with excellent elders and having a rich experience of the fashionable society. He is also blessed with a happy, warm family life. He is married to a lady of a distinguished family and of a devout religious mind. All these must have contributed to his magnificent and graceful character.

The people working in the Secretariat are brilliant people of various nationalities. But, since they are there recommended each by their own country, they cannot help being ambitious, too. Because people nowadays regard the Secretariat as the place of learning in foreign policy or of heroism in international politics, there are many aspirants for important posts in the Secretariat. I heard that the number of CVs sent to the office already reached some forty or fifty thousand.

In face of international rivalry and jealousy that might have place, Drummond has cut his way through a difficult situation for these ten years without ever being blamed or reproached by any one. That is a fact to be wondered at. His character played a main part in this feat, of course, but it would have been impossible without his outstanding ability as well.

At first when the League of Nations started, the post of Secretary-General was regarded in the Council as a mere office worker, and as such his seat was placed behind the table of the Council members. However, though the Council members were all veteran politicians each in their own country's government, international affairs were too new to them and, in the course of complicated discussion, they always relied upon the Secretary-General's advice. It was soon found very inconvenient for them to turn around each time they face difficulties. As a result, the Secretary-General's seat was moved from behind them to the side of the chairman. Thus they became able to ask him quite freely. And that was quite natural, for they found in him a person as impartial and disinterested as one could wish to have. A friend of mine, who recently stayed in Europe for seven or eight years and attended various international conferences, once said to me, "I have observed in various meetings people in the post of chief secretary or head official expressing their international mind in a magnificent way at the beginning but, once the discussion began to touch their own country's interest, betraying their narrow-minded egotism or chauvinism. Drummond was the sole exception to that. He alone kept his impartial attitude. He was admirable." I make it almost a rule, whenever I become friends with a person who has had a rich experience abroad, to put a question to him, "What great men did you meet?" I once put this question to a man, a diplomat of a certain country, who stayed as an ambassador in various countries and, coming back after the War, became the Foreign Minister of his country. After a little thinking, he answered, "They are mostly British people," and referred to great British politicians and men of letters. Britain is a fortunate country; there is no lack of talent there.

## (3) A Savant Who Calls Himself a Primitive: Gilbert Murray [Trans. by Editor]

>from *Great Men I Met*, published in 1931. Translated from *The Collected Works of Inazo Nitobe*, vol. 5: 482–485.

### Spiritual Power is Most Prevalent in Primitives

Gilbert Murray's name is not well known in Japan because his speciality, Ancient Greek literature, is not so familiar to Japanese people. But he is famous as a great scholar in the Western world. He is Professor of Oxford University, author of many books, and, as a man of character, quite influential in various fields other than his speciality, too. Even in the political world, it is said of him that he will be appointed Minister of Education if the Liberal Party takes over the government.

He is married to a lady who is as famous as he, not only as a daughter of a Duke, but also for her contribution to various social movements.

Her mother, too, was a famous person. When she devoted herself to Abstinence Movement, she opened all the casks of wine which had long been kept in the cellar in a great quantity as usual in an old family, and literally made a river of that wine in her garden. Daughter to such a mother, she keeps to the Total Abstinence Principle and is a vegetarian into the bargain. She keeps to her principle at any party. And Professor Murray, too, therefore, doesn't drink alcohol nor eats meat.

He has got a kind of spiritual power; he practices telepathy. As to this, I already wrote in my *East and West in Contact*.*

I once put a question to him about this topic, and his answer was:

---

*[See the next section.]

"Since my youth I have noticed this strange power in me, but I didn't try to develop it further by frequent practice. Still I sometimes use this power. I find myself especially successful when at home among intimate people. But this power is not something to boast of, for it is most prevalent among primitive people."

## Western Sages Order for Eastern Dinner

I was interested in the fact that an Oxford scholar has got a power peculiar to primitives. It was in London that I was first introduced to him. At that time we only exchanged words of greetings, and didn't have any special conversation. We met often afterwards and became intimate. We also had frequent correspondence to each other. But I think it was when I invited him with his wife to dinner that our relationship became a confidential one.

As I heard later, he, too, said to somebody that it was his first time to talk with a Japanese so intimately. A man who went back in the same car with Professor Murray and his wife on that night reported to me as follows:

"The other night when we went back from your house, Professor Murray was silent for some moment without a word, and then murmured, 'What a strange hybrid he is, to preach *Bushido* as a Japanese *samurai*, become a Quaker, and talk about ancient Greek literature!'"

Since then I was taught many things by him, not only in the field of his speciality but in other matters. His insight was always a good lesson to me.

I had a memorable incident when I invited him and M. Bergson to a luncheon in a hotel I was staying in. Immediately after we took our seats at the table, I was wanted by a telephone call. When I came back, I found them engaged in an intimate conversation without noticing my approach. I thought it might be some talk on personnel matters. I thought I had better not intrude upon them, and remained at the door for some time. It appeared, however, that they were talking about the anxiety of the Western civilization at its dead end and the necessity of adopting Eastern ideas. Feeling myself somewhat flattered by it, I went to them and took my seat, when they both opened their mouth and said,

"A great problem presented itself during your absence."
I said, pretending ignorance,
"About the menu?"
Professor Murray said,
"A thing more important than that."
"Is it? But it's past one o'clock already. I beg your pardon for keeping you wait for so long. You must be hungry. At such a time, what problem can be more important than the order for dinner?"

Then M. Bergson said,
"Nothing, indeed! Therefore we have been discussing which dish we should order for, Indian or Chinese, or, if Japan can offer a better one, we would like to hear about it from you."

This witty answer pleased us much and led us to the discussion of the problem in question. And I realized the fact that these two great scholars are not satisfied with the thoughts and ideas of modern Europe.

Of course, this was a light talk over lunch, and I don't think any deep insight was exchanged among us. But I was able to infer, from their general tone, how seriously they are thinking about the necessity of harmonizing East and West with each other.

I felt our talk was going a little too far to the extolment of East. So I could not help restraining myself a little, and expressed my opinion somewhat like this:

"Belonging to East like India and China, but situated at the far eastern edge of it, Japan has not contributed much to the formation of ideas and thoughts, regrettable though it is. As it may be known to you already, everything new came from the continent, and very few were invented by us. If we can boast of anything, it is in the field of practical things, such as social welfare, material gains, politics and economics, where we may be able to hope to rival other countries. When it comes to abstract thinking and idealistic thoughts, we are very poor. Probably, Japan can contribute to mankind best by adopting the continent's theories and ideas and examining their utility and applicability in the actual world."

## (4) Spiritual Phenomenon
[Trans. by Editor]

> from *East and West in Contact*, published in 1828. Translated from *The Collected Works of Inazo Nitobe*, vol. 1: 271-274.

I had entertained from my early youth a kind of superstitious belief in spiritual power. In my school days my friends laughed at it. But, of course, I was not so superstitious as to believe in spiritualistic media, fortune-telling, divination or suchlike things.

As modern psychology makes progress, it will more and more reveal the secrets of potential power working latent in the deep layer of our mind. And it will eventually discover the site (either in our heart or head) of that spiritual power which science has hitherto dismissed as inexplicable. It is a well-known episode in the history of English literature that Dr. Johnson walked round a graveyard, knocking gravestones one by one, just to see ghosts by his eyes. It is no wonder that he didn't find any ghost. It is not in graveyards nor among stone monuments for the dead that we can find ghosts. Ghosts or spirits exist in each person's hidden depth of existence. And it seems that spirit has no power to come out of our body and make its appearance before our senses; it only lies dormant with its heat and light shut up to no purpose, like a dying fire covered up with ashes, and goes off melting away. Even if it manages to appear in the external world overcoming many obstacles, since it must assert its power only through a corporeal body, its pure spirituality will inevitably be distorted in some way or other in the process, and, as a result, it cannot help appearing in a form which is unnatural to external eyes. There are some people who train and regulate their sentient body successfully to make easier the coming out of spirit. Also some people who believe in spiritual power pretend to have it or make too much use or abuse of it. Hence the general tendency to regard such people as mountebanks or charlatans.

I often asked M. Bergson's opinions about this topic. As a

philosopher he was deeply interested in it. He had been for a long time President of the so-called Society for Studies of Supernatural Phenomena. I thought his knowledge reliable in this, not only for its depth but also for its impartiality. Therefore I asked him. I found that he fully believes in spiritual existence. He also knows well that this subject is infested by many shams. Therefore when talking about mysticism he never forgets to add epithets such as "genuine" and "true." To my question whether psychology will some day explain the spiritual power revealed in Joan of Arc, his answer was that her power will never be explained by science; that her spiritual power is the greatest and rarest example of mystical phenomenon. He added that such powers may exist abundantly in the world but unfortunately due to our lack of power to recognize it, most of them are being overlooked.

I discussed this topic many times with Dr. Gilbert Murray of Oxford, too. It is well known at least in Britain that he himself is a possessor of this strange supernatural power. It was five or six years ago that an English newspaper caused a sensation among people by the following report:

> Professor Murray attended a small party of distinguished people. The conversation turned to mysticism. Lord Balfour, who was present at the party, said to Murray, "I heard that you have a power of clairvoyance. If it is true, why not show it in the presence of these people who are all eminent each in their own field?" Professor consented to this proposal with pleasure, and was conducted to a distant room separated from the party room by a long corridor. The members left behind agreed to decide on some idea which will never be dreamt of by Professor. The members were all intellectual people and they hit upon the following brilliant idea: Two hundred years ago, in the reign of George I, Robert Walpole was Prime Minister. The King was fond of learning and the Walpole, too, was a great reader. It is said that they very often enjoyed themselves in learned discourses whenever they could find time during their official work. Under a tacit understanding that all members will be thinking of this historical episode, Mr. Murray was called back to the room. They said to him, they are all thinking of one thing silently in

their mind. What is it that they are thinking of? Then, after some silence, Mr. Murray began to speak: I think I see some very decent person occupying a very high seat. He looks like a King as I often see in the theatre. By his side, a very sagacious-looking man is explaining something, looking at a voluminous book opened in front of him. But who that person is and what kind of book it is, are beyond my power to see. To a further inquiry about the details of his vision, Murray only answered that he cannot see further than that: that perhaps it is a scene of some royal person questioning to his counsellor about some matter of a great importance.

The newspaper article was not so minute as this. It reported only the outline of what happened there. The above is what I have pieced out from what I heard directly from him afterwards. He said to me that generally speaking this kind of power is strongest in primitive people and is disappearing from among people of civilized countries; that he is sometimes able to see clearly a thing too distant for anybody's sight; and that he feels this power most strongly especially when he is at home with intimate friends and family members. Mr. Murray once presided over a Society of Supernatural Studies in Britain, and has a wide knowledge of this kind.

My talk may not deserve psychologists' deep interest. This is nothing more than a mere idle talk. But I referred to these episodes just in order to suggest that belief in spiritual phenomena are not limited to superstitious people. I reported here as its evidence what I heard directly from the two great savants of our time.

## (5) Ignorance is Power
[Trans. by Editor]

> from *East and West in Contact*, published in 1928. Translated from *The Collected Works of Inazo Nitobe*, vol. 1: 211-213.

I think myself to be a very lucky man. Very often even my ignorance helped me become famous. If I have won some reputation, my successes were, in retrospect, mostly lucky hits coming from my ignorance rather than my true merits. The episode I tell here is a little comical one, but I will try to be frank with it.

It was a time when the League of Nations was newly established and its headquarters was still placed in London. The World Red Cross Society was going to have its meeting at Geneva, for which the Red Cross wished the League, too, to send its delegates. It was to be the first international conference after the Great War. It was decided that the League should send prestigious persons as delegates. One of the two persons appointed for this mission was Director of the Section which deals with various social problems, a British lady who had been awarded with a medal equivalent to the Japanese second-grade medal. And the other was me. We two started for Geneva, each accompanied by a private secretary. Persons attending the conference were expected to talk either in English or French. However, very few spoke English except British people, and those British, too, mostly understood French. So, all the speeches were made in French, and no one took trouble to translate them into English. I confess I am very poor at French even now. At that time I was as good as a mute. I could understand documents written in French, but to follow speeches made in French was almost impossible for me, especially when people talked fast.

We were given VIP treatment and seated in special seats while discussion was going on. That lady whispered to me from time to time, and then asked me to stand up and object to the motion under discussion because it is unacceptable to the causes of the League.

While I was asking my interpreter what is the purport of the discussion, one man stood up and objected to the subject, and the lady told me I need not speak since that objection would settle the matter. While I was feeling relieved, a representative of a certain country stood up and began to renew the motion. The lady told me that it is absolutely necessary this time for us to object to it. While I was asking her the reason, one man stood up and made an objection to it, and I was relieved of my responsibility. This was repeated three or four times. I entreated her to speak out and object to the proposal herself. She said that a lady had better be unobtrusive. Moreover, since my position in the Secretariat is higher than hers, my objection would be more weighty and effective, she said. That was a reasonable thing to say, I couldn't but admit. So I prepared myself to stand up and speak next time the occasion came again. But I hadn't grasped the point of the matter well enough, so I was still hesitant in my mind. But when a certain representative made a speech, and the lady told me that this is indeed a grave situation; that if we didn't stop it now, it would have a very bad effect, I stood up suddenly, throwing away all my hesitation, and asked for permission to speak in English. That being granted immediately, I made a brief simple speech, saying that as the representatives of the League of Nations we cannot agree to that proposal; that we wish the proposer should think it over again; and that we entreat them all not to agree to such a resolution. But, to tell the truth, I didn't know at all what I was making objection to. Taking my seat again, I asked the lady what was the result of my speech. But before she had time to answer, two or three persons stood up and supported my objection one after another, and the result was that the motion under discussion was rejected.

  The conference of the Red Cross Society was continued in this vein two or three days, and then we went back to London. Several weeks after the conference, I heard from one British person a comment made by a scholar of Edinburgh University, a great authority of physiology, on his way back to Britain after that Red Cross conference: "I had no Japanese acquaintance, but had long since heard that they are a far more sagacious people than any European. I saw the real example of it the other day. In one conference I attended, discussion became very complicated concerning some proposal. Then a Japanese representative (it appears that he mistook me for a delegate from Japan) stood up and objected to it with very simple words. The tone of his words was strong enough to encourage some two or three persons to stand up one after another to speak against that proposal, and in the event the resolution was rejected quite successfully. I was struck by the Japanese representative's effective speech which with simple and timely words overturned the whole drift of discussion and stopped the passage of the motion successfully at its critical moment. I could not but give enthusiastic praise to his skill and judgement." Indeed, my achievements, if any, were mostly more or less like this.

*III. The Time of Japan's Withdrawal from the League of Nations: 1932–1933*

## (1) Japan's Place in the Family of Nations

*December 1932. One of the speeches Nitobe made during his American tour 1932-1933. The Collected Works of Inazo Nitobe, vol. 23: 383-391.*

When the League of Nations was started twelve years ago it was received in different ways by different people according to their different temperaments. Broadly speaking, we may say that it was hailed by the idealistically inclined as the last stab dealt by Janus into the breast of Mars. On the contrary, to the cynics and pessimists, the League of Nations was only an instrument of obstruction to the free play of the natural and beneficent law of struggle for life and the survival of the fittest. Between these two ways of thinking, there was another: namely, that of men of affairs, who expected of the League some tangible results though these might be neither totally perfect nor perfectly good.

The idealist supported the League with enthusiasm as a flawless device for the prevention of war and for international coöperation. The cynic tolerated its creation as a harmless joke. Practical minds viewed it as a promising makeshift, capable of improvement, but sufficiently implemented for the sustenance of law and order among nations for the present. These three types of mind exist everywhere, in all countries, and among all peoples; and they come plainly to the fore, whenever great issues are at stake.

In Japan no subject of any consequence comes into the limelight without bringing these three typical shades of opinions into prominence. But as regards the League of Nations, there were three reasons peculiar to Japan, which made it an object of almost religious faith, of severe contumely and condemnation, or of doubt and indifference — according to the temperament of the men who took it up. Now of these three reasons:

1. The first was that the framers of the Covenant persistently refused to put into it the only proposition made by the Japanese

delegate in the Peace Conference. The proposition was simple and made without any ulterior motive. It was in reference to race equality — an exceedingly ticklish subject, to be sure, to be presented before the American and Australian statesmen. Japan, naïvely believing that the greatest men were gathered from the four quarters of the globe, honestly to usher in a new heaven and a new earth, proposed that either in the preamble or somewhere in the numerous articles that constitute the Covenant, the fundamental principle of human equality should be clearly stated. The Japanese spokesman expressly stated that it was not to serve as a basis for demanding for his countrymen free immigration into other countries. He admitted that the control of immigration is a matter for the internal legislation of any sovereign state. His motive for requesting the insertion of some brief phrase to this effect was national pride. Though the proposition was adopted by a large majority, it was turned down by the chairman, President Wilson, who declared that a resolution so important must have the unanimous assent of all present.

The rejection of the Racial Equality clause in the Covenant had a most unhappy repercussion on Japanese opinion regarding the League of Nations. The idealists suffered most. They began to doubt whether the League was really to be as good, fair, and just as they had hoped. The cynics pointed at the incident as the clearest evidence that the League was at heart intended to be another Holy Alliance of Western Powers, another concert of Europe joined by America, and that no good would befall Asia or the Far East in time of need. The liberal minded, bent on finding some practical way out of the world chaos, felt no small misgivings, made light of the unhappy incident, and forced themselves to believe that entrance into the League of Nations would at least be indirectly beneficial to their country if it would help the Western World. For the whole nation it was a hard pill to swallow. It estranged a large number of its adherent. We had the assurance, however, that by her steady endeavor a nation can disarm others of prejudice and suspicion and the best policy would be to conquer our pride and abide our time, and in the meanwhile to observe how other nations would treat us.

2. When, thus, with the best intentions, Japan joined the League of Nations, what was the surprise that awaited her in its earliest days? America would not join it! This fact was to Japan a blow no less hard

than the refusal to inscribe in its constitution the academic principle of racial equality. The latter is theoretical, the former material. If the one is of abstract character, the other is of substantial, diplomatic importance. A League minus the United States loses in the estimate of Japan more than one-half of its value. A general treaty of which neither Russia nor America is a signatory has very little use for Japan. It is, as we say, like a mass of flesh with the bones taken out — the whole thing ready to collapse at any time.

Again, the idealists were well-nigh in despair; but idealists are optimistic and they would not lightly give up the hope of America's coming soon into the fold. At this the cynics laughed in scorn, calling the whole thing another trick to deceive the Eastern races. Practical men, half confident that the United States would sometime find its way to coöperate with the League, and trustful that the best way to build up the incipient institution was to be a part of it, favored loyal memberships.

In the twelve years that have passed, Japan has been a faithful member of the League, fulfilling all the duties that were required of her. She had had little to complain of in her treatment in it. She had seen no indication of racial discrimination. She has watched with increasing satisfaction America's approach and coöperation. She has noted the great structure in Geneva growing broader and stronger at its base, higher and nobler in its form, richer and fuller in its content. Surely the whole world is better for the League, and Japan was second to none in her participation with patience and fidelity.

3. In all the years of its existence, there had never come under the purview of the League any subject relating to Japan as a principal party. This record was suddenly broken when China applied to it for protection of her territory from Japanese attack, which was made, according to her statement, without the slightest provocation. It was unfortunate that the League acted without full knowledge of the many provocative causes covering a period of over a decade, which precipitated the action taken by the Japanese troops stationed in Manchuria.

The Sino-Japanese issue got more and more complicated in the hands of the League, due partly to the emotional aspect it assumed, and partly to insufficiency of knowledge concerning the actual situation in the Far East. As Viscount Cecil said, the question was largely befogged because the delegate (the Japanese) spoke too little and the other (the Chinese) spoke too much.

I am afraid the League was not aware that China does not or cannot function as a sovereign state, a nation, in the modern sense of the term. The so-called national government, which is represented in Geneva, is the government of Nanking — just at present moved to Loyang — which exercises control over a very small part of the large geographical area known as China. Within that area are several states, independent to all intents and purposes of the Nanking government.

Owing to the circumstance just stated, China, in spite of her vast territory and population, is regarded as a secondary Power and as such has gained the sympathy of the smaller states members of the League. She poses as an innocent victim of a great marauding Power and appeals to the world as an under-dog. This complicates still more the Sino-Japanese issue pending in the League.

In its eagerness to solve the Sino-Japanese question, the League, under the pressure of small Powers, has been inclined to take a narrow and legalistic view of the Covenant, regarding it as a rigid constitution, forgetting the statement by Clemenceau, Wilson, and Lloyd George that "The articles of the Covenant are not subject to a narrow technical construction."

The principle of national equality, in spite of the rebuff it received in the Peace Congress when proposed by our delegate, is now being applied as an implement of indictment of Japan's action in Manchuria. According to press reports, four small Powers — Spain, Czechoslovakia, Ireland, and Sweden — seem to take the most prominent part in charging Japan with violating the peace treaties.

In the refusal to accept the Japanese proposal for incorporating the theory of equality in the Covenant was implied the belief that states are not equal in questions that involve vital interests, because their responsibilities are different. Should a great war break out — and we must remember that both the Covenant and the Peace Pact take it for granted that a war may break out — what can Small Powers do? The world has to depend upon Great Powers for the restoration of peace. If thus a distinction of Great and Small Powers is admitted, in a case where a Great Power is involved, expediency demands that her case should be studied and judged by her equals — namely, by Great

Powers.  Indeed, it is not only expediency but justice that demands it. Aristotle stated long ago that it is as unjust to treat equals unequally as to treat unequals equally.  A man — and a nation, too — must be judged by his peers.  Already, while the Covenant was under discussion, fear was expressed in some quarters that the League might be wrecked by the preponderance of Small Powers.  We remember that early in the nineteenth century, when Castlereagh was prime minister, he devised something like a league of nations, but he was sagacious enough to exclude in his scheme the presence of Small Powers.  Much water has since then passed under the bridge and democracy and equality among individual and among nations has made steady progress; but none the less is it practical and political wisdom to keep in mind that the psychology of Small and Great Powers is different because their responsibilities are different or vary in degree.

One may well ask — what about the Lytton Commission?  Was it not composed of distinguished members representing Great Powers?  Assuredly. Nobody can deny it.  My own personal opinion is that in most, but not in all, respects it is fair to Japan.  We contend that it is not fair when it states that Japan exceeded her rights of self-defense when she took the course that she did in Manchuria.  Common sense should convince one that drastic and speedy action be taken when a small army of 10,000 has to defend itself against an army of 200,000 — and that on foreign soil.  No third party can define self-defense.  As Mr. Kellogg remarked repeatedly, it must be left to each sovereign state.  We may recall the definition of it given by Mr. Elihu Root, as "the right of every sovereign state to protect itself by preventing a condition of affairs in which it will be too late to protect."  The American government has maintained the Monroe Doctrine under this definition of self-defense.  The Peace Pact has brought a new era in diplomacy; but has it also changed the concept of self-defense?

May I go a step further and ask — Has the League of Nations or the Peace Pact effected any change in the economic order of the world?  And without doing so, can it expect to make any change in the fundamental relations between nations?  Whence come wars?  An apostle asked and in his naïve but penetrating way answers — Greed, lust for riches, or, as we would say in modern phraseology, economic conditions.  The League of Nations knows it and it has been most actively engaged in paving the way for a more rational and equitable distribution of wealth. Take Japan as an example. Here is a country smaller than the single state of California, with a population of about half that of the entire United States. The country is so mountainous that only one-seventh can be cultivated. There are certainly countries more densely populated than Japan — England, Holland, Belgium. These countries can support themselves by industries, thanks to their access to raw materials either at home or near by. Japan has little coal or oil, iron or any other metal. Her emigrants are denied entrance to other countries, her produce is likewise debarred by tariff. If she finds a sparsely populated and undeveloped land near her borders and wishes to develop it, the whole world rises to impede her movements. The much vaunted new age will not be realized unless facts and realities of national existence throughout the world are taken into account.

Personally, I am an advocate of the League of Nations — and not in theory only. It is because I wish to see its high aims fulfilled that I call to your attention its short-comings. If the world really wants peace, if the nations of the earth sincerely desire to form a family, it is not sufficient for any one or ten or twenty or fifty to say to a hungry sister or shivering brother: "Go in peace." St. James admonished the Church against the folly and futility of lip service to peace and brotherhood.

The friends and advocates of the League are almost impatient with the present attitude of Japan. She has been called by hard names. She has been accused of being untrue to her promises and engagements. It was not so long ago that Mr. Elihu Root, when he was Secretary of State, spoke of Japan as the most trustworthy partner in diplomacy, or when Earl Gray in his *Reminiscences* bore the same testimony. Has Japan changed all at once? If she has, please, see if she has not some strong, solid reasons for her actions. See if some fundamental issues affecting her very life have not burst forth from her innermost being, like the eruption of her many volcanoes.

In the presence of problems that will decide her future, Japan has taken her fate in her hand. Her very existence is involved and her honor at stake in her present crisis. She has to deal with a country which is not an organized nation. She has to deal regarding a region which, if left to itself or if left to China, will fall an easy prey to another Power which threatened her before and which will threaten her again, and which will turn the Far East into pandemonium. Viewed from this angle, the steps Japan has taken in Manchuria are measures of self-defense according to Mr. Root's definition.

By insisting on her rights in the League of Nations, Japan, it is feared, may jeopardize the very existence of the League. I have far greater confidence in the Geneva institution. It is not such a fragile framework. Every trial and tribulation to which it will be subjected, will only strengthen it the more.

"The world's history is the world's judgment seat," said a great poet. Let us adhere to facts and realities. Let us survey the Far Eastern situation from a higher vantage ground of justice and fair play. Let us study, the permanent and basic facts that underlie the question now agitating the League of Nations — not the ripples or the billows on the surface, but what is contained in the ocean of teeming populations and what lies at the bottom of our conception of justice.

## (2) How Geneva Erred
"Time will come when League will realize its mistake; Is not Japan responsible for Geneva's ignorance?"

> *Speech made to an audience of more than 100 people, representing all nationalities, attending the luncheon of the Tokyo Pan-Pacific Club at the Imperial Hotel, Tokyo, on 7 April 1933. The Collected Works of Inazo Nitobe, vol. 23: 373–379.*

### (I)

Before I begin my speech, if I have a speech to make, I regret very much the absence of Mr. Carr, whose acquaintance it was my privilege to make in his city of Pasadena. I had heard much about him, read some of his articles in the *Los Angeles Times*, and had always been deeply impressed with the literary value as well as the profound ideas which he expressed in a special column devoted to his pen. He was going out to Australia, but I am more or less responsible for diverting his route. I suggested that instead of going to Australia first he should come here for two or three months, and I think I prevailed upon him to come here immediately and make the trip to Australia later. I saw him several times in Tokyo, but it was only a few minutes ago that I learned he is indisposed today. According to the well known logic of the greatest historical work of Confucius, I feel I am more or less responsible for his illness.

From the very kind words of introduction uttered by our chairman, I presume you expect me to say something about my latest trip to America. I left this country just about a year ago, and until then I was not at all disposed to cross the Pacific Ocean. In the presence of so many good American friends, I have to confess why I did not feel disposed to go.

## Admirer of U.S.

I consider myself one of the greatest admirers of America. I spent a few years in Baltimore when I was a young man, where I distinguished myself not when I was a student but about 50 years later, as a classmate of Woodrow Wilson.

Then I went to Germany for five years, and my foreign education was chiefly acquired in Germany. But none the less, having been deeply impressed by the study, though not very profound I assure you, of English history and English literature, I was very partially inclined to Anglo-Saxon ideas, both in politics and in the general view of life — philosophy, you may call it.

So after leaving the Agricultural College in Sapporo, I came to Tokyo to continue my studies in agricultural economics in the university here. When I asked for admission to the university, I told the dean I would like to study agricultural economics and English literature. He thought that a rather queer combination, because in all the vast literature on economics in the English language, there is not a word to designate "agricultural politics" — what the Germans call Agrarpolitik.

## Meeting with Dr. Saunders

I remember when I went to Canada I spent a day with a great agricultural authority there. Dr. William Saunders. He talked to me like an expert, and in about three minutes he found he was talking to a perfect stranger to agricultural science. My few replies betrayed that I was utterly ignorant about certain crops, fertilizers, and implements, and when he said, 'May I ask what department of agriculture you are interested in?', I replied that no wonder he asked, for there was no English word to designate the subject in which I was interested — agricultural politics. His answer was: 'Indeed! In our country we consider that the less politics we have in agriculture the better.'

When I told the dean of the university I wanted to take English literature for my minor subject, I said that I wished to be a bridge across the Pacific Ocean, a bridge across which western ideas could flow without obstacle or impediment to Japan, and over which oriental ideas could find entrance to America.

## Avocation not Abandoned

However far I have wandered from my original plan of agricultural economics, I have not strayed very far from my avocation to be a bridge across the Pacific. I have never lost sight of it, though for more than eight years I consistently declined to go to America on account of the Exclusion Law, by which our people of course are excluded. I respect the American law so well and so conscientiously that I thought I would not do injustice to America by treading on its sacred soil. Not another Jap should land there.

## (II)

That is why I declined about 10 invitations from universities and other institutions, and when I was in Geneva, though I had friends in America and my wife had relatives there, I always used the Indian Ocean route back to Japan, out of respect for that law which would not tolerate any inferior people to land. But when last year the sentiment in America became so bad against Japan, my friends told me it was high time I should desecrate that soil with my feet, because the questions involved were more serious than the Exclusion Law, and after thinking much about it, I decided to go. I am very glad that I went. I, like an ordinary human being, like darkness more than light, and America was dark, so I went there.

## Back into Darkness

In the same way I came back into darkness. I do not think the atmosphere in this country is very light. We have left the League of Nations. The League of Nations is an artificial institution formed by the consent and the will of the states members. Entrance into it is voluntary.

Now we have left it, and here let me say I am one of those inconsistent and self-contradictory people who believe that while Japan is justified at the present moment to leave the League, — still believe that the League is the greatest hope for the future welfare of the world. I still insist upon looking at the League as the greatest achievement of the human race, and it is a pity that we have had to leave it. The League, being a human institution, errs. To err is human. I think the League has erred in its too rigid interpretation of the Covenant of the League. The founders of the League, be it Wilson, Clemenceau, Lloyd George, did not look upon the League as a tight compartment — in fact these three men once wrote an official letter to the effect that the articles of the Covenant of the League are not subject to a narrow and technical construction. They are to be interpreted in a broad and statesmanlike manner.

But the arguments which were waged in regard to the Manchuria question showed that many small powers have interpreted the Covenant not in a broad and statesmanlike manner, but like lawyers, in a cheap way. What a pity! None the less, there will come a time when the League itself will find it has committed a grave error.

## Japan also Erred

At the same time, I believe Japan also has committed a grave error. We insisted that the League does not know sufficient of the causes and the reasons that underlie our action in Manchuria. We speak of the attitude of the League as being founded on ignorance, but who made the League ignorant? Are we not responsible for it? We have committed a grave error in being too reticent and uncommunicative, and I may say also unsociable, and the sooner we find out that error, the better for our future relations with the rest of the world.

Now we have left the League, which is an artificial institution, but we cannot leave the family of nations, which is a natural institution, and whatever rights we may have lost by our withdrawal from the League, we must make good by further attention to the family of nations. Our relations with the rest of the world must now be largely controlled by the idea of our membership in the family of nations, the natural, instinctive, warm, and more or less emotional institution. It is by attention to the duties demanded by our membership in the family of nations that we should guide our diplomacy.

## U.S. is Powerful Member

America is not a member of the League of Nations, but it is one of the greatest and at present perhaps the most powerful members of the family of nations, so our relations with that country must demand our deepest and most careful consideration. Therefore, though the clouds that hang over the Pacific at present are still quite dark, yet with an effort and a will to bring about better understanding, we shall, I hope, regain our position in the heart of the American people.

At present things look dark, but darkness will not last forever. The shouting and the tumult will die, and the captains and kings will depart.* Then we shall regain cooler judgment, and I do not think the time is far distant when this cooler judgment will come back. Then we shall see that on both sides of the Pacific there are many earnestly interested in our good relationship — I see many represented here this afternoon.

## Dawn over Pacific

I think we may look forward to such a time. May we not already congratulate ourselves in forming new ties! In such a gathering as this we are forming ties that will grow stronger, and that in the coming years will bring back the enjoyable and friendly relations which have been the tradition of the Pacific.

I thank you for this opportunity of greeting my friends, and I wish that this society may grow in importance and influence. We meet like ships in the night, but we rarely forget the ships that we pass in the night.**

---

\* [Rudyard Kipling, "Recessional," ll. 7-8:
   The tumult and the shouting dies;
   The captains and the kings depart:]
\*\*[Henry Wadsworth Longfellow, *Wayside Inn III. Elizabeth IV*:
   Ships that pass in the night, and speak each other in passing,
   Only a signal shown and a distant voice in the darkness,
   So on the ocean of life we pass and speak one another,
   Only a look and a voice, then darkness again and a silence.]

## (3) Great Hopes for the League of Nations

*from Editorial Jottings: The Osaka Mainichi, June 6, 1933. The Collected Works of Inazo Nitobe, vol. 16: 479.*

It cannot be too strongly emphasized that Japan's withdrawal from the League of Nations does not mean her indifference to world peace or a challenge to the principles of the League.

The League is an artificial organization and is subject to human frailties. In its handling of the Manchurian question it has committed a grave error. But this does not necessarily prove that it is useless or that it is undesirable. It is a most useful and desirable institution for the preservation of world peace and for carrying on international coöperation.

The League may before long find its own mistake and so revise its constitution or so interpret the Covenant as to make it possible for Japan to remain in it. Should such a step be taken, America and Russia may also be willing to join this great assembly of nations and make it a truly universal and effective organization.

The world is not yet entirely governed by quibbling lawyers who stick to the letter of the text and to abstract principles and talk of *de jure* recognition. There are statesmen who can see facts with the naked eye and recognize realities, however ugly they may sometimes be.

# PART TWO (COMMENTARY)

# BACKGROUNDS AND CRITICAL ESSAYS

# I. Introduction:
# The Historical Context of Inazo Nitobe

## Teruhiko Nagao

This essay is intended as a reassessment of Inazo Nitobe (1862–1933) and his world-wide best-seller *Bushido: The Soul of Japan* (1900), especially in reference to its historical significance. The ¥5000 bank note has his portrait printed on it, so everybody in Japan knows him. But his work is very little known even in Japan. He was Under-Secretary-General in the Geneva Headquarters of the newly-founded League of Nations from 1920 to 1926. He especially contributed to the establishment of the International Committee on Intellectual Cooperation in 1922, the forerunner of the present UNESCO. And, as such, he appears in a biography of Einstein, *Einstein: The Life and Times* by Ronald W. Clark. It was at that time of Einstein's life when his attitude to the Committee wavered after accepting the invitation to it, quite naturally in the strongly anti-Semitic atmosphere of the post-war Germany in 1922:

> Einstein wrote a brief letter to the League, brusquely stating that he felt it necessary to resign from the committee [International Committee on Intellectual Cooperation].... To Madame Curie Einstein wrote in more detail, explaining that he was resigning... because of anti-Semitism in Berlin and his feeling that he was "no longer the right person for the job...."
>
> While Madame Curie was writing to Einstein on a personal basis, the officials of the League had been thrown into despair, and desperate efforts to retrieve the situation were being made by the Secretary of the committee. This was Nitobe, a Japanese Samurai, born with the right to wear two swords, whose philosophic journey was to lead him into the ranks of the Quakers. On receiving Einstein's resignation Nitobe had cabled to Gilbert

Murray: "Einstein resigns giving no reasons stop important to have him stop fear his resignation will have bad effect stop grateful if you can use your influence." He also appealed to Bergson....[1]

(*underline added*)

There are many other documents still kept in the UN Library in Geneva telling of Nitobe's activities during his Geneva days. Nitobe's house in Geneva beside the Lake Leman became a meeting place for such eminent scholars and scientists of those days as appear in the above quotation. The young Einstein often played fiddle there.

This seems to me a remarkable thing, for even today (still less in his days) there are not many Japanese people who can play such an important role in international scenes. (In his days, Japan sent outstanding men as delegates to the League, but Nitobe himself observed at that time that "Reticent by training, and handicapped by the very meager linguistic talent given to them by nature, the Japanese cannot win the confidence of nations by word of mouth.")[2]

The underlined part of the above quotation gives us, I think, something of Nitobe's characteristics as at once a nationalist and an internationalist. It is my purpose to bring into relief this dual quality of Nitobe.

Nitobe's book *Bushido* can be described as the first expression of the Japanese nationalism. What I call the Japanese nationalism here dates from 1890s and ends in 1945. Nowadays Japanese people don't like to talk about nationalism. Nationalistic symbols, such as the Japanese Emperor, the national anthem and the national flag, are rather looked upon with an eye of suspicion, because these things have long been associated in the mind of Japanese people with that disastrous Pacific war ended in the atomic bombs.

Indeed, it would be a depressing thing to suppose that the whole nation rushed into that war with a single mind, inflicting many sufferings on other Asian countries. But the truth is, a different nationalism characterized by nobler aspirations existed before that. Nitobe's achievement is a testimony. In other words, nationalism in Japan had two aspects, a bright side and a dark side, different in nature but closely related historically, almost mixed with each other.

I feel I must first explain this relatively late date of the Japanese nationalism, as compared with the Western nations that experienced the awakening of some kind or other of nationalism much earlier.[3] For that purpose I will sketch the history of Japan briefly.

> A.D.300 The Imperial Court of "Yamato" (= ancestors of the present Emperor of Japan) sets out to unify the country.
> 794 Kyoto becomes the site of the Imperial Court till 1868.
> Frequent intercourse with the Continent (China and Korea) until the end of the 10th Century.
> After the 11th Century, a rise of nationalistic culture.
> 1192 [The Imperial Court continues to exist, but the ruling power is transferred to the head of the warrior-class, called "Shogun" (hereditary within each government) (until 1868)]
>
>> 1192 **Kamakura Government** (until 1333)
>> 1274;1281 Abortive attempts of invasion of the Mongolians under Kubla Khan.
>> 1333 Civil Wars (until 1338)
>> 1338 **Muromachi Government** (until 1573)
>> 1467 Civil Wars (until 1573)
>> 1573 **Nobunaga** (House of Oda) (until 1582)
>> 1582 **Hideyoshi** and House of Toyotomi (until 1603)
>> 1592;1597~98 Attempts to conquer Korea, resulting in the debilitation of the House of Toyotomi.
>> 1603 **Tokugawa (or Yedo) Government** (until 1867)
>> 1633 Ordinance pronounced closing the door to foreign influences.
>> 1853 American commodore Perry knocks the closed door of Japan.
>> 1867 Collapse of Tokugawa Government.
>>
>> "Restoration": The ruling power restored to the Imperial Court.
>> = The end of Feudalism.
>> = The beginning of Westernization (i.e., modernization or enlightenment)
>> = The beginning of international age for Japan.

Of course, Japanese history is hundredfold more complex and richer, but this skeleton of chronology will serve my purpose here. Comparing this with any Western country's history, I think, two things stand quite unique.

One is the extreme scarcity of international relations. Until the 10th century, influence of the classical China was conspicuous. But after that, Japan began to develop its own culture on that basis. And Japan experienced a danger from outside only once. It was Kubla Khan's attempted invasion in the 13th century. But his two consecutive attempts were repelled by strong tempests on the sea. After all, his power was that of a horse people, not of Vikings or a sea-faring nation.

On the other hand, an attempt to invade into the Continent was made also only once, toward the end of the 16th century. But this attempt quite debilitated the government, and it gave a lesson to the next government, Tokugawa Government. And this leads me to another uniqueness of Japanese history.

That is the long interval of peace and stability, some two hundred and fifty years, from the beginning of the 17th century to the mid-19th century. No danger from outside, nor any big civil wars within. The government took to the isolation policy. They knew well that the import of effective weapons, for instance, will threaten their stability. Also they sensed something dangerous and subversive in the doctrine of Christianity. The firearm (or "matchlock" of those days) was first introduced to Japan in 1543 by shipwrecked Portugueses, and as it happened to be the time of big civil wars with dozens of feudal lords competing with each other for hegemony, this western weapon much influenced the warfare of the period. It is said that Japanese craftsmen soon mastered the technology, but during the peaceful time that came after, their technology was turned, not into more effective weapons, but into fireworks ("fire-flowers" as they are called in Japan), which became an important popular culture of Japan, and still now Japanese craftsmen pride themselves on their skill as the best in the world.

The uniqueness of this second point is quite obvious if we compare it with the history of Western countries during the same period, that is, from the 17th to the mid-19th century.

And the result is also quite unique. While Western countries were undergoing drastic social changes, Japan remained a living fossil of feudalism. This fact was observed and recorded by Karl Marx. In the first book of *Das Kapital* (published in 1867), he wrote that feudalism could then be seen in living form only in Japan.

Remaining a living fossil had demerits, of course. It kept Japan for a long time from modernization and enlightenment. When Japan opened its gate to the Western world, they felt themselves to be a country of pigmies, due to the backwardness of their civilization and technology.

From a conservationist point of view, however, it has some merits or attractions. The sword, for example, remained to be the main weapon throughout the feudal age. And during the long period of peace of the Tokugawa Government, it was even detached from its original, practical purpose, and became a kind of symbol, and, as such, developed into an artistic craftsmanship. One can refer to Nitobe's description of it in Chapter 13. It is a craftsmanship unrivalled in the whole world.

It is during this period of long peace and stability that everything we now regard as peculiarly Japanese was formed. Everything tended to ceremony. Tea-drinking became a ceremony, fencing or swordsmanship became a ceremony. Japanese national sport is wrestling, "sumo" wrestling, and I think a foreigner will be bored to death to watch this wrestling. The fighting itself is done in half a minute, or in a second or two, in some cases. Before the real thing starts, one must watch with patience a long preparation, which is a ceremony.

Even such a horrible thing as an execution (beheading) was turned into a ceremony. I mean *seppuku* or *hara-kiri*, Nitobe's topic in Chapter 12. We have only to call to mind the execution of Charles I or the hanging of the dead body of Oliver Cromwell. No ceremony, no artistic beauty in that.

Also the Noh plays were strictly preserved during this peaceful time and handed down safe to us. As a result, we can fairly assume that we are watching the same performance, the same action, the same speech, the same tone that were heard some five hundred years ago — a situation quite different from that of Shakespeare's plays.

Let us now go back to the history of Japan.

The state of a living fossil came to an end in 1868 abruptly. The relatively minor, feudal lords of distant counties revolted against the central government, and they tried to justify their rebellion by pledging allegiance to the long neglected Imperial Court. That is why this is called Restoration.

No matter how we define this event, this was the end of feudalism, and the beginning of Japan's rapid modernization. Also it was the opening of an international age for Japan. Before that, nationalism didn't have any place, because other nations didn't come into their consciousness. If any existed, it might be called a blind nationalism, or an absolute nationalism, but not that kind of nationalism we are assuming here (they called their own country, not Japan, but the world, "the place beneath Heaven").

For some twenty years after the Restoration, Japan was busy adopting the results of Western modernization. Japan was as good as a colony, not politically, but in terms of culture, state of mind, and attitude. Everybody tried to imitate the Western style.

During those twenty years, two books became the Bible for the rising generation:

(1) Yukichi Fukuzawa (1834–1901), *Encouragement of Learning* (1872–76), written in Japanese. Every Japanese knows by heart its opening words: "God didn't create man above man, nor below man...," which was in fact a free translation from the opening paragraph of the American Declaration of Independence, which was in its turn the fruit of the European Enlightenment.

(2) Masanao Nakamura (1832–91), *Success Stories in Western Countries* (1871), which is a Japanese translation of Samuel Smiles's *Self Help*.

The sudden change also affected the whole system of education in Japan. The traditional education founded on Chinese classics was suddenly discarded; foreign teachers were hired mainly from America, notwithstanding the huge amount of money the new Government must pay for it. It is during this period that Nitobe received his higher education. In his childhood he was educated in the traditional form both at home and in school. After that he was trained in this new Western style. By the way, we might say that up to the time of Nitobe, Japanese people had never tried to learn foreign languages. Japanese scholars were able to understand Chinese classics perfectly well. But their understanding of the language was entirely for the written form. The same is true with the Dutch language which a handful of people mastered during the Tokugawa period. Therefore, if we assume with Otto Jespersen, that the essence of any language consists in its spoken form, rather than in its written form,[4] then we must say that Japanese people had never learned foreign languages (though, of course, there may have been exceptions).

The situation was different with Nitobe, for he was taught

entirely by living American and British teachers.

Now, after the twenty years of hectic imitation, there came a return wave, a rise of nationalism in Japan. And interestingly enough, it was younger people like Nitobe taught by foreigners who were to make this return wave of nationalism. With their command of English and other European languages, they began to assert the identity of the Japanese nation. Three authors are specially mentioned as "masters of English" in our history of English studies (mastery of English is regarded as such a rare feat in Japan):

(1) Kanzo Uchimura (1861–1930), *How I Became a Christian: The Diary of a Japanese Convert* (Tokyo & Chicago, 1895), written in English.

(2) Inazo Nitobe (1862–1933), *Bushido: The Soul of Japan* (Philadelphia, 1900), written in English.

(3) Tenshin Okakura (1862–1913), *The Ideals of the East* (London, 1903); *The Awakening of Japan* (New York, 1904); *The Book of Tea* (New York, 1906), all written in English.

Of theses three, Nitobe's *Bushido* is particularly worth reading and rewarding, due to its standing on both cultures like an amphibian. An interesting review was written by a Julian Hawthorne (who is the famous novelist's nephew) in 1905:

> Inazo Nitobe has edited an essay, a little more than a hundred pages long, which must be studied as well as read. and since it is fascinating as it is important, that is no hardship. This English which the professor writes is so singularly pure, easy and effective that no one would imagine it to be the work of a foreigner — and of a foreigner so very foreign as a Japanese. But that is little: The author seems to be the master of all the knowledge proper to a learned man of the West, as well as of that Oriental lore of which Westerners know not much.... You may read the book through in a couple of hours, but you may return to it profitably for years.[5]

Nitobe's method in this book is to compare the two cultures, Japan and the West. And his aim is always to emphasize, not the difference but the similarity, the common humanity. Let me quote one example:

> The sorrow which overtook Antony and Octavius at the death of Brutus, has been the general experience of brave men. Kenshin, who fought for fourteen years with Shingen, when he heard of the latter's death wept aloud at the loss of "the best of enemies." It was this same Kenshin who had set a noble example for all time in his treatment of Shingen, whose provinces lay in a mountainous region quite away from the sea, and who had consequently depended upon the Hôjô provinces of the Tokaido for salt. The Hôjô prince wishing to weaken him, although not openly at war with him, had cut off from Shingen all traffic in this important article. Kenshin, hearing of his enemy's dilemma and able to obtain his salt from the coast of his own dominions, wrote Shingen that in his opinion the Hôjô lord had committed a very mean act, and that although he (Kenshin) was at war with him (Shingen) he had ordered his subjects to furnish him with plenty of salt — adding, "I do not fight with salt, but with the sword," affording more than a parallel to the words of Camillus, "We Romans do not fight with gold, but with iron." Nietzsche spoke for the Samurai heart when he wrote, "You are to be proud of your enemy; then the success of your enemy is your success also."
> (*Bushido*: Chapter 4)(*underline added*)

This is his usual method. He picks up a well-known episode in Japanese history, and then refers to several similar episodes in the European culture including the classical Greece and Rome. For this reason this book is difficult for Japanese readers. Also I think it is challenging to European readers, for they will be tested in their knowledge of their own culture. Nitobe quoted freely from Western writers, but very often neglected to mention the sources.

It appears that this book was read by many people of the world. Nitobe reports as follows:

> I have been more than gratified to feel that my little treatise has found sympathetic readers in widely separated circles, showing that the subject-matter is of interest to the world at large. Exceedingly flattering is the news (which reaches me from a

trustworthy source) that President Roosevelt has done me the honour of reading the treatise and of distributing copies among his friends.

(*Bushido*: Preface to the 1905 Edition)

In this book, Nitobe gave expression to that blind nationalism or speechless nationalism that must have existed in the feudal Japan, during the period of a living fossil. Even at his time it was rapidly receding into the past, but he believed that the past is not an absolute past, that it is still living in the present, subsumed in it, underlying Japanese people's mentality.

Here, we must note that Nitobe first became an ardent admirer of the Western culture. He studied in America for three years, and after that in Germany for another three years. On his way to Germany he visited Britain, went straightway to Edinburgh, the utopian city of his mind, then came down to London, and straightway visited the Carlyle House in Chelsea.

Nitobe's nationalism was born out of his study of the Western culture — oozed, as it were, out of it. I call it "romantic" partly because it is strongly influenced by Burke and Carlyle. In the first place, the influence of Burke is quite obvious in Nitobe's *Bushido*. The whole book is based and modelled on Burke's eulogy on chivalry in his *Reflections on the Revolution in France* where Burke remarked that the French Revolution was an outrage against the spirit of the ancient chivalry which was the glory of Europe.[6] However, Nitobe's book was far from a mere imitation. Although Burke's observation makes sense in hindsight and looks almost prophetic, yet to speak of 'chivalry' in the late 18th-century England must have sounded a little anachronistic. In the case of Nitobe, who was born to a samurai family, the spirit of Bushido belonged to his living past. Even if it, too, was disappearing, the memory was still fresh and green.

The continuous peace for 250 years from the 17th to the mid-19th century gives Japan a unique status in the history of the world. While it kept Japan long from the way to modernization and enlightenment, it prolonged the age of feudalism and, during that prolongation, crystallized the feudalistic values into an ethical and even aesthetic system. For instance, military weapons long since lost their practical purpose and, instead of developing into more effective and more destructive instruments, became a kind of spiritual symbol. Valour, too, became a virtue to be pursued for its own sake, rather than the one proved and exercised in real fields. In a word, everything became a 'ceremony,' as I stated earlier. So much so that we can say that the feudalistic ideal has seen its ethical and aesthetic completion in Japan more than in any other part of the world. And this it was that Nitobe immortalized in his book. That is why his description of the Bushido precepts strikes us as a solid reality, while Burke's eulogy on chivalry ends in a vague expression of nostalgic sentiments; after all, in Burke's England, chivalry was a thing which existed only in the world of romance.

The influence of Carlyle is no less strong on Nitobe's book. Not only his writing but also his whole character-building was permeated by Carlyle, as he himself confesses it. His first encounter with Carlyle was in the autumn of 1879, when, as a youth of seventeen, he read a brief passage by Carlyle quoted in an American magazine. In an instant he realized that this sage should be his spiritual guide. However, no book-seller in Japan in those days knew the name of Carlyle. After many difficulties, he managed to get a copy of *Sartor Resartus* from an American missionary, and he says he read through the book more than thirty times. Most certainly this was the first case of the reception of Carlyle in Japan. The people before him had been too much dazzled by the Western industrialism with its technological achievements to pay due attention to its severe critic.

Nitobe was not uncritical of Carlyle's definition of History and estimate of Heroes, but the whole contention running through *Bushido* — the contention that a nation's power consists not in its materialistic resources but in the spiritual — was surely a lesson he directly learned from Carlyle. Also his richly figurative language is the style he learned from, and even improved upon, Carlyle's.

Another important aspect of Carlyle's influence was the eulogy on George Fox in *Sartor Resartus*, Book III: Chapter 1. This initiated Nitobe at an early stage to Quakerism, which was to play an important part in Nitobe's subsequent career. Born to a samurai family, he became a devout Christian, a devout Quaker. Nitobe's *Bushido* is a strange hybrid-sort of book. Though written in English, it will be a difficult book for present-day Westerners, too, not because it tells of a distant Far-Eastern country, but because of its wide reference to the

Western culture. It consists of a constant juxtaposition, or bringing together, of two distinct cultures, East and West, overlapping the Bushido ideals with the concepts of Christian gentleman, and Nitobe always emphasizes the common features of the two, not their disparities. Thus his *Bushido* was quite in keeping with his later activities in Geneva, his belief being that East and West can be reconciled, in spite of the famous and too often misquoted lines from Rudyard Kipling's poem.[7]

Not only East and West, but also nationalism and internationalism blend into one in Nitobe's *Bushido*. Towards the end of his life, he often expressed his belief that nationalism is one and the same with internationalism. Nitobe's earlier book was an embodiment of this belief. Thus his nationalism is entitled to be called "romantic" again for its high and noble aspirations:

> The antithesis of patriotism is not internationalism or even cosmopolitanism, but Chauvinism. Internationalism is the extension of patriotism. If you love your country, you must needs love other countries without which your own country cannot exist and loses its raison d'être. If you love the world, you must, perforce, love best that part of it which is nearest to you.
> (*The Osaka Mainichi*, June 7, 1930)

> A good internationalist must be a good nationalist and *vice versa*. The very terms connote it. A man who is not faithful to his own country cannot be depended upon for faithfulness to a world principle. One can serve best the cause of internationalism by serving his country. On the other hand, a nationalist can best advance the interests and honour of his country by being internationally minded. (*The Osaka Mainichi*, May 16, 1933)

However, the time was to come when Nitobe's romantic nationalism proved fragile before a stern reality — here we note is another common feature of Romanticism. It was soon taken place of by another kind of nationalism, characterized by national pride and military power. Japan was to withdraw from the League of Nations. It was coincidentally Nitobe's last year, 1933. His speech at the time is so impressive, so touching that I am tempted to quote almost the whole of it, running the risk of a digression. His speech was made to an audience of more than 100 people, representing all nationalities, attending the luncheon of the Tokyo Pan-Pacific Club at the Imperial Hotel, Tokyo, on Friday, April 7, 1933. And it was entitled "How Geneva Erred" when published as an article in *The Osaka Mainichi*, April 12 and 13, 1933.

> ... From the very kind words of introduction uttered by our chairman, I presume you expect me to say something about my latest trip to America. I left this country just about a year ago, and until then I was not at all disposed to cross the Pacific Ocean. In the presence of so many good American friends, I have to confess why I did not feel disposed to go.
>
> I consider myself one of the greatest admirers of America. I spent a few years in Baltimore when I was a young man, where I distinguished myself not when I was a student but about 50 years later, as a classmate of Woodrow Wilson.
>
> Then I went to Germany for five years, and my foreign education was chiefly acquired in Germany. But none the less, having been deeply impressed by the study, though not very profound I assure you, of English history and English literature, I was very partially inclined to Anglo-Saxon ideas, both in politics and in the general view of life — philosophy, you may call it.
>
> So after leaving the Agricultural College in Sapporo, I came to Tokyo to continue my studies in agricultural economics in the university here. When I asked for admission to the university, I told the dean I would like to study agricultural economics and English literature....
>
> When I told the dean of the university I wanted to take English literature for my minor subject, I said that I wished to be a bridge across the Pacific Ocean, a bridge across which western ideas could flow without obstacle or impediment to Japan, and over which oriental ideas could find entrance to America.
>
> However far I have wandered from my original plan of agricultural economics, I have not strayed very far from my avocation to be a bridge across the Pacific. I have never lost sight of it, though for more than eight years I consistently declined to go to America on account of the Exclusion Law, by

which our people of course are excluded. I respect the American law so well and so conscientiously that I thought I would not do injustice to America by treading on its sacred soil. Not another Jap should land there.

That is why I declined about 10 invitations from universities and other institutions, and when I was in Geneva, though I had friends in America and my wife had relatives there, I always used the Indian Ocean route back to Japan, out of respect for that law which would not tolerate any inferior people to land.

But when last year the sentiment in America became so bad against Japan, my friends told me it was high time I should desecrate that soil with my feet, because the questions involved were more serious than the Exclusion Law, and after thinking much about it, I decided to go. I am very glad that I went. I, like an ordinary human being, like darkness more than light, and America was dark, so I went there.

In the same way I came back into darkness. I do not think the atmosphere in this country is very light. We have left the League of Nations. The League of Nations is an artificial institution formed by the consent and the will of the states members. Entrance into it is voluntary.

Now we have left it, and here let me say I am one of those inconsistent and self-contradictory people who believe that while Japan is justified at the present moment to leave the League, — still believe that the League is the greatest hope for the future welfare of the world. I still insist upon looking at the League as the greatest achievement of the human race, and it is a pity that we have had to leave it.

The League, being a human institution, errs. To err is human. I think the League has erred in its too rigid interpretation of the Covenant of the League. The founders of the League, be it Wilson, Clemenceau, Lloyd George, did not look upon the League as a tight compartment — in fact these three men once wrote an official letter to the effect that the articles of the Covenant of the League are not subject to a narrow and technical construction. They are to be interpreted in a broad and statesmanlike manner.

But the arguments which were waged in regard to the

Manchuria question showed that many small powers have interpreted the Covenant not in a broad and statesmanlike manner, but like lawyers, in a cheap way. What a pity! None the less, there will come a time when the League itself will find it has committed a grave error.

At the same time, I believe Japan also has committed a grave error. We insisted that the League does not know sufficient of the causes and the reasons that underlie our action in Manchuria. We speak of the attitude of the League as being founded on ignorance, but who made the League ignorant? Are we not responsible for it? We have committed a grave error in being too reticent and uncommunicative, and I may say also unsociable, and the sooner we find out that error, the better for our future relations with the rest of the world.

Now we have left the League, which is an artificial institution, but we cannot leave the family of nations, which is a natural institution, and whatever rights we may have lost by our withdrawal from the League, we must make good by further attention to the family of nations. Our relations with the rest of the world must now be largely controlled by the idea of our membership in the family of nations, the natural, instinctive, warm, and more or less emotional institution. It is by attention to the duties demanded by our membership in the family of nations that we should guide our diplomacy.

America is not a member of the League of Nations, but it is one of the greatest and at present perhaps the most powerful members of the family of nations, so our relations with that country must demand our deepest and most careful consideration. Therefore, though the clouds that hang over the Pacific at present are still quite dark, yet with an effort and a will to bring about better understanding, we shall, I hope, regain our position in the heart of the American people.

At present things look dark, but darkness will not last forever. The shouting and the tumult will die, and the captains and kings will depart. Then we shall regain cooler judgment, and I do not think the time is far distant when this cooler judgment will come back. Then we shall see that on both sides of the Pacific there are many earnestly interested in our good relationship — I see many represented here this afternoon.

I think we may look forward to such a time. May we not already congratulate ourselves in forming new ties! In such a gathering as this we are forming ties that will grow stronger, and that in the coming years will bring back the enjoyable and friendly relations which have been the tradition of the Pacific.

I thank you for this opportunity of greeting my friends, and I wish that this society may grow in importance and influence. We meet like ships in the night, but we rarely forget the ships that we pass in the night.

Probably, Nitobe in his last sentence alludes to Henry Wadsworth Longfellow's poem,[8] and this explains the queerness of his expression. His style was literary to the last. Note that, two paragraphs above, he cited without inverted commas from Kipling's poem "Recessional": 'The tumult and the shouting dies; The captains and the kings depart.' Longfellow's poem he now refers to is *Wayside Inn III. Elizabeth IV*:

Ships that pass in the night, and speak each other in passing,
Only a signal shown and a distant voice in the darkness,
So on the ocean of life we pass and speak one another,
Only a look and a voice, then darkness again and a silence.

There might have been a better time for us to meet, Nitobe is saying, but, as it is, we are met in the dark, like 'ships that pass in the night.' However, such is the life, isn't it? Then, let us make much of this chance meeting; it will give an inspiration to a new age, when there will be enough of lightness and sweetness to realize our dreams. — Here, we see the author of *Bushido* addressing himself, like a prophet, to all the internationalists of the world.

Around the same time he reported on his conversation with Roy W. Howard, then head of United Press, visiting Japan:

I met with the famous reporter, Howard.... he said to me, "Because your country left the League of Nations, it is going to collapse." "You should not say such things. I (Inazô) think that because of that the League of Nations will grow stronger. The League is at fault.... When they realize this, the League of Nations will be restructured and then your country, too, will become a member. Russia will join, and Japan, and the League will truly become a League of Nations of the world." "Do you really think so?" "Of course I do." "You are an optimist." "Is it possible to live on this small globe, filled with suffering, and not be an optimist?" "Yes I see what you mean," he said, and we parted.[9]

Now, going back to the original topic, I say the two nationalisms (romantic nationalism and military nationalism) are almost sheer opposites. But strangely the two were closely related in Nitobe's case. Nitobe's book became world-famous especially around 1905, the year of Japan's victory over Russia. Japan's victory attracted the world's attention to Japan, and with it to Nitobe's book. Also this great internationalist was lucky enough to get an important position in the Headquarters of the newly born League of Nations in 1920. Why? Again, it was Japan's growing power, military and economic, after the first World War.

After Nitobe's death, when the military authorities began gradually to usurp the government, his name and the title of his book "Bushido: the Soul of Japan" were made use of to raise the morale of soldiers. If they had read through the book, Nitobe's call for the world peace would have been obvious, but, as I said before, it was a difficult book for Japanese readers. As a result, only his title was taken up and changed into a warlike catch-phrase appealing to the national pride. What a misunderstanding! And that is why Nitobe was long neglected after the nightmare of the Pacific War. Nowadays there are not so many who misunderstand him, but then there are still very few who truly appreciate his achievements, which, if reconstructed in its true shape, will surely give us a valuable orientation for the new age of true internationalism in this twenty-first century. That is what I in my feeble effort aimed at in this reassessment of Nitobe's *Bushido*.

**Notes**
1. Ronald W. Clark, *Einstein: The Life and Times* (New York: Avon Books, 1971; 1999), p. 432.
2. John F. Howes (ed.), *Nitobe Inazō: Japan's Bridge Across the Pacific* (Boulder & Oxford: Westview Press, 1995), p. 189.

3 This paper was first read to a conference *Romantic Nationalisms 1750–1850*, held at the University of Surrey Roehampton, London, 28 June to 1 July 2001.
4 Otto Jespersen, *Essentials of English Grammar* (London: George Allen & Unwin, 1933), p. 17.
5 John F. Howes (ed.), pp. 13–14.
6 Edmund Burke, *Reflections on the Revolution in France* (1790; London: Penguin Books, 1986), pp. 169–74 & *passim*.
7 'Oh, East is East, and West is West, and never the twain shall meet' ("The Ballad of East and West," l. 1.)
8 Cf. *Editorial Jottings*, "Longfellow's Midnight Bridge" (August 6, 1932).
9 Uchikawa Eiichiro, *Nitobe Inazô: The Twilight Years* (Tokyo: Kyobunkan, 1985), p. 151.

# II. Nitobe's *Bushido*: A Western Perspective

## Norman Page

*Bushido: The Soul of Japan* is a work that presents several curious features of which the first and perhaps the most striking concerns the circumstances of its original publication. For here is a Japanese classic that was written in English and appeared from a Philadelphia publishing house in the significant year of 1900. It became an instant best-seller and by 1905 was already in its tenth edition in English (its twenty-fifth if we also count translations). Later it could be described with justice as "one of the most widely read books about Japan". The author's introduction refers to "foreign readers", and the implied audience is cosmopolitan: evidently the purpose of this book written by a Japanese author in the English language was to explain Japan to foreigners. Hence, it is to be hoped, this western view of *Bushido* needs no justification or apology. At the same time, a century after its first appearance, it is possible for our perspective to be temporal as well as spatial, historical as well as cultural.

But there are other features of the book that may strike the reader as curious. The author was himself cosmopolitan and internationalist by virtue of his experience and outlook, yet his subject is Japanese tradition; he was also a Christian — specifically, a member of the Quakers, who have a long association with pacifism — yet he writes about the military tradition and seems at times to celebrate nationalism and the arts of war. (As we shall see later, by a curious irony his title has come to be synonymous, at least in the field of contemporary popular culture, with the practice of martial arts.)

The explanation of these ambiguities and ambivalences must be that Inazo Nitobe has two distinct purposes. His book was written partly to answer the questions of foreigners who wished to learn more about Japanese traditions and customs. But as well as defining traditional morality — what he refers to as the "ethical system" enshrined in Japanese traditions — he explores ways in which this can be adapted to the needs of a rapidly changing world. Born into the age of Darwin, he is interested in the evolution of Bushido and its ability to survive in a radically different environment from that in which it has previously flourished.

On the threshold of the twentieth century, then, he looks both to the past and to the future. In this respect he has something in common with such English Victorian moralists or "sages" as Matthew Arnold, John Ruskin and William Morris, who similarly sought to preserve and transmit the values of the past at a time when the world was changing more rapidly and radically than ever before in history.

The book is divided into seventeen chapters, and these comments will focus on only a selection of them. The opening chapter is concerned with the code of morality practised by "knights" (that is, samurai). The western reader will here be tempted to draw a parallel with the ideals of European chivalry in the Middle Ages, as defined, for instance, by Chaucer in his portrait of the Knight who stands first among the pilgrims described in the General Prologue to the *Canterbury Tales*. There is, however, an analogy much closer in time, suggested by Nitobe's own reference to (and quotation from) Thomas Hughes's novel *Tom Brown's Schooldays*. This Victorian story, intended for young readers, is set at Rugby School in the time of its great headmaster Dr Thomas Arnold (father of Matthew, already mentioned), and Arnold was in effect the creator of the modern English public school system, which trained and disciplined the ruling class of Victorian England in a manner not dissimilar from that in which the young samurai were trained and disciplined in Japan. Not only the medieval knight, therefore, but the Victorian gentleman seem to offer themselves — as Nitobe must have been fully aware — as parallels to the Japanese "knights" with whom this opening chapter deals.

Politeness would certainly have been deemed to be one of the hallmarks of a Victorian gentleman, and this attribute is the subject of Nitobe's sixth chapter. "In its highest form," he tells us, "politeness almost approaches to love." He is well aware that this quality, viewed more superficially, is one of those especially associated with the Japanese nation in the minds of foreigners; but he insists that the word should convey more than mere outward and conventional behaviour, and has indeed a "spiritual significance". The problem here, it should be pointed out, is partly a semantic one. Words that have once carried considerable force tend to weaken through long usage, just as people weaken through old age, and this may be particularly true of terms that once denoted firm moral and ethical concepts. "Courtesy" and "decorum" are other examples of words that formerly implied something more substantial than correct social behaviour or etiquette. It is in this spirit that the seventh chapter proceeds to relate politeness to sincerity.

It is clear by this stage that Nitobe's method is to identify, define and examine various key-concepts that he regards as major aspects of the code of Bushido, and one of those that comes under his scrutiny is "self-control" (Chapter 11). He notes that the Japanese have been widely regarded as possessing "a national trait of apparent stoicism", and makes it clear that this is closely related to "politeness" and indeed a logical consequence of it, for politeness requires us "not to mar the pleasure or serenity of another by expressions of our own sorrow or pain". For the western reader it is interesting that the term "stoicism" used in this context by Nitobe derives from the name of a school of philosophy in ancient Greece, and, in terms of western culture and aesthetics, self-control is clearly an attribute of the classic rather than the romantic temperament. In English literary history a figure such as Lord Chesterfield may be viewed as representing the quality to which Nitobe is drawing our attention.

In Chapter 14 the author turns to a theme that has become intensely topical in our own time: the training of women and their position in society. He acknowledges that in the samurai tradition the role of women was regarded as being primarily domestic, but quickly adds that this attitude is by no means confined to Japanese tradition. It is revealing, for instance, that the English word "wife" (which originally meant "woman" and not just "female spouse") is etymologically connected to the domestic activity of weaving, just as "daughter" originally signified "milkmaid". In contemporary Germany, he adds, the Kaiser himself famously defined the province of women as consisting in devotion to home, children and church. Again, it is striking to observe how readily Nitobe turns to western analogies in order to make a point about Japanese traditions.

Chapters 15 and 16 raise broader questions: what has been the enduring influence of Bushido, and does it have a future in the modern world? As already noted, Nitobe is conscious of writing at a period when Japanese society and culture are about to experience sweeping changes. His first-hand knowledge of the western world has taught him that the Industrial Revolution and its aftermath have transformed ideas and beliefs as well as material life in the West, and the question in his mind is whether the essence of the Bushido tradition, which has helped to mould the Japanese national character, can be preserved, even with modifications, to meet the needs of a newly emerging world.

The western reader of Nitobe is bound to be reminded of the great Victorian moralists and sages, and of twentieth-century writers such as E. M. Forster and George Orwell who have inherited their mantle. Like Nitobe, they were preoccupied by the question of what can be preserved from the past at a time of ideological cataclysm. Matthew Arnold traces the contribution of "Hebraism" and "Hellenism" to European culture, in contrast to the "philistinism" that threatens to engulf these long-established influences; John Ruskin examines the nature of Gothic and its relationship to an age of almost universal religious belief that has now been succeeded by an age of widespread unbelief and materialism; William Morris relates the work and society of the Middle Ages to the industrial age in which he lived; Orwell, writing in 1941 (*The Lion and the Unicorn*), analyses "the English genius" at a time when the very survival of the nation seems threatened.

Readers of Nitobe's book — and not only western readers — are likely to be struck by the fact that, although his subject is centrally and distinctively Japanese, his frame of reference is highly eclectic and truly international. In particular, there are many allusions to English literature, ranging from Shakespeare and Wordsworth to Burke, Carlyle, Ruskin, and T. H. Huxley, as well as the American Emerson, and the cosmopolitan Lafcadio Hearn. The Bible in translation, both Old and New Testaments, is also frequently alluded to. These references have the effect of creating a kind of dialogue between Japanese and western cultures: for the non-Japanese reader, the unfamiliar is rendered more accessible and more intelligible as a result of this frequent placing of the Eastern subject-matter within a frame of Western ideas as mediated through the work of great writers.

There are other ways in which Nitobe draws on his close knowledge and experience of the West in his elucidation of aspects of Japanese tradition. We have already seen, for instance, how readily he turns to the etymology of certain common English words in his discussion of the role of women in society. It is revealing, again, that when he refers in Chapter 13 to the initiation ceremony for young samurai, he should refer to this as "this first ceremony of 'adoptio per arma'" — using a Latin phrase (meaning, approximately, the taking up of arms) to define a crucial stage in the education of a Japanese boy. Implicitly the Japanese and the Roman traditions are brought together and, despite Kipling, East and West seem to meet.

As noted earlier, the closest parallel in European civilization to those who embodied the ideals of Bushido would probably have been such medieval figures as Chaucer's "veray parfit gentle knight", and Nitobe would obviously have been well acquainted with this tradition through his reading of western literature and history. He himself, however, was a product of the nineteenth century, and that was, in England, the period during which the concept of the "gentleman" became fully defined. (It was also, incidentally, the period in which, through Tennyson's very popular *Idylls of the King*, the ideals of medieval knighthood became once again familiar to a wide public.) Nineteenth-century English literature furnishes many examples of such figures, from Jane Austen's suggestively-named Mr Knightley (*Emma*) and Thackeray's Dobbin (*Vanity Fair*) to Trollope's Mr Harding (*The Warden*). Towards the end of the century, notably in the fiction of Thomas Hardy, the ideal is shown as being betrayed by such spurious "gentlemen" as Fitzpiers in "The Woodlanders" (selfish and immoral despite his aristocratic origins) and Alec d'Urberville (a member of the nouveau riche capitalist class). Anyone reflecting on these examples, and others, is likely to ask the same question that Nitobe is asking: can this type adapt itself successfully so as to survive in the modern world? An English writer who, a generation or so later than Nitobe, asks the same question is Evelyn Waugh.

One hundred years after the original publication of this work, can Bushido be said to have survived as a valid and viable concept? Certainly a search of the internet — that ever-expanding encyclopaedia of universal knowledge — yields some curious and somewhat discouraging results. The first item thrown up by "Bushido" is

"Bushido Martial Arts and Kickboxing", closely followed by "Bushido Aquatic Club", "Bushido Karate-do", and several other items in similar vein. There also exists, it seems, a company offering "samurai t-shirts". All this is a very long way from the refined intellectualism of Nitobe, and it looks as though, at any rate in the popular mind, Bushido has been appropriated by those who are more interested in the cultivation of the body than in mental enquiry. Against this, however, must be set the fact that a new edition of Nitobe's book appeared as recently as 1998. There is evidently still an audience for Inazo Nitobe's thoughtful and richly informed reflections on the traditions of his country, and western readers who turn to his book will continue to find much to interest and stimulate them. Their position — on the threshold of a new century and in a period of extraordinarily rapid and disconcerting change — is after all remarkably similar to his own.

# III. *Bushido*: Romantic Nationalism in Japan

## Simon Edwards

Karl Marx suggests that in periods of revolutionary change the experience of history undergoes a qualitative shift. The long *durée* of feudal or, even, pre-feudal time, with its slow quantitative accumulation of economic and political growth — a new technology here, a palace coup d'etat there — is suddenly transformed. Event follows event, change multiplies change, and consciousness itself is made new: 'All that is solid melts into air.' Marxist literary and cultural critics like Georg Lukacs and Walter Benjamin have in turn attempted to interpret the exceptional quality of the cultural production of such periods as manifestations of that *qualitative* leap. Inazo Nitobe's *Bushido* seems to invite such an approach. On the surface a meditation on the samurai code of feudal Japan, it may better be read as a fusion of ideas and images that draws from both a repertoire of Western culture and thought and an intimate understanding of Japanese history.

Some qualitative shift of the kind which Marx describes must have been the experience of many in late nineteenth century Japan, the time of Nitobe and that wider circle of intellectuals formed in the hotbeds of the Christian missions in the 1870s, not least that of Hokkaido. This remains the case even if the changes in Japan do not quite correspond to any revolutionary model to be found in Marx. Given that the Meiji Restoration has its origins in counter-revolutionary politics, we may be reminded of that revisionist view of the English Revolution of the seventeenth century which attributes it to the work of a disaffected provincial aristocracy rather than an emergent capitalist class. At least one influential aspect of contemporary Marxist historiography, associated with Tom Nairn and Perry Anderson, has notoriously insisted on the incompleteness of England's bourgeois revolution. This, in turn, may suggest some productive analogies between the histories of these two island empires.

At the very outset of *Bushido* Nitobe himself cites Marx's *Das Kapital*, on 'the peculiar advantage of studying the social and political institutions of feudalism, as then to be seen in living form only in Japan.' The particular vitality of those institutions in Japan, differing so radically from what, elsewhere, Marx describes, dismissively, as 'the Asiatic mode of production,' derived from the ways in which the Japanese had wilfully excluded the rest of the world from their development. This unprecedentedly successful system of autarkic political and economic development (paradoxically anticipating, as it does, the attempts of the European powers to achieve something similar in the capitalist world during the 1930s), enabled Japan to form a unique consciousness of itself. This consciousness echoes and corresponds to the new *nationalist* cultures that had been constructed so deliberately in the West over the previous hundred years, where a more distant medieval past had to be either recovered or invented. This was the fertile ground from which *Bushido* grew. It is those *national* formations which were to prove the major articulation of political life through the rest of the world in the twentieth century in the wake of the great programmes of *imperialist* expansion which had already began in Britain, France, Russia, Germany, the USA and which were to be joined, so rapidly, by Japan itself. Indeed it is nationalism and imperialism, as popular ideologies, that will provide the dominant counterpoint to the Marxist diagnosis of modernity. Both are equally fatefully inscribed with the new theories of racial difference and discrimination, underwritten by the 'science' of Social Darwinism with its misappropriation into the cultural sphere of the biological theory of natural selection and its assertion of 'the survival of the fittest.' Social Darwinism makes itself felt in so many late nineteenth century Western writers that we might think of it as a *leitmotif* of cultural modernism, in writers as diverse as Wells, Shaw, Zola, Hardy, Dreiser, Lawrence and Forster. Anxieties about *hereditary degeneration* occur alongside Utopian, or, dystopian, fantasies of *selective breeding*. One might cite here as typical of these contradictory responses two novels by H. G. Wells: *The Time Machine* and *The War of the Worlds*.

Nitobe was not free from these categories of thought and, given the impact of Social Darwinism's most pervasive apologist, Herbert

Spencer, (invoked, from time to time, by Nitobe) on the Japanese intelligentsia of the period, this is hardly surprising. A contemporary Japanese historian, Hirakawa Sukehiro, refers to this phenomenon by citing George Sampson's *Japan: A Short Cultural History* (1932):

> It was unfortunate that, when at last the Japanese had time to consider the nobler efforts of the Western mind, it was the dreary ratiocinations or the homiletic of men like Benjamin Franklin and Samuel Smiles which seemed best to stay their intellectual pangs. (*Cambridge History of Japan: Volume 5*. Chapter 7, Hirakawa Sukehiro, "Japan Turns to the Past.")

The same historian estimates that Nakamura Masanao's 1871 translation of Smiles's *Self Help* sold one million copies. The literature of the Victorian work ethic may have found congenial soil in the culture of loyalty and duty that Nitobe sets out to describe in *Bushido*. It would have been reinforced by the local 'frontier' experience of his adolescence in Hokkaido. It is worth remembering too that *Bushido* was written in California, then a frontier state, even if now we identify it as the apotheosis of post-modernity.

For Nitobe, however, the Victorian work ethic was always mediated by the more subtle ideas he found in Carlyle's early writing. A close reading of *Bushido* suggests that he was always happily agnostic towards the kind of racist rhetoric to which Carlyle himself had succumbed by the 1860s. The text remains remarkably free of what clouds so much reflection on nationality at this time. This confirms, I think, that Nitobe's agenda of Western literature was drawn up from very different sources and thus different principles from those which shaped so much other late nineteenth century thinking. Nitobe was also a Christian (not that this has done much to inhibit racist beliefs), and while he wears his faith lightly enough throughout *Bushido*, this also seems to have given him access to an alternative model of the relations between the individual and society in his account of the samurai code.

Nitobe was a contemporary of Lafcadio Hearn, one of the first Western 'readers' of Japanese culture, in whose work we find an almost utopian quality ascribed to the daily life of the Japanese people in the 1890s. We find descriptions that we might equally find in William

Morris's *News from Nowhere* or, indeed, in Wells's account of the playful and diminutive Eloi in *The Time Machine*. Just as in Wells the life of the Eloi is measured against the dark sustaining forces of the brutal subterranean Morlocks, the underside of the industrial system, so Hearn observes, quite dispassionately, the processes whereby Japan becomes a modern industrial and military power: the wars with China and Russia, the occupation of Korea. All these mark Japan's entry on to the the stage of world history, a stage on which Nitobe himself was soon to become a troubled actor.

This utopian strain in Hearn, suggesting a sensibility shared with both Morris and Wells, is to be found in *Bushido* too. It may be thought to derive in equal part from the actual experience of contemporary Japanese history and a pre-existing set of responses to cultural crisis that Nitobe found in the Western writers with whom he was absorbed.

In order to establish this aspect of Nitobe's work, I want, briefly, to compare *Bushido* and its reflections on the inception of Japanese imperialism with those we find in an almost exactly contemporary work, Joseph Conrad's *Heart of Darkness*. Conrad's novel resembles *Bushido* in offering a double vision in which heroic stoicism marches alongside the vulgarization of all civilised ideals. Thus Marlowe, the narrator of events, lives by a code of personal integrity associated with English naval service, analogous in some way to the anecdotes that Nitobe provides to illustrate the samurai code of honour and loyalty. The two books, however, project very different conclusions about the nature and future of imperial expansion. Whereas Conrad's contempt for the European imperial adventure is unwavering, Nitobe is only fitfully dismissive of what he finds degraded and dishonourable in modern Japan. Perhaps the latter's very different response to what in Europe is a moment of *fin de siecle* world is determined by his great sustaining metaphoric comparison. Japan's emblematic cherry blossom is evanescent and exquisite, while the flower of European chivalry, the rose, that ripens as slowly as it rots on the stem. Conrad's vision is one of vast organic decay that links the primeval swamp of the Congo with the origins of England as a barbaric province of Rome and the dark prosperity of contemporary London as the sun sets, as if for ever, over the Thames. Conrad's is just one version of the persistently recurring trope within Western modernism of the innate corruption of material progress. Indeed the incorporation, by contrast, of aspects of Japanese visual and dramatic art, embodying what Hearn saw as the sense of 'play' in Japanese life, into European aesthetic theory and practice during the 1890s may be thought of as one of the few positive and joyful symptoms of what is otherwise a culture of overriding revulsion and despair.

There are then 'native' reasons for Nitobe's meditation on this moment in Japanese history as something more than a version of the nightmare from which the archetypal modernist, James Joyce, insists that the artist must try to awake. Of equal weight, however, is the fact of his indebtedness to a pre-modernist Western literary culture. Thus I should want to argue that both his strategies and sensibilities are those we find in the 'tradition' of the Culture and Society debate, classically identified by Raymond Williams in his 1960 study. Williams's version of that tradition has been subsequently much elaborated and revised, and although he continues his original analysis down to 1950, the bulk of its discussion is reserved for the nineteenth century. Like Nitobe he begins with Edmund Burke.

He goes on to include William Cobbett, the populist political agitator and pamphleteer of the 1820s and 30s, whose work is a continuous celebration of an old agrarian order against the destructive energies of capitalist production. He discusses Samuel Taylor Coleridge, as journalist as well as poet, famous, like his erstwhile friend and collaborator Wordsworth, for his apostasy from the French Revolution; Robert Owen, the millionaire factory owner, socialist and philanthropist who founded the utopian industrial community of New Lanark; Thomas Carlyle, endorsed by Marx and Engels as the first great critic of the industrial system, the first indeed to describe it as a system: Matthew Arnold, poet, journalist and school inspector, and the first to invoke the term 'culture' as Williams uses it; Benjamin Disraeli, novelist and Tory politician; John Ruskin, art historian and critic, painter and lecturer; William Morris, architect, designer, poet and revolutionary socialist. He also pays attention to the work of those novelists who specifically addressed the formation of industrial society: Dickens, Eliot, the Brontës, Gaskell and Charles Kingsley. It is clear that these figures do not make up a liberal tradition since their politics are as diverse as they are volatile. Williams wrote about them, too, in the shadow of his involvement with the British Labour Movement and its own uneasy relations with the intellectual legacy of European Marxism that manifested itself so differently in Germany, France and Italy. What all these writers do have, however, is a quality of engagement, whereby they understand both their work and their lives as interventions in the social and political realms. In that sense they may be seen as continuing the artistic, cultural and political project that we associate with Romanticism. It is a project that insists on the possibility of human self-determination in history, that seeks to define and then open the grounds on which men and women can live most fully. It takes the achievements of the past as the source of potential blueprints for what may still be achieved. And thus, like Nitobe's work, it returns in complex ways to an account of the feudal past. 'Romanticism,' thus conceived, is a distinctive re-reading of Western history, one no longer rooted in the primacy of classical civilisation (though writers like Arnold remained absorbed by the legacy of Greece and Rome). It might be argued that it is in a constant state of dispute with that model of Enlightenment history, Edward Gibbon's *Decline and Fall of the Roman Empire*, which for English readers set the seal on a judgement of the European middle ages as the site of darkness, misery and superstition. It is, paradoxically, from Gibbon that Nitobe takes his examples of early Christian martyrdom which he compares with the rites of *hara-kiri* and *seppuku*. Nitobe must also have seen that this Romantic tradition was absorbed by the legacies and promises of Christianity, while recognising how little purchase such theological positions could have on either the daily life of ordinary Japanese or, increasingly, the citizens and subjects of the secularised West.

I am claiming Nitobe, therefore, for a tradition of European romanticism, a tradition that is as sensitive to the nuances of local and cultural difference as it is to the bewildering imperatives to be found in the totalising sweep of modern history.

To illustrate in more detail this strategic thrust of *Bushido* I want to conclude by glossing the first chapter. Here we have allusions to not only Burke and Marx but also Ruskin, Thomas Hughes's *Tom Brown's Schooldays*, and the French poet Lamartine. But these are never mere allusions, but rather examples of Nitobe's own literary method. From Burke throughout he takes his fundamental rhetorical technique, the great sweep of metaphor and allegory as in his use of the cherry blossom and the rose, or in the chapter on the Soul and the

Sword. Perhaps the more detailed evocation or, indeed, invention (as some contemporary Japanese scholars have argued) of the samurai past is more directly indebted to Carlyle's precise rendering of the life of the monastery of St Edmundsbury under Abbot Jocelin in *Past and Present*. But Nitobe begins with Chivalry and here his indebtedness to Burke is explicit as he concludes his first paragraph:

> It is a pleasure to me to attempt to reflect upon this subject in the language of Burke, who offered the well-known touching eulogy over the neglected bier of its European prototype. (Chapter 1)

That elegy occurs in the *Reflections on the Revolution in France*, the text whose prophetic diagnosis of the consequences of the Revolution became a kind of touchstone for so much later nineteenth century social thought, even for Burke's enemies. It is Burke to whom Nitobe returns at the end of *Bushido* when he speaks not simply of the formal abolition of feudalism in Japan in 1870, but focuses on that telling detail of the 1875 edict prohibiting the wearing of swords. In an echo of Burke's theatrical dismay that not one sword was raised in the defence of the Queen of France, for Nitobe this edict rang out, in Burke's own words, the old 'unbought grace of life, the cheap defence of nations, the nurse of manly sentiment and heroic enterprise,' and it 'rang in the new age of "sophisters, economists and calculators".' (Chapter 17)

From Burke Nitobe turns, as has already been noted, to Marx. Then, in the manner of one of Ruskin's adventures in etymology, he teases out the literal meaning of Bu-shi-do (literally Military-Knight-Ways), as part of a speculation that distinguishes nicely between the German *Gemuth*, the English *gentleman*, and the French *gentilhomme*, before turning his attention to the terms *samurai*, *Bu-ke*, and *Bu-shi* (Fighting Knights). This discussion of the gentlemanly/knightly code leads him, as it led so many Anglophiles of the period, to *Tom Brown's Schooldays*.

> "Fair play in fight!" What fertile germs of morality lie in this primitive sense of savagery and childhood.... We smile (as if we had outgrown it!) at the boyish desire of the small Britisher, Tom Brown, "to leave behind him the name of a fellow who never

bullied a little boy or turned his back on a big one." And yet, who does not know that this desire is the cornerstone on which moral structures of mighty dimensions can be reared....

(Chapter 1)

Ian Buruma, a contemporary Western 'interpreter' of Japanese culture, has recently turned his attention to the study of European Anglomania in *Voltaire's Coconuts* (1999). He confirms the remarkable influence achieved by Hughes's frankly simple-minded novel. It is apposite perhaps, here in Sapporo, the city of the Winter Olympics, to recall Pierre Coubertin, the founder of the modern Olympic movement. In the aftermath of the Franco-Prussian war, this Frenchman conceived the idea of sublimating and renewing the old military codes that he saw as underpinning Europe's civilisation. Discredited by the defeat of modern France as much as by the new technologies of war, they might return at the level of international sporting competition. For Coubertin, as for other French anglophiles like Hippolyte Taine, the English public school provided a useful, perhaps the best, model of how this might be done. In the figure of Thomas Arnold, the reforming headmaster of Rugby School, the setting of Hughes's novel, there seemed to be an appropriate hero. When Coubertin finally visited Rugby and saw Arnold's grave in the school chapel, he recalls that he fell on his knees and wept (or, perhaps, suggests Buruma, that is what he felt like doing had it not been less than manly). We can see what the public schools offered in other ways. If they became the training grounds for Imperial administrators, they were also intended to bring together the sons of landed gentlemen with those of industrialists, bankers and professionals to forge a common culture and solidarity between social classes which in nineteenth century Britain were still culturally and politically hostile. Tom Brown's own father, in the novel, is a Berkshire squire unremittingly contemptuous of the railways and all other manifestations of modern industry. The emphasis on both sporting prowess and team spirit was conducted in a world of ascetic, even brutal discipline in spite of the high material privilege enjoyed by the families from which these boys came. The microcosmic world of suffering and comradeship was intended to force different elements of the British ruling class, at a susceptible age, into a shared sense of social responsibility. Just as Nitobe says of the samurai code, fighting skills were always valued above learning and culture. So organised games always took precedence over both at Arnold's Rugby as Hughes conceived it.

We know that Nitobe was familiar with the work of Arnold's own devoted son, Matthew, the failed poet who advocated the pursuit of 'sweetness and light' as the true goal of those who wanted to resist what he believed to be the dubious secular forces of democracy and material progress. It was Matthew Arnold who gave us the term 'Philistine' to describe all who lie beyond the reach of superior sensibility and cultural sensitivity, and who threaten to dominate the new bourgeois universe. It is odd then how the unlikely hero of such a slight novel, both the apparent embodiment of philistine values, came to haunt so powerfully the consciousness of those who, like Nitobe, endeavoured to transform them. This may be the final paradox of nationalism itself at the end of the nineteenth century: that it must make philistine brutality the basis of the nation's claim to a superior sensibility, as part of the rationale of those colonial programmes that Japan was about to emulate. We know these terrible contradictions to be at least part of Nitobe's own tragic destiny. They may also still help us to understand the self-destructive energies unleashed by Japan itself, as part of a wider movement of human history, in the first half of the twentieth century that Nitobe's *Bushido* so eloquently and humanely ushers in.

# IV. A Bridge Across the Pacific: Nitobe's Knowledge of English Literature

## Teruhiko Nagao

What I'd like to emphasize here is the centrality of English literature in the wide scope of Nitobe's learning. His famous words, 'a bridge across the Pacific,' were uttered, when he was young, in answer to the question why he wishes to learn English literature. He called it his avocation, and in his final year's speech, "How Geneva Erred,"[1] he said he was always true to this avocation, while his vocations changed from one to another.

And yet, in the Nitobe studies, contributions from literary field have been relatively few. The reason seems to me three-fold. First, when Nitobe says literature, it covers a wider range than that of present-day literary scholarship. It is not limited to fictional literature, but extends and merges into history, philosophy and religion; it meant, to borrow Matthew Arnold's words, 'the best that has been thought and said in the world.'[2]

Secondly, as a disciple of Thomas Carlyle, Nitobe believed that the end of man is an action, not a thought. He turned to literature, not like a literary critic who is going to write academic papers about it, but like a man trying to put the bookish knowledge into practice. And this leads to the third reason.

The bookish knowledge must be turned into actions, and, as a result, the knowledge itself must recede to the background; that is to say, it must remain an avocation, giving priority to actions which constitute vocation.

These three factors — the wider range of literature, the priority of actions to writing, and the subsidiary status of literature as avocation — these three have been concealing the fact that Nitobe was a great scholar of English literature.

As this city Victoria[3] was the final place for Nitobe's earthly existence, Sapporo the city where I came from was the place of Nitobe's intellectual awakening.[4] And Nitobe's close friend Kanzo Uchimura reports about him that his tendency was literature when they were students in Sapporo.

The Shakespeare text, the central canon of English literature, seems to have been memorized in his head almost like a computer. Allusions to the Shakespeare text permeate Nitobe's English writing. Nitobe's *Bushido*, for example, is a treasure box of Shakespeare quotations. He very often neglects to footnote the reference, as was usual with literary scholars of his days. As a result, the Japanese translators of *Bushido* very often miss the point because of their failure to recognize his Shakespearean allusions.[5]

Nitobe's lecture entitled "What the League of Nations Has Done and Is Doing"[6] is a very important lecture, and I think it marks the climax of Nitobe's career. The League of Nations started officially in January 1920, according to the Versailles treaty. But the secretariat itself was set up provisionally in London the previous summer, and Nitobe had been busy collaborating with Eric Drummond, the Secretary-General. Beset with many objections, cynicisms and skepticisms, 'it was necessary for the League to sell itself in advance of its inauguration. Nitobe increasingly took on the lecturing mantle on behalf of the League of Nations team, both in Britain and on the continent.'[7] It was in this context that Nitobe presented this lecture. It was given several times but most memorably at the International University in Brussels on 13–14 September 1920. Even by that date the League had already dealt with a number of international problems. One of which is the suppression of the epidemic in Poland. Typhus was raging in the devastated Poland just after the war. International aid was essential, and the League of Nations raised a sum of two million pounds by contributions from different countries. Nitobe states proudly as follows:

> This is a gigantic scheme of philanthropy: when it requires a vast sum of money to be raised from countries far from the seat of danger, an appeal can be made only to their generosity. Participation in such a labour of love adds to the work of the League a 'touch of nature that maketh the whole world kin.'

The source of quotation is not indicated, but it is from Shakespeare's play *Troilus and Cressida*.[8] Every Shakespeare scholar will admit that this play is the most difficult text in the whole Shakespearean canon. However, considering that Nitobe is now engaged in an urgent task — the task of defining this newly established organization — we must conclude that the quotation came spontaneously from his memory. We can't conceive that he had time to open his Shakespeare on the desk, looking for some relevant quotation.

Literary allusions are not limited to Shakespeare. The most memorable one to me comes in his luncheon speech of the Tokyo Pan-Pacific Club, 1933, Nitobe's last year. The topic is "How Geneva Erred." Here he regretted the League of Nations' insufficiency in dealing with the Manchurian affairs, and also Japan's failure to explain herself to the world. Japan left the League of Nations for which Nitobe had so enthusiastically worked. He says:

> Now we have left it, and here let me say I am one of those inconsistent and self-contradictory people who believe that while Japan is justified at the present moment to leave the League — still believe that the League is the greatest hope for the future welfare of the world. I still insist upon looking at the League as the greatest achievement of the human race, and it is a pity that we have had to leave it.

The time was moving toward darkness. But still he appreciated this opportunity of speaking to the people of so many nationalities and talking about the peace in the future. He concludes his speech as follows:

> I thank you for this opportunity of greeting my friends, and I wish that this society may grow in importance and influence. We meet like ships in the night, but we rarely forget the ships that we pass in the night.

No quotation mark is here, but I think the last sentence is a subtle allusion to Longfellow's poem. It is so subtle that very few people may notice it, but all the more moving for that subtlety. Longfellow's lines are as follows:

> Ships that pass in the night, and speak each other in passing,
> Only a signal shown and a distant voice in the darkness,
> So on the ocean of life we pass and speak one another,
> Only a look and a voice, then darkness again and a silence.
> (H. W. Longfellow, *Wayside Inn III. Elizabeth IV*)

If these lines can be evoked in our mind, then Nitobe's words become an eloquent message: 'There might have been a better time for us to meet,' Nitobe seems to be saying, 'but, at present, we are met in the dark, like "ships that pass in the night." However, such is our life. All that we can do may be small and trivial, but to do it here and now is our mission on this earth. Then, let us cherish this chance meeting; it will give an inspiration to a new age, when there will be enough light to realize our dream.'

Literary allusions thus lend a beautiful embellishment to Nitobe's style. Nurtured by literature, Nitobe's English has elegance and beauty, and it is this that made him the top spokesman for the League of Nations at the time of its inauguration. Japanese people are mistaken in this point. They are too apt to think that the secret of Nitobe's success was a mere matter of language skill.[9]

The influence of literature doesn't stop at embellishment, of course. I think his firm belief in peace and love, which was in him not a mere ideology but the heart-felt truth, was nurtured by literature. In the concluding passage of his lecture, "What the League of Nations Has Done and Is Doing," Nitobe says:

> Let the League fulfil its mission. Guided by high principle as laid down in the Covenant, advised by expert knowledge and fortified by enlightened public opinion, I trust the League will so act as to justify its creation and existence, until a higher form of world organization, <u>foreshadowed by poets and philosophers</u>, shall have taken its place for the perpetual reign of justice and peace on earth.     (*underline added*)

Nitobe says, 'foreshadowed by poets and philosophers.' Here we are reminded that justice and peace, especially peace, is the eternal message from great literature. Homer's *Iliad*, the great epic dealing with the Trojan War, is bound up with a moving appeal to peace and reconciliation. The same is true with Shakespeare's drama *Henry V*, the nationalistic play that celebrates England's victory over France at Agincourt.

In this connection, most important for Nitobe was the influence of Thomas Carlyle. As I said above, Sapporo was the place of his intellectual awakening, and there he discovered the fountain-light of his career — Thomas Carlyle. In his later reminiscence, he talked about this episode in his youth — rather incorrectly, as quite natural after so many years. He says that in the library of his school he found Carlyle's words quoted in an old American magazine. It was the autumn of 1879. Nitobe's biographers have so far been unable to identify that magazine.[10] Hokkaido University has all the books and magazines of the library of Nitobe's time preserved. And after a search and consideration, I have concluded that the magazine he read must be the April number of 1874 of *Harper's New Monthly Magazine*.[11] In that number the magazine contains an article on Carlyle written by a James Grant Wilson, and the relevant passage is as follows:

> Though not the safest of guides in politics or practical philosophy, his value as an inspirer and awakener can not be overestimated. It is a power which belongs only to the highest order of minds, for it is none but a divine fire that can so kindle and irradiate. The debt due him from those who listened to the teachings of his prime, for revealing to them what sublime reserves of power even the humblest may find in manliness, sincerity, and self-reliance, can be paid with nothing short of reverential gratitude. As a purifier of the sources whence our intellectual inspiration is drawn, his influence has been second only to that of Wordsworth, if even to his.
> ..........
> To another aspirant for literary fame, who was compelled to submit to the drudgery of teaching a small school for a livelihood, and who appealed to Carlyle in a querulous and desponding spirit, the sage of Chelsea gave the following admirable advice in a letter dated November 17, 1850, and which I am not aware has ever before been in print. It was copied for me last summer from the original by an English literary friend. "Apparently," writes Carlyle, "you are a young man of unusual, perhaps of extreme, sensibility,

<u>and placed at present in the unfortunate position of having nothing to do.</u> Vague reverie, chaotic meditation, the fruitless effort to sound the unfathomable, is the natural result for you. Such a form of character indicates the probability of superior capabilities to work in this world; but it is also, unless guided toward work, the inevitable prophecy of much suffering, disappointment, and failure in your course of life. Understand always that the end of man is an action, not a thought. Endeavor incessantly, with all the strength that is in you, to ascertain what — there where you are, there as you are — you can do in this world; and upon that bend your whole faculties, regarding all reveries, feelings, singular thoughts, moods, etc., as worth nothing whatever, except as they bear on that, and will help toward that. Your thoughts, moods, etc., will thus, in part, legitimate themselves, and become fruitful possessions for you; in part fall away as illegitimate, and die out of the way; and your goal will become clearer to you every step you courageously advance toward it. No man ever understood this universe; each man may understand what good and manful work it lies with him to accomplish there. 'Cheer up, there's gear to win you never saw!' So says the old Scotch song, and I can say no more to you."[12]

*(underline added)*

I can't enter into detail here, but the writer of the article says, 'As the purifier of the mind Carlyle is second only to Wordsworth.' Now at this time Nitobe was in a mental crisis which would remind us of John Stuart Mill's youth.[13] Just as John Stuart Mill turned to Wordsworth's poems, Nitobe decided to read Carlyle to overcome his mental crisis. But the library of his school had no single book by Carlyle, nor any bookstore in Tokyo, as he found to his great disappointment. Then by a sheer luck, half a year later, he found Carlyle's book *Sartor Resartus* (1833-34) at the house of an American missionary who was just leaving Japan. Once in his possession, Nitobe says, he read this book avidly — more than thirty times.

And placed in the middle of that book by Carlyle is the famous diatribe against war. It runs as follows:

What, speaking in quite unofficial language, is the net purport and upshot of War? To my own knowledge, for example, there dwell and toil, in the British village of Dumdrudge, usually some five hundred souls. From these, by certain 'Natural Enemies' of the French, there are successively selected, during the French war, say thirty able-bodied men: Dumdrudge, at her own expense, has suckled and nursed them; she has, not without difficulty and sorrow, fed them up to manhood, and even trained them to crafts, so that one can weave, another build, another hammer, and the weakest can stand under thirty stone avoirdupois. Nevertheless, amid much weeping and swearing, they are selected; all dressed in red; and shipped away, at the public charges, some two thousand miles, or say only to the south of Spain; and fed there till wanted. And now, to that same spot in the south of Spain, are thirty similar French artisans, from a French Dumdrudge, in like manner wending: till at length, after infinite effort, the two parties come into actual juxta-position; and Thirty stands fronting Thirty, each with a gun in his hand. Straightway the word 'Fire!' is given; and they blow the souls out of one another; and in place of sixty brisk useful craftsmen, the world has sixty dead carcasses, which it must bury, and anew shed tears for. Had these men any quarrel? Busy as the Devil is, not the smallest! They lived far enough apart: were the entirest strangers; nay, in so wide a Universe, there was even, unconsciously, by Commerce, some mutual helpfulness between them. How then? Simpleton! Their Governors had fallen out; and, instead of shooting one another, had the cunning to make these poor blockheads shoot. (Book II, Chapter 8)

Later, the same sentiment was taken over in a much amplified form by another man of letters of the 19th century, John Ruskin. It was in a lecture given to the young soldiers of the Royal Military Academy in 1865 (about thirty years after Carlyle's book). Paradoxically and surprisingly, however, Ruskin begins his lecture, praising the merits of war.

When I tell you that war is the foundation of all the arts, I mean also that it is the foundation of all the high virtues and faculties of men. It is very strange to me to discover this, and very dreadful, but I saw it to be quite an undeniable fact.... I found, in brief, that all great nations learned their truth of word and strength of thought in war; that they were nourished in war and wasted by peace; taught by war and deceived by peace; trained by war and betrayed by peace; in a word, that they were born in war and expired in peace.[14]

This was not a mere lip-service to those young soldiers to whom he was addressing. He had long been invited to talk before them who he thought were not likely to take any interest in an art critic's talk. Then he was struck by a strange relationship that exists between war and art. Though dreadful, it is a fact. If human beings had not had war at all, literature, for example, would have lost more than half of its subject matter. More than half of great literature would have gone. Thus, Ruskin's passage sounds almost like a worship of war. But just as the eternal message of great literature is peace even when it deals with dreadful wars, Ruskin's true intention, here, is a continuation of Carlyle, that is to say, a vehement accusation against all kinds of war. He quotes that passage of Carlyle in the middle of his lecture,[15] and the whole lecture is an amplification of it.

And the third person that took it over was Nitobe (again after about thirty years from Ruskin). In the footnote of the first chapter of his *Bushido* (1899), Nitobe quotes this passage of Ruskin,[16] and starts his exploration of the Bushido ethics in a similar fashion. Just as Ruskin says, art is born out of war, and yet its appeal is to peace, Nitobe says that the Bushido ethics is born out of war, and points to peace. We may remember, in the thirteenth chapter of *Bushido*, Nitobe says that the Japanese sword is a dreadful weapon, but its best use is not to use it, not to wield it. However paradoxical it may be, Bushido or the way of the warrior can and did coexist harmoniously with his Quaker principle of pacifism.

Literature is especially rich in this kind of paradox and contradiction. Perhaps, it is because, of all disciplines, literature is the closest to life and our immediate experience. Literature tries to intensify experience, while other disciplines try to abstract it and impose upon it their own systems. In his 1933 luncheon speech, Nitobe says that he is 'one of those inconsistent and self-contradictory people.' That is what he was, as a great lover of literature. And as a great lover of literature, his belief in peace and love was a deep-rooted feeling. And this made him a true League of Nations man.

## Notes

1 A speech made to an audience of more than 100 people, representing various nationalities, who attended the luncheon of the Tokyo Pan-Pacific Club at the Imperial Hotel, Tokyo, on 7 April 1933 — the time of Japan's withdrawal from the League of Nations. *The Collected Works of Inazo Nitobe* (Tokyo: Kyobunkan, 1969-87), vol. 23: 373-79. See above pp. 99-103.
2 "Literature and Science," a Rede Lecture at Cambridge in 1882.
3 This paper was first read to the 18th Annual JSAC conference in Victoria, Canada, October 15, 2004.
4 Nitobe both studied (1877-81) and taught (1891-97) at the Sapporo School of Agriculture, the forerunner of the present Hokkaido University. The school was started by the government. Teachers were all English-speaking foreigners invited by the government with great cost. The school had two great attractions, at least for the first several years. At the transitional time of the Meiji Restoration, the traditional education based on Chinese classics, though a splendid one in its own way, was being acutely felt to be outdated; it was thought that young people with ambition should study English. Also the school offered to each student the board and lodging with even monthly allowances. It was a time when many samurai families, the former ruling class, had lost their position and income, and their children were poor for all their brilliant and ambitious mind. Thus the school attracted brilliant youths, mainly from the best schools in Tokyo — a kind of brain-drain. Interestingly, the government's hope was to train pioneering engineers to develop this northern island, very important in their eye to protect the whole country from the threat of Russia, but the teachers coming from America emphasized the Christian gentleman's education rather a little too much. The result was that, rather than engineering pioneers, the school produced many outstanding intellectual pioneers for the modernizing Japan.
5 For example, the translators of *Bushido* since 1938 have committed, without exception, a chronic error of mistaking a character in Shakespeare's play for a poet, probably misled by the verse form of the speech quoted in Chapter 9. If they had read Shakespeare's historical play *Richard II*, they would have noticed their error quite easily.
6 A lecture delivered in various places in Europe 1919-1920; published 1921 in London. *Collected Works*, vol. 15: 371-400. See also above pp. 4-25.
7 As Ian Nish puts it. See below p. 172.
8 III. iii. 176-177: 'One touch of nature makes the whole world kin: /That all with one consent praise new borne gaudes.'
9 Recently two books were published praising Nitobe's proficiency of English: Toshifumi Saitou, *Great Masters of English in Japan* (Tokyo: Chuoukouron shinsha, 2000); and Naoyuki Agawa, *Did You Find Out America? — The*

*Pre-war Era* (Tokyo: Toshoshuppan, 1998), but, as it seems to me, their emphasis is a little too much on the language skill side. For example, the former expresses a wonder at the fact that Nitobe at seventeen had enough language skill to understand Carlyle's abstruse passage. But it is not a mere matter of language skill that enabled Nitobe to understand and appreciate Carlyle's thought. Also the latter carelessly ascribes Nitobe's proficiency in English to his marriage with an American lady. The fact was the other way round. Nitobe's language skill matched with his deep knowledge of Western culture persuaded his wife to follow him as a partner in life.

10 In one of his reminiscences made around 1907 (*Collected Works*, vol. 5: 156), Nitobe mentions the name of the American magazine as "Independent." But according to *Poole's Index to Periodical Literature 1802–1906*, the *Independent* (New York) was a magazine issued from 1892 to 96, that is to say, not yet extant in the year 1879. In tackling with this problem we must sift grain from husk, because Nitobe's reminiscences are not always correct.

11 *Harper's New Monthly Magazine* (New York: Harper & Bros., 1850–1899) absorbed *International Monthly Magazine*, and was continued by *Harper's Monthly Magazine*.

12 This passage fits in well with one of Nitobe's reminiscences (made around 1928: *Collected Works*, vol. 1: 184): 'It was in the autumn evening. I still remember well. I was desultorily reading in the study room of our dormitory, when my eyes met with the words of Carlyle quoted in an old American magazine. I found his words had described my own state of mind exactly as if in a photograph. Then I realized that I am not the only person; that there are other minds who are troubled in the same way.' It also fits in with another reminiscence (*Collected Works*, vol. 5: 156): 'I was much intrigued by Carlyle's words quoted in it. I was struck by the ingenuity and loftiness of the idea.'

13 John Stuart Mill, *Autobiography* (1873), Chapter 5.

14 John Ruskin, "War," Lecture III in *The Crown of Wild Olive* (1866; 1873), Section 94.

15 *The Crown of Wild Olive*, Section 99.

16 *Bushido*, Chapter 1. In his excellent book *Inazo Nitobe as a Bridge Across the Pacific* (Tokyo: Misuzu shobou, 1986), Yuzo Ota seems to be worried about this quotation. Nitobe is quoting from such a worshipper of war, and Nitobe's own theme, too, is the ethics nurtured among the war-making people. Thinking in that way, he casts a grave doubt on Nitobe's pacifism. His statement runs somewhat like this in translation: 'Nitobe is very often spoken of as a pioneer of pacifism, democracy and liberalism in modern Japan. But such words as the following, for example, even though uttered borrowing other person's mouth, can be labelled almost as an encomium of war' (p. 79). However, the stance adopted by Ruskin is that of irony: he starts with the words of praise for war but his real intention is an accusation against all kinds of war. Yuzo Ota either failed to grasp this stance so common in literary

discourses, or didn't read the whole essay, judging Ruskin only from this single paragraph, whereas we can easily imagine Nitobe reading through the whole essay most avidly.

# V. Chinda Sutemi, 1857-1929:
# Ambassador in War and Peace

## Ian Nish

[Reprinted with the permission of the Japan Society, London]

Historians have a penchant for examining the origins of war. That is very proper because it is important to learn the art of preventing wars. But the aftermaths of war are equally worthy of study because it is there that things go wrong for the future and the decisions have often to be taken at breakneck speed in fast-moving situations. This requires adaptability, flexibility and vision on the part of decision-makers.

This was nowhere more needed than in the case of Japan and the Paris peace conference of 1919 which brought an end to the 'first world war'. In spite of the description, it had been primarily a European war; and Japan had kept herself on its fringes. She had grown prosperous as a result of it. Without doubt she had made a contribution to allied victory, mainly as a result of her naval actions. But she had not suffered many casualties which for many nations was to be the criterion by which their contribution to the war effort was judged. This left the Japanese with a seat at the top table at the Paris Peace Conference where the peace was negotiated — one of the members of the Council of Five Great Powers but outside the Council of Four in which many of the critical decisions were vested. Japan had advanced on to the world stage and had much to do to adjust to her new role.[1]

Chinda Sutemi as ambassador to Britain from 1916 to 1920 was one of those who had to attend the Paris conference and address these new international problems. He had a role in the preparation of Japan's peace terms, took his share in steering through the negotiations and conducted important business during the first two years after the armistice.[2]

Born in Mutsu, Aomori-ken, Chinda graduated at an American

university and joined the Foreign Ministry in 1885. After a variety of consular posts, he became minister to Russia briefly in November 1900. He then returned to the ministry as vice-minister under Komura Jutaro in 1903 and served throughout the stressful days of the Russo-Japanese war. Because of Komura's frequent illnesses and his absences at Portsmouth, New Hampshire, and Beijing, Chinda was effectively in charge at critical junctures. He had close relations with the British ambassador who reported confidentially to London in 1908: 'Chinda is considered by some to be a man of exceptional ability. The Baron speaks excellent English but is very reticent.'[3]

In June 1908 he went to his first ambassadorial post, succeeding Inouye Katsunosuke in Berlin. He then moved to Washington from November 1911 where he had a long stint of five years. He enjoyed cordial relations with the British ambassador there; Sir Cecil Spring Rice.[4]

## Chinda in London

Chinda was appointed to the London embassy in the middle of the first world war and arrived at his post at a critical juncture on 1 August 1916. It was a strange coincidence that he should succeed Inouye whom he had earlier replaced in Berlin in 1908. It was rumoured that he had turned down the post of foreign minister in 1915, a sign that he was approaching the pinnacle of his career. He came to London at a depressing time for the Allies before the United States joined them in April 1917. China which was even more a matter of concern for Japan entered the war in August of that year. While Britain was preoccupied by the changing fortunes of the fighting, Japan was looking ahead to the bargaining which would take place at the peace-table.

In October 1916 the Okuma cabinet resigned, making way for the cabinet led by General Terauchi Masatake. The foreign minister appointed was Motono Ichiro, the former ambassador to Russia who had played a large part in formulating the Russo-Japanese alliance which had just been concluded in July. Motono came to the post dissatisfied with the lack of clarity over Japanese policy towards the war. Basically Japan was at war against the Central Powers of Germany and Austro-Hungary, and should cooperate with the Entente to the fullest degree. But the situation, Motono wrote, was full of uncertainties:

> Peace terms should include Japan's retention of Tsingtao and occupied islands in the Pacific and acquisition of rights possessed by Germany in Shantung province.... But, if victory does not go either to the Alliance or the Entente, it is likely that Germany will reject Japan's claims.... If the war ends in victory for the German Alliance, it will be even more difficult to get approval for Japan's claims.... Even if the Entente are victorious, they will probably expect the country that made the least sacrifice in the war [i.e. Japan] to be modest in its demands.... Hence we should give the Entente countries as much help as possible in material, finance etc.[5]

Clearly from Japan's perspective, all contingencies were being explored. But Motono was seeking clarification and proposing a radical shift of emphasis away from a policy which would not send troops to the western front and hitherto declined to send war-ships beyond Singapore. The Japanese cabinet agreed that, now that the war was finely balanced, it was desirable that Japan should more explicitly throw in her lot with Britain and her Entente partners in the hope of securing the prizes on which she had set her sights.

Such was the policy which Chinda had to apply in the months ahead. Almost as soon as he reached London, the naval situation in the Atlantic took a turn for the worse because of German submarine attacks. Britain reiterated to Chinda her appeals for naval assistance and Japan responded by requesting a number of undertakings. These included a postwar guarantee for Japan's retention of Shantung and Germany's insular possessions in the Pacific which were already occupied by Japan. Japanese naval authorities were probably itching to go beyond the confines of the China seas; and Chinda indicated that there would probably be no difficulty in securing their cooperation. On 2 February 1917 Japan agreed to make available the necessary naval assistance. The *Tsushima* and *Niitaka* were to go to Cape of Good Hope, while the *Akashi* and two flotillas of destroyers were to be despatched to the Mediterranean.[6]

The British war cabinet duly responded by confirming the necessary guarantees on 14 February. Britain agreed in rather careful language that she would support Japan's claims in regard to the disposal of Germany's rights in Shantung and possessions in the Islands North of the Equator on the occasion of a peace conference, it being understood that Japan would '... treat in the same spirit Britain's claims to the German islands South of Equator.' This last phrase was included in order to create the impression of parity between the two sides. But this was spurious since Britain was in this instance the mendicant, desperate to obtain Japanese naval assistance regardless. Where this formula was devised is not clear. Probably in London; but Chinda's role in this negotiation is not completely clear. He was a newcomer to the post, compared to Sir Conyngham Greene who had been ambassador in Tokyo since 1913 and was, of course, able to lobby the naval establishment there direct.[7]

Over the next issue Chinda took a more personal interest. A telegram from Deputy Foreign Minister Alfred Zimmermann in Berlin to Mexico on 19 January 1917 had been intercepted and successfully decoded by British intelligence.[8] The thrust of the message was that 'if war broke out between Germany and the United States, Germany would offer Mexico an alliance and try to persuade her into operations against the United States, with the ancillary suggestion that the Mexican president should mediate between Germany and Japan and request Japan to take part in their alliance.' This obscure speculation was dynamite. The intercept was passed over by Britain to Washington; by President Wilson to the press; and by the newspapers to an astonished American public. Germany was on the point of starting unrestricted submarine warfare in the Atlantic and wanted to dissuade the United States from declaring war. In April, however, the Americans severed relations with Germany because of her threat to make these submarine attacks against both enemy and neutral shipping.

The air between Washington and Tokyo was already hostile; and those suspicions were greatly intensified by the inclusion of Japan's name in the Zimmermann telegram. Chinda at Washington had had the additional responsibility as envoy to Mexico and was already familiar with the problems there. Japan had sold a considerable amount of arms to Mexico; and the arms dealers were a source of constant embarrassment to the Japanese government. Chinda was able to tell Britain with considerable authority that Japan was keeping her distance from the Mexican government. She published denials that she would have had any hand in such a deal and emphasized that there was no way that Mexico of all states could persuade Japan to make peace with Germany.

On 5 May Viscount and Viscountess Chinda were invited to spend two nights at Windsor Castle as royal guests. During their visit the king spoke to them of the need for Japanese destroyers to sink German submarines because of the battle of the Atlantic Ocean and the need for arranging convoys. At this stage Japan asked in return for the supply of special materials required for the construction of naval ships, in other words, steel. Britain had to say that she had none to spare and urged Japan to approach the United States where she was again refused.[9]

American entry to the war on the Entente side was succeeded by the decision of the government of China to follow the same path. This had long-term consequences for Japan as the Motono statement above has shown. It was now inevitable that China would send plenipotentiaries to the ultimate peace conference and dispute the major Japanese claim.

## Paris Peace Conference

When the war ended in 1918, Chinda as ambassador to Britain was chosen alongside Matsui Keishiro, ambassador to France, and Ijuin Hikokichi, ambassador to Italy, as Japanese delegates to the peace conference. The initial idea was that Japan would rely on those who had expertise from the Portsmouth conference of 1905 which ended the Russo-Japanese war. Viscount Chinda arrived in Paris on 11 January 1919. On the 18th the main delegation led by Baron Makino Nobuaki, a former ambassador and foreign minister, arrived *via* the United States. For the critical first six weeks Makino conducted negotiations as de facto chief. Chinda was in effect second in the pecking order, slightly higher than Matsui and Ijuin. Chinda had some advantages over the other Japanese delegates: his English was superior; and he was 'robust in argument'. More importantly, he knew most of the American delegates who had been members of the Wilson administration and had had dealings with them and with the British. He was, in particular, familiar with Arthur Balfour who as foreign secretary was a chief British negotiator. When Prince Saionji arrived on 2 March to head the mission, not much changed since he was content to keep a low profile and be consulted behind the scenes.[10]

Nonetheless conference diplomacy was a novel experience for which Japan as a whole was ill-prepared. The Portsmouth negotiations of 1905 had been no real preparation. Similarly the international conference at Beijing of 1900-1 to sort out the Boxer problem, while it was truly international, dealt only with a limited and well-defined subject. This was a problem for the delegates who were to be pitied because their instructions were strictly laid down from Tokyo. They were formulated not only by the Foreign Ministry but sometimes by the Gaiko Chosakai, an extra-parliamentary group of politicians with strongly-held views and without exposure to the arts of international negotiation.

That left much of the business of the delegation to be conducted by what one Japanese scholar calls the 'Makino-Chinda *kombi*'. That is, the two tended to combine as a team and lobby together on all substantial issues. Cooperation between Makino and Chinda was to be a special feature of the Japanese delegation's actions at Paris; and it worked well.[11] They had a broad mandate from Prime Minister Hara to follow the line taken by the British and Americans. But this was not easy to implement because they found that Anglo-Saxon feeling was generally in favour of China and this was shared by conference participants as a whole.

Japan was negotiating as one of the victors. In the initial stages of the conference Japan lost out over the racial equality clause.[12] There was a fierce determination therefore not to give in over her most precious demand, the transfer to Japan from Germany of the former German leased territory in Shantung province in China. This issue became an acute embarrassment to the Council of Four, all the more so as Italy had already left Paris dissatisfied and in disgust. Chinda was at his most threatening at this stage, suggesting that Japan would not join the League of Nations. On 16 April he met Balfour to see if any compromise could be worked out over Shantung. Balfour told him that the United States and France were supporting China. Chinda assumed not inaccurately that Britain, while ready to act in accordance with her agreement of 1917, was endeavouring to induce Japan to reduce her demands in order to secure a compromise acceptable to other delegations. But he would not agree. When the Versailles treaty was signed, it transferred the residue of the German lease of Shantung to Japan, in spite of China's pleas. But, in order to secure her prime demand, the Japanese delegates, not least Chinda, had to give some assurances of the vaguest kind that Japan would ultimately restore some of Germany's rights to China. That assurance was probably given in good faith but it was not publicly endorsed by the Tokyo government.

The Paris Peace Conference left a lot of loose ends. This was particularly true of the far eastern field and the issue of Shantung. Since it had not been possible to resolve this to the satisfaction of the powers, it was left to the Foreign Office and the State Department to pursue the issue with Japan on a bilateral basis. These were awkward days for Chinda who was summoned to meet the acting foreign secretary, Earl Curzon, on 18 July for this purpose. Curzon reported that he had told Chinda that 'it was unwise of Japan to insist upon the technical rights secured to her by her agreement with China in respect of Shantung. I was aware that a declaration of her intentions had been made by Japan to other Allied Powers in Paris; but this action which was to a large extent a justification of the action taken by the Powers had never been published to the world.... The whole policy of Japan was wrapt in a mist of doubt and suspicion which was creating very general alarm.' In response, the ambassador (as described in the flowery language of Curzon) 'intervened with an almost impassioned defence of the action of his country and his Government, the fervour of which in no wise abated until our conversation lasted for nearly an hour and a half.... Arguments which were again and again reiterated with great vigour.'[13] Something of the personality of Chinda comes out in these exchanges. He was not inexperienced in diplomacy and was not prepared to be browbeaten by Curzon. Loyal to his government, he stood up to the imperious foreign secretary.

Chinda continued to be actively involved in the politics of Europe after the Versailles treaty. It was one of the consequences of Japan's enhanced role in international affairs that her representatives had to be involved in the various conferences held around Europe in order to implement and expand on the findings of the Versailles treaty. There were also meetings of the nascent League of Nations of which Japan was a founder member. For example, Chinda had to attend a special meeting of the League Council which was summoned for St James Palace on 14 June 1920, London acting for the time being as the headquarters of the world body. The press were calling for the highest possible representation by prominent politicians so that the League of Nations could be launched strongly. Alas, 'apart from Lord Curzon for Britain and Viscount Chinda for Japan, other representatives lacked distinction,' it was reported. Chinda was punctilious in attending to these public duties. Japan wanted to be seen as cooperating in the League Council which was the prime international body of the time; and Chinda played his part.[14]

## Departure: End of the Alliance

Chinda's term of office in London was fast coming to an end. One item of business which he wanted to resolve before he left his post was the future of the alliance, the third treaty being due to lapse on 13 July 1921. There was no doubt that Hara Kei as prime minister was committed to the continuation of the alliance and carried his cabinet with him. But, as in Britain, there were discordant elements outside the cabinet. Some thought that Britain was a symbol of old-style imperialism which had been further displayed in the terms of the Versailles treaty and was not to be trusted by Japan. Others in intellectual circles were broadly favourable, taking the view that the United States had become so hostile to Japan during the war that Britain was the only great power that could be relied on to be moderately sympathetic to Japan.

Apart from xenophobic distrust which is natural to all countries, what divided the two allies in 1920 was the relation of the alliance to the newly-founded League of Nations. To the Japanese the issue was simple: the alliance was stable and tested in time, while the League was experimental and its future unpredictable. British opinion-makers looked at it differently: the world had moved on from the days of alliances towards world organizations and so the alliance would have to take second place to the covenant of the League. The London embassy found it necessary to inform Tokyo of the existence of two contrasting strands of opinion within the British Empire: those for extending the alliance (*domei encho ronsha*) and those opposed to continuing it (*hikeizoku ronsha*). To the Japanese, however, it was a nonsense to think of a contradiction existing between the League and the alliance; the two would complement one another in achieving stability in east Asia. The end-result was that a formula had to be found which would preserve the alliance and would see the League through its teething period.[15] That formula was approved by the cabinet and the Gaiko Chosakai.

One of Chinda's last acts was to sign along with Curzon at the Spa conference on 8 July 1920 the following document:

[Our agreement of 1911] though in harmony with the spirit of the Covenant of the League of Nations, is not entirely consistent with the letter of that Covenant. [The two governments agree] that, if the said Agreement be continued after July 1921, it must be in a form which is not inconsistent with that Covenant.

In order to get this formula through the Privy Council where opposition was expected, it was necessary for the Ministry to append lengthy explanations.[16]

Before Chinda left his London post, there was a large number of farewell functions for the retiring ambassador. Of course, he was entertained by the Japan Society of London of which he had been president. But he was widely feted by the political establishment. In spite of all the doubts and dismays in diplomatic circles, the Japanese were generally popular in Britain in 1920. The Chindas were the symbolic beneficiaries of this affection.[17]

In particular, Chinda met with Britain's leaders. On 17 August Chinda called on the British prime minister, Lloyd George, whom he had known well from the various postwar conferences that they had attended together. While exchanging parting greetings, they discussed first the future of Russia and later the Anglo-Japanese alliance. Chinda, raising the alliance issue, said that Japan wanted to continue the former Anglo-Japanese relationship which was in the interest of both countries and also in that of the world. While he was due to retire, he said he would strive for that relationship to the best of his ability. Lloyd George asked how Japanese opinion thought about continuing the alliance. Chinda said he had no doubt that the majority of the responsible intellectual classes agreed to the continuation of the alliance. The prime minister pointed out that he believed that British public opinion also favoured continuing the alliance but he had to consider the views of dominions overseas and of the United States. In his opinion, if it were possible, there would be advantages in adding the United States to the parties to the alliance. But, considering the present difficulties of the American administration, it would be absolutely impossible to attempt to negotiate on this problem. Following this, Chinda made his farewells to Curzon and found him very cordial. On the alliance he took the same view as the prime minister.[18] These views were not expressed out of politeness because they were repeating views like these to their cabinet colleagues.

Chinda, accompanied by Viscountess Chinda who had played a large part in her husband's success, sailed from Tilbury on 24 August by the *Kitano-maru*. He was succeeded by Hayashi Gonsuke. This was at roughly the same time as the arrival of Sir Charles Eliot as the new ambassador in Tokyo. So there was a change of pilots in both capitals. Exhausted after four years of wartime and postwar diplomacy which had taken their toll on his health, the departing ambassador returned to Japan early in October.

Chinda was as good as his word to the British ministers and gave his views on the alliance in a conversation in the Foreign Ministry on 15 October, explaining how he saw British opinion:

> since the alliance had been in existence so long, it would raise all sorts of important issues for it to be abrogated without very special reasons. Besides, turning to the future of the League of Nations, the whole British nation was feeling a bit disturbed. By and large, there were no obvious objections on the part of the government to continuing the alliance. But Japan must try to avoid some cases which whipped up anti-Japanese feeling like the arrest of Shaw and the issue of Shantung and Tsingtao and make her viewpoint clearer. Britain's major problem was to take into account the opinion in the United States and the Dominions.[19]

This was a broadly accurate interpretation of British thinking. Perhaps Chinda placed undue emphasis on the views of Lloyd George and Curzon which did not wholly represent those of the people at large and the Foreign Office secretariat. But he clearly identified the intense feeling of British subservience to Washington. There was not much that Japan could do for the present while the election campaign was being fought out in the States or, in the case of the British Dominions, until the imperial conference was held during the summer of 1921. Japan should, however, avoid provocative actions which would stir up a damaging press campaign against her. This was a recognition of a new truth about the power of public opinion and the media in post-Versailles foreign policy-making in Europe. Japan could well understand that the future of the alliance would not be a simple legalistic matter such as had been the case with the renewal in July 1920 but was likely to become a major issue of international affairs.

Viscount Chinda was made a count on 7 September 1920 for services during the first world war. Whether this was a reward for his work at the London Embassy or at the Paris and other conferences is not stated. It was merely one of a number of elevations announced at the same time.[20] Chinda was appointed to the Privy Council and in 1921 joined the Imperial Household Ministry. He played an important part in promoting the notion of international cooperation through various activities of the Japan League of Nations Association [*Nippon kokusai remmei kyokai*], a branch of the global organization set up to win support for the cause of League.[21]

Chinda was further honoured by his appointment to accompany the Crown Prince during his state visit to Britain commencing on 9 May 1921. It was not a political mission insofar as it was designed primarily as part of Hirohito's education and coming of age. Chinda's role was not to negotiate but to instruct him on the niceties of protocol and steer him through the byzantine rituals of the British court. He is to be seen in the photographs of the visit, a diminutive figure standing protectively close to the young prince. He only surfaces in one instance where the Prince of Wales, thinking that the Crown Prince should come closer to the British people, was alleged to have proposed that he should travel on the London underground. When, however, this madcap proposal was raised, Chinda was the one that had to veto it, or rather (to avoid *lese majeste*) to discourage the enterprise. Overall, the itinerary ran smoothly thanks to Chinda; and Curzon as foreign secretary saluted the prince's visit as 'a uniform and conspicuous success'.[22]

The culmination of Chinda's career in London has to be measured in two respects. First, as ambassador to London. Like his predecessor, he came without early training in London or a previous London posting. By the time he left in 1920 he had been won over to Britain and, in spite of the verbal knocks he experienced at the hands of Earl Curzon, he appears to have genuinely enjoyed his last few months. *The Times* saluted him for taking his share of the heat and burden of those anxious days.[23] Second, he has to be measured against the changing face of world diplomacy. Chinda was at the centre of things at the Paris Peace Conference and in the postwar round of international conferences. Conference diplomacy required linguistic ability and political flexibility, not qualities that Japan had conspicuously shown in the past. Nonetheless Chinda, in combination with Makino, did his best at Paris in a new and difficult role. Kimura Eiichi, a Foreign Ministry official attached to the plenipotentiaries there, described Chinda as showing great fighting spirit with special reference to the Shantung question at Paris and general coolness in negotiation.[24] While Makino appealed more to foreign observers as a man of ideas ready to explore and discuss new approaches, Chinda was a more conventional bureaucrat but he emerged as a firm believer in the League of Nations. *The Times*' editorial summed up his qualities on his departure, saying that he had 'a fixed and unswerving loyalty to the immemorial traditions of his country [which went] hand in hand with a sympathetic understanding of the problems and growth of Western democracy'.[25]

## Notes

1 The best general treatments of the subject are R. H. Fifield, *Woodrow Wilson and the Far East*, New York: Crowell, 1952; and Bruce Elleman, *Wilson and China: A revised history of the Shandong question*, Armonk, NY: M. E. Sharpe, 1984.
2 Kikuchi Takenori (ed.), *Hakushaku Chinda Sutemi-den, 1857–1929*, Tokyo: Yumani-shobou, 1938.
3 *British Documents on Foreign Affairs*, Part I, Series E, vol. 8, Maryland: University Publications of America, 1989, p. 69.
4 Honda Kumataro on 'Chinda and Spring Rice' in Kikuchi, p. 288.
5 Kajima Morinosuke, *Diplomacy of Japan*, Tokyo: Kajima 1980, vol. 3, p. 203 (my parenthesis). See also *Nihon gaiko bunsho*, Taisho 6/3, doc. 667 [hereafter cited as 'NGB']
6 Professor Seki Eiji in his book *Nichi-Ei domei*, Tokyo: Gakushu Kenkyu, 2003,

devotes chapters 2 and 3, pp. 71-179, to Japan's Mediterranean expedition and Malta experiences.
7 There are new studies of this topic by Yoichi Hirama and Ian Gow with John Chapman, *History of Anglo-Japanese Relations*, vol. 3, 'The Military Dimension', Basingstoke: Palgrave, 2003, while the older study by G. Nakashima, 'Japanese Navy in the Great War, 1918-20' in *Proceedings of the Japan Society of London*, 31 (1917) is still useful.
8 See C. Andrews and D. N. Dilks, *The Missing Dimension*, London: Macmillan, 1984, pp. 144 and 147. Barbara Tuchman, *The Zimmermann Telegram*, London: Macmillan, 1983.
9 NGB Taisho 6/3, docs 106 and 110.
10 Margaret Macmillan gives a good pen portrait of Saionji and how his role puzzled foreigners. *Peacemakers*, London: John Murray, 2001, pp. 316-19.
11 Kimura Eiichi as quoted in Kikuchi, pp. 220-22. This view is generally supported by Naoko Shimazu, *Japan, Race and Equality*, London: Routledge, 1998.
12 Japan's claim for mandates over the Pacific islands which is sometimes depicted as a failure was eventually settled in her favour. The allocation, initially made at the Paris conference, was confirmed at the San Remo conference of 1920 and later by the League-Japan agreement in 1922.
13 Fifield, pp. 546-47 contains only the shortened version passed to the Americans. For the full version, *Documents on British Foreign Policy, 1919-39*, London: HMSO, 1 (vi), doc. 429. [hereafter cited as 'DBFP']
14 George Scott, *Rise and Fall of the League of Nations*, London: Hutchinson, 1973, p. 56.
15 NGB Taisho 9, vol. 3/2, doc. 882.
16 NGB Taisho 9, vol. 3/2, doc. 884.
17 Kikuchi, pp. 214-15.
18 NGB Taisho 9, vol. 3/2, nos 888-89; Kajima, vol. 3, p. 427.
19 NGB Taisho 9, vol. 3/2, doc. 986. George Shaw was an Anglo-Chinese merchant with business interests on the Yalu river. He was arrested by Japanese police in Korea on what seemed to Britain to be flimsy charges.
20 *The Times*, 7 Sept. 1920.
21 Ogata Sadako in Dorothy Borg and Shumpei Okamoto (eds), *Pearl Harbor as History*, New York: Columbia UP, 1973, pp. 462-63. Japan League of Nations Association was formed on 23 April 1920 and grew rapidly
22 DBFP, 1 (xiv), docs. 277 and 287. Ian Nish, 'Crown Prince Hirohito in Britain' in Ian Nish (ed.), *Biographical Portraits*, vol. I, Richmond: Japan Library, 1997. Dealt with also in F. S. G. Piggott, *Broken Thread*, Aldershot: Gale and Polden, 1950, pp. 123-31 and Philip Ziegler (ed.), *Diaries of Lord Louis Mountbatten*, London: Collins, 1987.
23 *The Times*, 18 August 1920.
24 Kikuchi, pp. 222-25.
25 *The Times*, 18 August 1920.

# VI. Nitobe and the Secretariat in London 1919

## Ian Nish

### Nitobe in London

In the spring of 1919 Nitobe Inazo (1862-1933) was touring the United States and Europe as escort and interpreter for Baron Goto Shimpei. They had known each other since Goto had been Governor-general of Taiwan in 1901-3 and Nitobe had served as an adviser on agriculture there while acting as professor of colonial policy at Kyoto Imperial University. Goto had since advanced in political circles to become the most talented member of the Terauchi cabinet (1916-18). He had held the portfolios of Home Minister and, after the death of Motono Ichiro, of Foreign Minister also. Having been replaced by Hara when he became prime minister in September 1918, Goto decided to go on an extended Grand Tour round the world and survey the state of postwar affairs. The group set off on 4 March, reaching San Francisco at the end of the month. It was not unnatural that Goto should include a number of linguists in his party and that Dr Nitobe should be chosen to accompany him. They were joined in California by Mary Nitobe, his American-born wife, for the journey through the United States. They left Mrs Nitobe at her home on the east coast. The party reached London on 8 June for a stay of three weeks during which they had an audience with King George V at Buckingham Palace and an interview with the acting foreign secretary, Lord Curzon of Kedleston. Nitobe dutifully prepared a letter of thanks to Curzon on 27 June 1919.[1]

The party reached Paris as the deliberations on the German peace treaty were at their height. Of the many issues which this generated, we need only consider the origins of the League of Nations, the creation of which had been approved in principle on 25 January 1919. A commission was set up to consider the drafting of the covenant and was eventually presided over by President Woodrow Wilson. Its relevance for Japan was over the subject of racial equality about which she wished to insert a clause in the covenant of the League. While this was out-voted in the commission, it was suggested that it could be worked on after the League came into being. On 28 April the draft of the covenant was adopted by a majority vote.[2]

Once the League had been agreed in principle, much of the initiative would depend on the speedy establishment of a permanent secretariat and the selection of its personnel. Soundings were made for the post of secretary-general from February onwards. The appointment of Sir Eric Drummond, a former British diplomat who had been in Paris for the negotiations, was made in April in a rather cavalier manner. Accounts differ. Nitobe himself thought that it was the choice of Wilson while some attributed the selection to Arthur Balfour, the British foreign secretary whose private secretary Drummond was and others to Georges Clemenceau.[3] After this appointment there was a sense of urgency to get things under way in view of the difficulties which President Wilson was already facing, from a hostile American Congress. An organization committee [soshiki iinkai] was set up with Baron Chinda Sutemi as Japan's representative. At its second meeting on 9 June Drummond put forward proposals for the structure of the secretariat. He assumed that the posts of under-secretary-general would be drawn from among the nations which had participated in the Big Five deliberations at Paris; but that, since most of the League's business would be 'European', representation would be from the countries of Europe. Drummond approached the Japanese representatives suggesting that they should put forward names for the post of director [bucho] rather than under-secretary-general. Chinda and his colleagues felt that in these circumstances Japan would be isolated from decision-making on world affairs and asked that Japan should have an appointment as under-secretary-general. As a result Drummond amended his proposal to include a Japanese at the higher level. It had in any case come to be accepted in Paris that Japan should be allowed to sit on all conference committees 'whenever questions particularly affecting her were under consideration.'[4]

After winning this behind-the-scenes battle for recognition, the

Japanese plenipotentiaries who were in Paris for the German peace-treaty came under pressure to put forward a name urgently in order to ensure that Japan was given a role commensurate with her standing at the Paris conference. They had to bear in mind that the person should be a person of distinction and should ideally be available in Europe for immediate appointment without having to travel from Japan and arriving when the groundwork had been completed. They were anxious to appoint someone with good linguistic skills and a good knowledge of world affairs.[4]

Nitobe's name was mooted for the post some weeks before the Goto party turned up in Paris on 30 June. He himself understood that the first step had been taken by Viscount Chinda Sutemi, one of the plenipotentiaries. But it appears to have been done without consultation with the nominee. From an international standpoint, Nitobe was ideally suited for the job. He was not a politician or a diplomat. He was an accomplished linguist in English and French. He was fairly well-known in the English-speaking world for his books on Bushido. He was recognized as a liberal internationalist, though he had not taken a strong position on the various League issues which had arisen in the early months of 1919. In religion his Quaker beliefs made him very suitable for an institution which was aiming at preserving world peace. Dr Nitobe had been a professor at Tokyo Imperial University, Japan's most prestigious university, since 1909 and had the high status of a senior academic with official experience. He seemed likely, therefore, to be acceptable to those who had to be entrusted with making the appointments. It was still assumed that the United States would take a large role in the League so the fact that he had been educated there and had married an American wife would count in his favour.

In Japanese eyes also he was an ideal candidate. Makino Nobuaki who was the *de facto* head of the Japanese delegation and was an enthusiastic supporter of Japan belonging to the League had known Nitobe when he was minister of education in 1906. It was he who had then successfully persuaded Nitobe to accept the post of principal of Ichiko, the prestigious First National College in Tokyo. The most influential plenipotentiary in Paris, Ambassador Chinda, was also favourable. Needless to say, Goto when he was consulted was also in favour. This was important for the success of the appointment since

Goto had good contacts with the military in Japan. So the recommendation from Japanese quarters in Europe was unanimous.

Strangely enough the procedure in Tokyo was not entirely clear. The process of making a League of Nations appointment was a delicate one. It was not a matter where the Tokyo government selected its nominee. The appointment was to be made by the League but discreet enquiries were to be made to establish that it was acceptable to the home government of the candidate. Japan's delegates asked Tokyo for extreme urgency. Apparently Nitobe's name was deemed acceptable for the post on 19 May. It appears to have leaked out in *Osaka Mainichi* newspaper on 28 May that Nitobe had been appointed to the post of under-secretary-general and director of the international bureau of the League, while continuing on the establishment of Tokyo Imperial University for the present [Teidai zaikan no mama].[5]

In fact this announcement was premature since the Paris committees had still to make the appointment and offer the post to the nominee. It was only after further travels on the continent and the return of the party to London on 17 July that Chinda informed Goto three days later that Nitobe's name had been officially approved and asked him to encourage the candidate to accept. Nitobe was initially guarded in his response, claiming that he was ill-qualified for the post. But eventually, after receiving strong recommendations that Drummond would be easy to work with, Nitobe public-spiritedly took on the job but added that his vision was to be 'a bridge over the Pacific'.

The treaty of Versailles was signed on 26 June. During the following month Drummond formed his permanent international secretariat. The newly created posts of under-general-secretary were assigned to Jean Monnet (France), Inazo Nitobe (Japan), Raymond B. Fosdick (USA) and Italy which did not put forward a nominee until January 1920. It was hoped that, by appointing an American to high office, the United States could still be induced to become a founder-member of the League. When it refused to join, the incumbent ultimately resigned in April 1920.

## The London Interlude

The covenant which was approved as an attachment to the treaty laid down that the seat of the League would be established at Geneva and that the permanent secretariat would be located at 'the seat of the League' (Articles 7 and 6).[6] The secretariat could now proceed to the next stage. The League established its secretariat temporarily in London in mid-summer, in spite of opposition from the French who felt that the world's political leaders had been located in Paris for the previous six months and that Paris was a more natural home until the headquarters moved to Switzerland as the covenant laid down. Japan was a signatory to both the treaty and the covenant and thus a founder member of the League. Although it was a considerable disruption to his family and academic life, Nitobe settled in the British capital to take up his duties under Sir Eric Drummond without delay. He was inspired by the thought of taking on an international role and decided to forego the possibility of returning to Japan to tidy up his affairs. Instead his wife Mary who had been left in the States undertook the journey to Japan to settle family affairs in preparation for a prolonged absence. She found the task a hard one and the prospect of continued separation even harder. She was sympathetic, however, to his accepting the post and joined him in London as soon as she could.

The League secretariat set up its temporary headquarters in Sunderland House, 117 Piccadilly W1 (an address sometimes described as 'Curzon Street'). It is described as a large but uncongenial house at the corner of Piccadilly and Down Street.[7] Coincidentally, it stands close to the present Japanese embassy at 101 Piccadilly. Of course London was only a makeshift headquarters for the organization. As early idealism wore off and the prospect of American financial largesse did not materialize, the League leaders had to cut their coat according to European measures of cloth. Accordingly the headquarters were transferred to Trafalgar House in Waterloo Place, Lower Regent Street, SW1, in 1920. Nitobe himself took up his personal residence at 66 Holland Park.

Switzerland commended itself to the delegates in Paris as the home for the League because it was a neutral country and the home of the International Red Cross. After considering and rejecting Lausanne, its government had selected Geneva; but it had found that Geneva was not as yet equipped to accommodate such a large and growing international institution as the League. So the secretariat stayed in war-ravaged London for over a year as arrangements were made to find suitable premises in Geneva.

The League could not be formally inaugurated until January 1920 when the Versailles treaty came into force. But there was plenty of preparatory work to do. The problem for the newly-appointed officials was that they were breaking new ground and had no prototype on which they could rely. Nitobe was able to play his part in planning the general affairs of the organization.[8] It was during this time that Nitobe who confessed to being lonely in London seems to have formed a cordial relationship with Eric Drummond. He fitted in well with the concept of international civil servants which Drummond was forming in his head, that is, of a body of men who were devoted to the League and prepared not to be browbeaten by pressure from their home country. Whereas others among the League officials were very conscious of their national affiliations, Nitobe was appreciated by Drummond for steering clear of this. The Drummond team settled down to the task of building an administrative structure, a novel experience but one for which Nitobe with his educational background had some past experience. By contrast, Drummond, coming from a Foreign Office background, had less background about office organization and office discipline (hours of work etc.).[9]

It was necessary for the League to sell itself in advance of its inauguration. Dr Nitobe increasingly took on the lecturing mantle on behalf of the League of Nations team, both in Britain and on the continent. It has to be remembered that the atmosphere in Europe generally was one of scepticism, firstly, about the Versailles treaty and, secondly, about the potential of the League. Even Britain, in spite of the fact that she was to be the leading member of the League Council, had many cynics. The reasons were that the League was showing more evidence of idealism than of realism; the covenant did not please the pragmatists; the conservatives felt that it was better to leave postwar problems to be solved by existing experienced bodies. Thus one British critic wrote:

> The Secretariat is merely an international Foreign Office and presents most of the ideas to the Council instead of making the Council do the work.... Our Foreign Office is jealous and refuses to have anything to do with the League.[10]

So there was a case for defenders of the League to answer and it was recognized that the members of the secretariat would have to travel around and speak convincingly to audiences. Like Drummond, Nitobe had to try to clear away the common misconception that the League was a type of super-state with a domineering bureaucracy whereas in fact it was an association of countries trying to build up international cooperation. It was in this context that Dr Nitobe presented one of his earliest lectures, 'What the League of Nations has done and is doing'. This was given several times but most memorably at the International University in Brussels on 13–14 September 1920. Even by that date the League had already dealt with a number of international troublespots such as the Saar Basin, the Free City of Danzig, the Aaland Islands and general items like opium traffic, the spread of disease and reparations.[11]

Nitobe was a much sought after lecturer in English. His name was already familiar in London because his books were well-known. His presence was valued by the Japanese embassy, where Chinda remained the ambassador till August 1920. In some of his initial lectures Nitobe concentrated on Japan. 1919 had been a bad year for Japan's reputation in Britain, particularly over her treatment of Korea and China. There had been sustained criticism on these topics both from the Foreign Office and from the British press. He spoke to the Japan Society of London on the subject of 'Japanese Colonization' on 17 December 1919. [text available: see Appendix] He described the wide range of Japan's colonial enterprises 'whether it be in tropical Formosa, or temperate Korea, or half-frigid Saghalien'. While economic factors were the immediate reasons for Japan's national expansion, 'her chief motive was national security.' A major concern was that 'with the steady advance of Russia southwards from Siberia the necessity of protecting Japan's northern frontiers became urgent, so began in the 1870s the colonization of Hokkaido (Yezo). Saghalien, a bone of contention between Russia and Japan, was exchanged for a group of 31 Kurile islands.' He remarked of Japan's efforts in Korea that it would be highly interesting to compare them to developments in Wales — or Ireland!'[12] In short Nitobe's standpoint could be described as apologetic but also conservative and defensive. It was, therefore, a bold topic for him to choose even for an audience so pro Japanese as the Japan Society of London.

His address was obviously popular with his audience because he was invited back to give the main toast 'Success To the Japan Society' at the 21st annual dinner of the society on 18 May 1920 at the Princes' Restaurant. On this occasion he was accompanied by his wife.[13]

He also spoke to the 'British Budokwai' at its headquarters in Grosvenor Place on 13 October 1919. His subject was 'the Japanese concept of loyalty'. His argument was that, with the disappearance of Japan's feudal system, 'the Emperor took the place of the feudal lord as the object of devotion of the Japanese people.'[14]

Apart from these lectures about his home country, Nitobe was a stout defender of the League in general and of (what he called) 'the permanent international secretariat' in particular. He was insistent that the secretary-general should be respected and seen as sitting alongside the president in a place of honour. As under-secretary-general he was proud of his special role in charge of the League's international bureaux. But he had in fact a much broader remit. Describing his work, he wrote:

> I am rather busier with other matters, a rubbish heap as it were, for problems which did not properly belong in any of the other sections all come to me.... I am the most easily found out person in the Secretariat.[15]

For example, educational problems had no special section within the League bureaucracy and landed on his desk. He claimed that he was much busier than other officials whose homes were more accessible and who were inclined to be absent from headquarters. Because he could not readily escape to Japan, he was the official who had to take on emergency duties.

## Transfer to Geneva

On 10 January 1920 the Versailles Treaty came into force; and the League started officially. By this time there was some reluctance on the part of officials in London to move to Geneva and transfer all the archives which had hitherto been lovingly accumulated. Who would bear the expenses of League officials who moved their households there in the new climate of economy? Out of the 11 meetings of Council held in 1920, only the last two were held in Geneva. They had all been held in various capitals where satisfactory meeting facilities were available. Nonetheless the leaders were firm about the transfer; and the secretariat made the move early in October in order to prepare the way for the inaugural Assembly of the League which was due to take place in the Salle de la Reformation, Geneva, on 15 November.[16]

Eventually Nitobe moved to Geneva though he had like most members of the secretariat been travelling back and forward to the continent for some time. What his particular views on the move were cannot be found. But he seems to have settled into a comfortable family life there beside the shores of Lake Leman. The Japanese government, unlike some others, decided to establish a permanent delegation to the Council with Ishii Kikujiro, the ambassador in Paris, in nominal charge. It would have an office (kokusai remmei no jimukyoku) with Sugimura Yotaro as the diplomat in charge. This gave Nitobe some interesting Japanese companionship. He and his companions were hoping to confirm the image of Geneva as the symbol of world peace the 'spirit of Geneva' — Geneva no kuki.[17]

From the start Nitobe had been concerned with international and social matters. Now he became more specialized in taking on the work of the committee on International Cooperation to which such presentday institutions as UNESCO and semi-government bodies like the British council and the Japan Foundation trace their origins. In other words, he and his committee of scholars had to assess the role of culture in international relations. In this connection Nitobe wrote a number of reports, including that on 'The language question and the League of Nations' dealing with the question of an international language and also 'The Intellectual Life of Various Countries'.

Much positive work had been done in London in the early days of the League and Nitobe had assisted Drummond greatly to lay its foundations. He had the seniority which gave it prestige. When Nitobe was appointed he was 57 years of age and was older than Drummond (aged 43) and most of the other officials like Jean Monnet (aged 31). Moreover, his modesty and his pleasing personality attracted those around him. Through his presence he ensured that Japan had the standing in the League to which it was entitled. Nitobe was a symbol of his country's commitment to the peaceful resolution of international conflicts. Even if Japan herself was not directly a party to the conflicts of the immediate postwar period which mainly affected Europe and the Middle East, Japan was called on to play her part. Nitobe was at one level an international civil servant but at another level he was a custodian of Japanese interests and a nationalist.

There could not fail to be an element of disappointment for Dr Nitobe, in the way the League developed. When he accepted the appointment in mid-1919, he must have thought that he would be near the centre of an organization in which the United States would lead the rest of the world. Nitobe had always been inclined to believe in the notion of the 'Americanization' of the world which seemed to come to realization with Wilson's appearance in Paris. Initially he had said that his acceptance of the League appointment was in order to build a bridge across the Pacific. But disillusion was bound to set in after the American Senate refused to ratify the terms of the peace treaty and the covenant of the League in 1920. Thus he wrote

> A League minus the US loses more than one-half of its value in the estimate of Japan.... A general treaty of which neither Russia nor America is a signatory has very little use for Japan.[18]

These were strongly expressed views which probably reflected Tokyo's standpoint. For Nitobe personally also American withdrawal was regrettable. Still he was loyal to the League institution without America and was able to adapt to its less idealistic European demeanour. There is no evidence that his period in Britain was anything other than pleasurable for Nitobe. He valued his cordial relationship with Eric Drummond and British officials. As a member of the Quaker movement, he may have felt some rapport with a country which had given birth to the Society of Friends in the 17th century. Even after President Wilson, the arch-idealist, had departed from the scene, there was still enough residual idealism left in League circles in Britain to make Nitobe's task a satisfying one.

**Notes**

1 On Goto's journey, Tsurumi Yusuke, *Goto Shimpei*, 4 vols, Tokyo, 1937. Fujiko Hara, *The Autobiography of Ozaki Yukio*, Princeton: UP, 2001, pp. 323–24. We learn from Kobayashi Tatsuo (ed.), *Suiuso nikki: Ito Miyoji bunsho*, Tokyo, 1966, that Goto absented himself from the gaiko chosakai deliberations from March 1919 till January 1920.

General studies of Dr Nitobe and the League include Unno Yoshiro, *Kokusai remmei to Nihon*, Tokyo: Hara Shobo, 1972; and Thomas Burkman, 'Nitobe Inazo as Under-Secretary General of the League of Nations, 1920–6' in *Journal of International Studies* [Sophia University, Tokyo] 14 (1985), pp. 77–93.

2 Peter Beck, 'Introduction' to *British Documents on Foreign Affairs*, University Publications of America, 1992, Part II, series J, vol. I, pp. xiii–xviii. Naoko Shimazu, *Japan, Race and Equality*, London: Routledge, 1998. R. H. Fifield, *Woodrow Wilson and the Far East*, Hamden, Conn.: Archon, 1965.

3 Marle-Renée Mouton, *La Sociète des Nations et les Interets de la France, 1920–4*, Bern: Peter Lang, 1995, pp. 14–15. Margaret Macmillan, *Peacemakers: Six months that changed the World*, London. John Murray; 2001. Unno, *op. cit.*, p. 16.

4 Fifield, *op. cit.*, p. 307. Unno, *op. cit.*, pp. 19–20.

5 Quite properly, there is little evidence of how Japanese leaders approved the nomination of Nitobe. *Nihon gaiko bunsho* and *Hara nikki* say nothing. *Suiuso nikki* suggests that members of gaiko chosakai were not consulted either. Seki Shizuo, *Taisho gaiko*, Kyoto: Minerva, 2001.

6 Ruth B. Henig (ed.), *The League of Nations*, Edinburgh: Oliver & Boyd, 1973, appendix I.

7 George Scott, *The Rise and Fall of the League of Nations*, Glasgow. Hutchinson, 1973, p. 67.

8 Unno, *op. cit.*, p. 20.

9 Nitobe, 'A typical British gentleman: Sir Eric Drummond'. See above pp. 77–78.

10 Hankey diary, 13 June 1920, quoted in Stephen Roskill, *Hankey: Man of secrets*, 3 vols, London: Collins, 1972, vol. II, p. 165.

11 The lecture was later published from Harrison (London, 1920, 21pp.). For the text, see above pp. 4–23.

12 As reported in the *Morning Post*. "The Japanese Colonization," *The Collected Works of Inazo Nitobe*, vol. 23: 111–120.

13 Japan Society of London, *Proceedings*, 1920, p. 186.

14 *The Times* [of London], 19 Oct. 1919.

15 See above p. 55

16 Speaking in Brussels on 13 September 1920, Nitobe confirmed that 'Its headquarters are at present in London; but they will be removed to Geneva within a few weeks.' See above p. 10.

17 This phrase is used in Ishii Kikujiro (ambassador to Paris) in *Gaiko yoroku*, Tokyo: Iwanami, 1930, ch. 7/1. Surprisingly he makes no mention of Nitobe.

On Sugimura, Ian Nish, 'A Japanese diplomat looks at Europe, 1920–39' in Nish and Dunn (eds.), *European Studies on Japan*, Tenterden: Norbury, 1979, pp. 134–39. *Gaimusho no 100-nen*, vol. 2, Tokyo: 1969.

18 See above p. 94.

# Appendix: Japanese Colonization By Dr. Inazo Nitobe

[Reprinted from *The Japan Society of London Proceedings 1919*; also *The Collected Works of Inazo Nitobe*, vol. 23: 111-120]

The nineteenth century is pre-eminently an age of nationality and of national expansion. All nations, large and small, were awakened to a strong sense of their own importance, so much so that not a few of them were obsessed with it. Those that wisely adapted their national self-consciousness to the law of organic growth, became conquering or colonial Powers, while those who, like the Foolish Virgins of the parable, were not ready to act at this call of the century were bereft of their independence. The merciless law of the survival of the fittest first announced in the middle of the century, has only justified the expansion of virile nations. So much for the universal tendency of the age just passed.

If we examine the more immediate reasons for national expansion, we shall find them to be largely of economic character, such as the growth of the investment of capital, the growth and migration of population, the necessity of command over the supply of raw materials, the desire to acquire markets for home products. None of these reasons is absent in the colonial enterprise of present Japan, whether it be in tropical Formosa, or temperate Korea or half-frigid Saghalien. But in its earliest form of modern Japanese colonization the chief motive was national safety — the safeguarding of territorial boundaries, the security from foreign invasion; and this reason has been present even in its later stages. Let me explain.

Modern Japan began her career late in the sixties of the last century. That was the period which Mr. Kidd has, in his recent book, called the age of Great Pagan Retrogression. It was the period when force was freely displayed and conquests unscrupulously made in the backward places of the globe. For some three centuries Japan had shut herself up in a shell; but when she first opened the lid and gazed upon the world, what was the sight she beheld? The Union Jack was firmly planted in India and was moving eastward to Singapore, Hong-Kong, and there was some probability of it marching on to

China. Why not to Japan too? The French Tricolour was also to be seen floating over Cambodia, Annam, and Tonkin, and nobody could tell how far north or east it would fly. More alarming than these, the Muscovite Power, like a huge avalanche, was steadily descending southwards from its Siberian steppes, crushing everything on its way. The necessity of protecting our northern frontiers was most evident and urgent. So began, in the seventies, the colonization of the long-neglected island of Hokkaido (Yezo). Saghalien, a bone of contention between Russia and Japan, was exchanged for a group of some thirty-one Kurile Islands (6,000 square miles). The colonization of Hokkaido was not fraught with great difficulties, as the natives — the Ainu — were a timid and fast-vanishing race. There was at first a reluctance on the part of the Japanese, who, being essentially a southern race, but for generations bred in the genial clime, were averse to move north. Colonial enterprise had therefore to be largely led by the Government. An immense amount of money was spent before the work was voluntarily taken up by the people. The island — 30,500 square miles, just about the size of Scotland — can nowadays scarcely be called a colony, being more a part of Japan than Algeria is of France. At present the chief motive of immigration from the south is not for the defence of frontiers; it is economic. Its agriculture, fisheries, and coal mines are very profitable. Its beans are of much better quality than those of Manchuria. Barley for brewing can be grown only there. Its herring, cod, and salmon are exported in vast quantities. It is rich in timber, oak and walnut. The population has now risen to over 10 millions, and it will prove an important granary to the rest of the Empire.

This sole colonial training in this northern island, though it proved of great use when Russia returned in 1905 the southern half of Saghalien, an area of some 13,000 square miles, and a population of 70,000, and valuable for its fishery, coal, oil, and timber, was inadequate to cope with the conditions of a tropical colony of Formosa, inhabited by 3.5 millions of the Chinese race and some ferocious head-hunting tribes. We acquired Formosa in 1895 after the war with China largely because we could not get anything else. To this rich island of 14,000 square miles, twice as large as Wales, there was attached at first no great economic value, neither was it considered indispensable for the defence of our realm But its strategic importance proved later very great during the war with Russia. China was apparently exceedingly willing to get rid of it, because of the chronic obstacles, as Li Hung-Chang said, in administering it on account of (1) brigandage; (2) epidemics; (3) aboriginal savages. Sure enough the island was for a while a white elephant to Japan, and its sale was even discussed at one time. Later on, under the able administration of Kodama and Goto, brigandage was put down, plague and malaria almost suppressed, and Malay head-hunters kept within bounds by hundreds of miles of electrified wire fence. The last device, let me explain, is not to kill the savages. Setting aside humanitarian reasons, it does not pay to do so. The interior of the island, so rich in camphor, must have labour, and this is reason enough to do everything to entice the aborigines to peaceful activity. When they are cut off by the fence they begin to suffer from want of salt. It is then that we offer salt in exchange for their weapons, and on their surrendering those we give them buffaloes and agricultural implements and the fence is moved, as it were, over their heads so that their village comes within Japanese protection. Every year an advance of ten or twenty miles is thus made. They are confined among mountains, while on the plains and along the shores the Chinese population ply their trade and industry. After the suppression of brigandage, the Japanese Government turned its attention to the development of island resources. The tropical climate, which was at first a terror to our people, was soon turned to good account. Irrigation and agriculture are encouraged; sugar production has increased nearly tenfold; cadastral surveys have increased the amount of Government revenue; rice culture has improved and the Oolong tea production has increased. Railways and harbours have been constructed, and the introduction of sewage systems in the larger cities, the gradual abolition of opium-smoking under strict regulation, the Government monopoly of the camphor industry, have been some of the more prominent features of the Formosan administration. The number of Japanese is steadily increasing, but they cannot compete with the Chinese in labour or in small retail business. Formosa is still an investment colony, but with the opening up of the higher altitudes in the interior, which is sure to follow the subjugation of the head-hunters and with the general sanitary improvement, I believe our people can settle without detriment to health. Already the island, thanks to camphor and sugar, is self-supporting. Indeed, the Home Government derives no small revenue from the heavy consumption tax on sugar and from Customs duties on her trade with China.

In its rather short history, Formosa has been under Portuguese, Spanish, Dutch, French, and Chinese rule. With such changes of masters there is little patriotism among the people, who nevertheless are intelligent, hard-working, and law-abiding. We do not hear of self-determination there. It is quite otherwise with Korea.

This country prides itself on being one of the oldest nations of the earth. Oriental pride in mere age is shared by our people too: but I am afraid that in the Occident old age is identified with senility, decrepitude, and dotage. However that may be, Korea was once a powerful and advanced nation, from whom Japan learned most of her ancient arts and craft.

The Korean Peninsula, jutting out into the Japan Sea, was like a phial, from which was poured milk and honey into the mouth of Japan. But as to Korea's political independence in the past, there are grave doubts how much she had ever enjoyed it. For centuries she was virtually under the suzerainty of China, paying tribute to Peking and receiving Chinese envoys as messengers from her over-lord. After a war in the sixteenth century we claimed Korea as our protégé. And later in the nineteenth century Russia was bent upon absorbing the kingdom, and was on the fair way to success. As long as Korea remains a really independent country, strong and well governed, it may well be a buffer State; but when it is now under China, and now under Russia, there can be no security for peace in the Far East nor safety for Japan. We can easily change the geographical metaphor, and liken the Peninsula to a sword-blade aimed at the heart of Japan. Suppose Belgium were a weak and vacillating country, to fall at any moment under the sway of Germany, what guarantee is there for the peace of Europe and the security of Great Britain? I wish Korea had been as strong and well ordered as Belgium, for in that case there would have been no need of three Powers (China, Russia, and Japan) preying upon her, nor any necessity on the part of Japan to annex her. Here again it was as a condition of self-preservation that Korea was taken under our rule.

I am not a believer in the Will to Power, or in the doctrine of the Divine Right of Might, but I do not believe it is the right of every people to do as they will, regardless of consequences to their neighbours. A nation that cannot keep order has as little right to absolute independence as a nation that has only power has to conquer another. As a matter of fact the old Korean kingdom had forfeited its right to independence when it was treated as a shuttlecock between China, Russia, and Japan. Lord Curzon wrote some years ago:

> "The spectacle of a country boasting a separate, if not an independent, national existence for centuries, and yet devoid of all external symptoms of strength; inhabited by a people of physical vigour but moral inertness; well endowed with resources, yet crippled for want of funds — such a spectacle is one to which I know no counterpart, even in Asia, the continent of contrasts."

As another English statesman has said, what India and Egypt want is a self-government, and not a good government; and though I believe that self-government is a sure means to good government, there is a proper time to begin it, and this depends upon the political maturity of the people who ask for it. As long as they resort to assassination, to terrorism, to appeals to third parties, to calumnies, childish methods of playing at governments on foreign soil — well, English people have had enough experience with this kind of demonstration! I count myself among the best and truest friends of Koreans. I like them. I do not share such unfavourable views as were expressed by Captain Bostwick, Archibald Little, George Kennan, or Professor Ladd, and other writers on Korean character. I think they are a capable people, who can be trained to a large measure of self-government, for which the present is a period of tutelage. Let them study what we are doing in Korea, and this I say, not to justify the many mistakes committed by our militaristic administration, nor to boast of some of our achievements. In all humility, but with a firm conviction that Japan is a steward on whom devolves the gigantic task of the uplifting of the Far East, I cannot think that young Korea is yet capable of governing itself. Let them study, I repeat, what we are doing.

Mr. Wickham called the Korean "the pale ghost of what a Chinaman was a thousand years ago," and Mr. Kennan called him "the rotten product of a decayed Oriental civilisation." Indolence was the badge of honour. The first lesson to instil into him is to work.

Before annexation was formally proclaimed, in August, 1910, Korea had been a protectorate for four years (1906-10) under the Residency of our foremost statesman, Prince Ito. It was in the early years of this régime that I called on him in Seoul. My mission was to induce him to accept a plan of settling Japanese farmers in Korean villages as demonstrators of better systems of cultivation. The old Prince refused to endorse my plan, insisting that Korea was for Koreans. But when I asked him how he could supply the decreasing population — of which there were several local indications in different parts — he still insisted in his opinion by saying, "Under better government, which I inaugurate, population itself will increase." By better government he meant more than the elementary functions of government — viz., legal security of life and property.

Certainly, a government to be better than a self-government must provide a substantial economic basis. A glance at the table showing the amount of agricultural produce grown in 1910 and 1915 needs no comment.

|  | 1910. Bushels. | 1915. Bushels. |
|---|---|---|
| Rice ... ... ... | ... 40,000,000 | 60,000,000 |
| Wheat and barley ... ... | ... 17,500,000 | 33,000,000 |
| Beans ... ... ... | ... 12,000,000 | 17,500,000 |
|  | lbs. | lbs. |
| Cotton ... ... ... | 11,000,000 | 45,000,000 |

Mining, fishery, and manufacture have advanced in the corresponding scale. The bald mountains have been covered with young trees. Trade has increased by leaps and bounds, foreign trade increasing from 60,000,000 to 108,000,000 yen. Railway mileage has nearly doubled. The peninsular Government can support itself without subsidies from the central exchequer. Schools, hospitals and savings banks are being built in all the larger towns and villages. The school attendance has more than doubled in 1910-15. And let me state here, with all emphasis, that there is perfect religious liberty. A strange rumour is now and then started by misguided missionaries or by malicious Koreans, that there is a Christian persecution by the heathen Government of Japan. May I add that the Chief Judge in Korea — a

Japanese — is one of the most earnest Christians; a Director of a Department is another, and the late Director of Education still another — not to cite other instances I am not personally acquainted with. Last summer we read in papers that a church was bombarded by Japanese gendarmes. That sounds bad enough. As far as I understand, this was done, not because it was a church, nor because good Christian people gathered there for worship — but because a dozen instigators of insurrection hid themselves under its roof. When a building is used, not for a religious purpose but for harbouring lawbreakers, it forfeits its sanctity. On questions like these it is exceedingly difficult to be absolutely impartial and fair. Distortion of facts by interested and hostile parties is only human and too frequent. I can well imagine, however, that Japanese authorities — or more probably the lower officials, civil and military — may exercise their functions awkwardly, to say the least, and sometimes too zealously. When a colonial administration as experienced as the British commits errors in Egypt or in Jamaica, it is not to be wondered at that novices like us are not free of them.

What is vital in any colonial scheme seems to me to be the right answer to this question: Do we govern an unwilling people for their sake or for our own?

As to the general unwillingness of any colony — not excluding India, Egypt, the Philippines, Indo-China, etc. — to be governed by a Power alien to it, there is little doubt. A colonial government has received no consent of the governed. Nor is there much reason to believe that a colonial Power, white or brown, bears the burden at a sacrifice simply to better the lot of the people placed in its charge. The history of colonization is the history of national egotism. But even egotism can attain its end by following the simple law of human intercourse — "give and take." Mutual advantage must be the rule, for the old doctrine of "colonial pact" holds no more. Korea must not be regarded as a mere boundary-line nor as a field for exploitation, much less its habitants as food for powder or as a labour supply. Certainly, two races so closely allied as the Korean and the Japanese must come to a better understanding, and such a time will be accelerated more by Japan's approach than by Korea's. To an English student of colonization it will be highly interesting to watch the development of Korea to a Wales or — to an Ireland.

# VII. Nitobe Inazo at the League of Nations: 1919–1926

## George Oshiro

*A man to be internationally minded must first have his feet planted firmly on the ground of his native soil. He then lifts his head and looks round upon the wide world, and finds where he is standing and whither he must go.*
    Nitobe Inazo, Editorial Jottings (June 7, 1930)

On January 25, 1919, representatives of the victorious allies gathered at Paris agreed that "a League of Nations be created to promote international cooperation, to insure the fulfillment of accepted international obligations and to provide safeguards against war."[1] They appointed a commission, chaired by Woodrow Wilson, with members from fourteen nations, including Japan, to work on the project. After several months of deliberations involving many meetings and compromises, the text of the Covenant was formally adopted at a plenary session of the Peace Conference, on April 28, 1919.[2]

The Japanese delegates, though conspicuous among the five great powers for their silence at the Peace Conference, were more outspoken on the League of Nations Commission. Her representatives, Makino Nobuaki, chief delegate, and Viscount Chinda, the Ambassador to London, participated actively in discussions dealing with disarmament, arbitration and racial equality.[3] Though the racial equality clause that Japan urged be inserted into the League's Covenant was rejected by the commission, Japan did not leave the Peace Conference empty-handed. She had won significant concessions. At the expense of the Chinese, Japan was allowed to stay in Shantung, as well as hold trusteeship over the Micronesian islands. Satisfied with her gains, Japan agreed to work with the European powers to build a new framework for conducting diplomacy which was based on the League of Nations with its concept of collective security to maintain peace.[4]

The League was officially created on 26 January 1920 when the Versailles accords were deposited at the French Foreign Office in Paris. In its quest to achieve its idealistic goal, the League developed many new institutions and adopted novel measures. Its activities were all encompassing and dealt with politics, economics, health, labor, culture, and education.[5]

But from its very beginning the League suffered under serious constraints. First and foremost, it was a creature of the national states which viewed it with ambivalence. Jealous of their sovereignty, they never gave the League the effective powers to carry out its mission. Moreover, the responsibilities of member nations were never fully spelt out. Eventually, this weakness would prove to be the League's undoing. A second obvious weakness was the aloofness of the United States. Without its participation, the League was hindered from the very outset. Notwithstanding the pessimism held by many on the prospects of success, and in spite of these serious handicaps, the League survived its birth and, after a few stormy years, managed to expand and prosper.[6]

The leaders of Great Britain and France, Ramsay MacDonald and Edouard Herriot, attended the Assembly in 1924, thus setting a diplomatic precedent of great importance: legitimizing the League as an international forum for debating and resolving the chief political issues of the day. Since then, foreign ministers of the major powers gathered regularly in Geneva for Council and Assembly meetings.[7]

In the mid-twenties, the League achieved several noteworthy successes, using conciliatory measures, which heightened its prestige. In the Spring of 1926, Germany was admitted as a member. Even the United States, which was cool to the organization in the first years, began to cooperate in non-political activities. By 1929, the League had reached the zenith of its influence. Only after the outbreak of the Manchurian Crisis in 1931 would the League's limitations be starkly revealed.[8]

## The Path to the League: Travels with Goto Shimpei

The press in Japan was filled with news of the latest developments in Paris after the opening of the Peace Conference in January, 1919.[9] Nitobe, who was busy writing his articles on democracy for the *Jitsugyo no Nihon*, took a keen interest in the latest news from abroad. When Goto Shimpei asked him to come along on a trip to view the postwar changes in America and Europe, Nitobe agreed. Taking a leave of absence from the Imperial University, he and Mary and several disciples joined the Baron. They left Yokohama and arrived in San Francisco on May 21st, 1919.[10] In the next seventy-two days, they toured the country and met leading public figures.[11]

In California, they met the world renowned botanist Luther Burbank and were interviewed by the Chief Editor of the *Los Angeles Express*. In Chicago, they were honored guests at a luncheon hosted by the University Club of the University of Chicago whose members Nitobe had addressed eight years before. At another luncheon a few days later in Springfield, Illinois, the birthplace of Abraham Lincoln, Goto delivered a keynote speech in Japanese which Nitobe interpreted into English. Passing through Detroit, they met Henry Ford and toured the burgeoning automobile plant. They then made New York their home base, but took frequent excursions down to Washington and Philadelphia. Nearly every day, they met with a great variety of business, academic, media and political leaders, among them the publisher Frank Doubleday, Thomas Edison, Sidney Gulick, William McAdoo, Alonzo Hepburn and the chief editors of the *New York Times*, the *New Republic* and *The Nation*. On May 7th, they visited Charles Evan Hughes, the future Secretary of State, and spoke about America's attitude toward the League of Nations.[12]

After a grueling forty days on the East Coast, Goto, Nitobe, and his four disciples, Tsurumi Yusuke, Kasama Akio, Tajima Michiji, and Iwanaga Yukichi travelled to Halifax, Nova Scotia, where they embarked for England on May 31st.[13] Six days later, the group arrived at Southampton and entrained for London. They spent June in London sightseeing and visiting such luminaries as James Bryce, whom Nitobe had met in 1912, and Robert Cecil, the leading spokesman for the League of Nations Union. Goto's impression of Cecil was that "he was like General Nogi." Three days before they left England, they had an audience at Buckingham Palace with King George V.[14]

They embarked for Paris on June 30th. And the day after they arrived, they went to see the Japanese Peace Conference delegates, headed by Saionji Kinmochi, at the Hotel Bristol.[15] From this meeting springs an apocryphal story about Nitobe which has now attained the status of a myth. The story goes that the delegates were wracking their brains to find a suitable candidate for the position of Under-Secretary General. Just then, Goto and his party walked in.

Makino, spying Nitobe, cried out "a, koko ni ita!" (why, here he is!).[16] Dramatic though it may sound, it appears that the reality was different and a bit more complicated.

Nitobe's name had already been submitted to Eric Drummond, the Secretary-General, almost two weeks earlier.[17] However, his name was submitted without prior knowledge of what the rank would be. Drummond apparently wanted the post to be on a director's level, but he succumbed to pressure to raise it to that of Under-Secretary General, for "it would create a very unfortunate impression if Japan of the five powers was put on a grade lower than the other four powers."[18]

It seems that Nitobe was unaware of what was taking place. The delegates kept quiet on the selection procedure, and even Goto was not privy to the appointment. After spending a few days in Paris, which included a meeting with Clemenceau and a tour of the famous Palace at Versailles, the group left to visit the battlefields of the War. Then they continued on to Brussels, where they paid a courtesy call on the King of Belgium. Next, after visiting Waterloo, they recrossed the channel on July 18th and returned to London.[19] Two days later, Chinda visited Goto from Paris to break the news of Nitobe's selection as Under-Secretary General and requested Goto's approval for the move. Goto consented, and only then was Nitobe himself notified.[20] He reported the momentous news to Anna Chalce in Providence, Rhode Island, on August 12th:

> I have been most unexpectedly and unsoughtly appointed Director of a Section, and one of the four Under-Secretaries General. When I think of the change in my career, I feel afresh that there is a Guiding Hand above me. I confess I do not trust in my ability but the cause which I serve is certainly deserving of all my energy. When the offer was pressed upon me by Viscount Chinda and Baron Makino, our Peace delegates, and by Baron Goto and by younger friends Tsurumi and Tajima, they were absolute in their assertion that this is the career for which my past experiences and my domestic life have been pointing.[21]

His *ichiko* student, Konoe Fumimaro, travelling as Saionji's secretary, chanced to run into Nitobe on the streets of London around this time and had lunch with him. Nitobe told him of the appointment.

The prince recollected later that he had never seen Nitobe so happy.[22]

## Work in the International Secretariat

The Secretariat was one of the three main organs of the new League of Nations.[23] Its function was to conduct the daily administrative duties of the organization, planning and preparing the agenda for the League's Councils, collecting data, and co-ordinating the work of the Council and the Assembly. And the Secretariat served as the liaison for the League in its dealings with national and international bodies. It was headed by a Secretary-General, whose duties were primarily that of an administrator, rather than a politician or chief of state.[24] Sir James Eric Drummond, a career official in the British Foreign Office, was appointed the first Secretary-General. He had a staff of Under-Secretaries General and Directors of Sections, each with his own personnel. Members of the Secretariat were independent from any national government; their allegiance was to the League alone from which they drew their salaries, and to which they were fully accountable.[25]

Drummond began his work immediately. Even before the League was formally launched, he started the difficult task of laying the groundwork for the organization. Setting up his Headquarters in London, he appointed two subordinates, an American Raymond Fosdick and a Frenchman Jean Monnet. To fill out the rest of his high level staff, Drummond did not have complete freedom, since his appointments had to be made from the candidates recommended by the respective member national governments.[26] Though Drummond may not have been pleased with this system of recruitment, the men who initially gathered around him did not disappoint him. Frank Boudreau describes the sort of persons who comprised the original staff in the Secretariat:

> In the first years, when no one could foresee how the League would succeed it appealed to persons imbued with the spirit of adventure. It took courage to give up good positions at home for the unknown abroad. Hence early recruits to the staff possessed the attributes which are commonly found in those of an adventurous disposition. They were devoted more greatly to the

cause of the League than to their own advancement; they brought to their work the energy and enthusiasm of the pioneer, and what some of them may have lacked in training and knowledge they made up for in zeal and devotion.[27]

But much of the success for the League's Secretariat lay with Drummond himself. In his own plodding but meticulous way, the former private secretary to Arthur Balfour had transformed a motley group of men and women from different parts of the world into an effective working unit of over six hundred men and women — the world's first international civil service.[28] In the Directors Meeting, he exhorted subordinates to behave in so impeccable a way that critics of the League could find no fault with which to attack the League. "Even outside office hours," he stressed, "we ... continue to be a corporate body, and the credit of the whole [is] affected by the act of [the] individual."[29]

In this closely knit but protocol-conscious organization, Nitobe ranked, as Under-Secretary General, only behind Drummond and Jean Monnet, the youthful French Deputy Secretary-General. He equalled Fosdick. At fifty-seven he was much older than they — Drummond was forty-three, Fosdick thirty-six, Monnet thirty-one — and he commanded a special respect.[30] In the Secretariat, and in Geneva at large, he was addressed as "Dr. Nitobe." Colleagues looked at him as a fatherly-figure and saw in him a wisdom garnished over many long years. Frank Walters, who served with Nitobe from the very first and later became an Under-Secretary General and Director of the Political Section, recalled Nitobe in these words:

> [His] qualities as a colleague were indeed exceptional: unfailing kindness and cordiality; a devotion to duty and to the ideals of the League which knew no bounds; a wise judgment, often all the more illuminating because it seemed to come from deeper sources than those which inspire most people's opinions on political or administrative questions.... those who came to Geneva with the purpose of finding the true principles of international cooperation — writers, teachers, and thinkers, who cared less for the immediate problems of the days than for underlying truths and ideals of the League — never failed to find instruction and

inspiration from Inazo Nitobe; and this was equally true whether the seeker came from his own Asiatic continent, or from Europe, or from the New World.[31]

Though esteemed and respected by many, Nitobe had his share of critics. Sugimura Yotaro recollected that two Directors, "a certain Mr. R and Mr. H did not like him."[32] His Section within the Secretariat appears to have run very well. According to Walters, "[t]here was no office in which more visitors were received or more work done...."[33] His private secretary Irene Stafford recalled:

> He was a friend of all. If at first sight he did not take to a certain person, he would go out of his way to cultivate his acquaintance in order to discover the good points of his character. 'Malice toward none, charity for all' was a maxim which he carried out in spirit and letter, and one could say of him with truth that he loved his neighbor better than himself.[34]

Nitobe's career background with no previous experience in politics or diplomacy relegated him at the League to work on non-sensitive projects. Unlike William Rappard, head of the Mandates section, or Fridjof Nansen, the charismatic explorer and Nobel Prize winner who directed the Refugee Section, or even his Japanese successor to the Under-Secretary General's position, Sugimura Yotaro, who was a trained diplomat, Nitobe's work at the League was not of the first order. Dealing with culture and thought, they were seen as peripheral to the more important political and economic tasks that faced the League. But this does not seem to have disturbed him since his inclination was not politics. Political questions had never really interested him, though he kept up with the more important day-to-day developments.[35] From the very beginning, along with his Under-Secretary General's status, he was entrusted with the Directorship of the International Bureau of the League whose function was outlined in Article 24 of the Covenant.

> There shall be placed under the direction of the League all international bureaus already established by general treaties, if the parties to such treaties consent. All such international bureaus

and all commissions for the regulation of matters of international interest hereafter constituted shall be placed under the direction of the League.[36]

Nitobe threw himself wholeheartedly into his work upon his entry into the Secretariat. With two lieutenants, Lloyd and Koeckenbeeck, he visited the Union des Association Nationales in Brussels to investigate how it fared the war. And on his way back, he stopped by the Hague to see the International Intermediary Institute.[37] He spent the next year busily developing a workable umbrella organization for all international organizations. But financial problems and neglect hindered much of his efforts. On one visit to Paris to inspect the groups there, he reported that of the fifteen he had seen, "nine proved to be defunct," and "only two or three were flourishing."[38]

With only a tiny budget and a small staff, the work that his International Bureau could do was limited.[39] In the first two years, Nitobe concentrated the bureau's resources on service as an information center for the various international organizations. His office sent out hundreds of letters to all known organizations, governmental and private, and compiled the information into a volume, *Handbook of International Organizations*, which was published in 1922.[40] It contained data on some 312 international groups, established privately or by governments, with a summary of its history, objectives, and general activities. It served for over a decade as the standard source of information on international organizations and was revised several times; the last edition appearing in 1937.[41]

Nitobe's energies were also expended on those organizations wishing to come under the auspices of the League. His first major success was the establishing of the International Hydrographic Bureau, whose purpose was to co-ordinate the work of several nations on the study of ocean currents and other maritime phenomena.[42] But Nitobe's most famous accomplishment, and the source of his greatest pride in his seven years at the League, was the Committee on Intellectual Cooperation.[43] The germination of this project lay in a proposal by the representative from Belgium on the League of Nations Commission who proposed that "international intellectual relations" should be included within the Covenant. Though ignored at that time, the idea was discussed in the First Assembly of the League. Later, at a Council meeting, Le Bourgeois, the French representative, moved that a committee to deal with "questions of intellectual co-operation and education" be set up. The practical working machinery was turned over to the Secretariat, and Drummond gave the project to Nitobe.[44]

Nitobe worked on an agenda for the Council to deliberate, and an appointed rapporteur was selected to preside over the work. Twelve scholars of diverse national and intellectual background, including several world renown for their individual accomplishments, were appointed to the commission. They included D. N. Banerjee, Professor of Political Economy at the University of Calcutta; Henri Bergson, Honorary Professor of Philosophy at the College of France; Kristine Bonnevie, Professor of Zoology at the University of Christiania; A. de Castro, Dean of the Faculty of Medicine at the University of Rio de Janeiro; Mme. Curie-Sklodowska, Professor of Physics at the University of Paris; J. Destree, former French Minister of Sciences and Arts; A. Einstein, Professor of Physics at the University of Berlin; George Halle, Professor of Astrophysics at the University of Chicago; Gilbert Murray, Professor of Greek at Oxford University; G. de Reynolds, Professor of French Literature at the University of Bern; F. Ruffini, Professor of Ecclesiastical Law at the University of Turin; and L. de Torres Quevedo, Director to the *Laboratorio Electrimecanico* in Madrid.[45]

To pull this diverse group together into a working unit became Nitobe's task. Between January 1922, when the Council decided to appoint the committee, until August 1922 when the committee met for the first time, he busily corresponded with these scholars. Madame Curie was reluctant to take the job, for she feared that it "would take too much time from her work." A good deal of persuasion by Nitobe convinced her that the task was worthwhile.[46] When Einstein quit for no apparent reason, Nitobe, realizing the prestige the German physicist would lend to the committee, enlisted Gilbert Murray and Henri Bergson to use their influence to persuade the German physicist. Einstein served for a few years.[47]

The Committee for Intellectual Cooperation met for the first time in July 1922. There a decision was made to support three subcommittees: (1) Intellectual Property; (2) Bibliography; (3) Universities. Over the next few years, it expanded its activities.[48] By 1930, three additional sub-committees dealing with other aspects of intellectual life were added. And the number of members on the Committee increased to fifteen. The biggest boost in the Committee's work came in 1924 when the French government allotted funds to to set up an Institute for Intellectual Cooperation in Paris, which was attached to the Committee. Also, subsequently, in different countries, national organizations for intellectual cooperation appeared.[49]

Nitobe spent most of his last years with the League, until his retirement in December 1926, working with the Committee for Intellectual Cooperation. At the Directors Meetings, he reported on the progress of the various programs of the sub-committees; when travelling or busy with other matters, he sent a subordinate, either his Japanese assistant, Harada Ken, or another member of his office, M. Orestru, to present the section's report to Drummond and the other directors.[50] From time to time, he attended conferences on Esperanto and represented the League's Secretariat at meetings pertaining to educational matters, such as the Educational Conference held in Edinburgh in summer 1925.[51] Through his position at the League, he also became acquainted with many private international groups, such as the Quaker International and the International Women for Peace, to whose Executive Secretary, Emily Balch, he sent encouraging letters of support.[52]

## Spokesman for the League

In the early years, to publicize the League and its work to citizens of all member nations was deemed an indispensable task. Only by winning their support could the League be assured of its survival. She had many champions initially. In America Woodrow Wilson fought hard, without success, to persuade an obstinate Congress of the League's virtues. After much static on capitol hill, he turned to a different strategy: direct appeal to the American people. But his dramatic actions were all in vain; the country rejected his idealistic message of internationalism and peace to return to its traditional isolation.[53]

But elsewhere other prominent leaders carried on the League's banner. Two of the most notable were a South African Boer, Jan Smuts, and an English aristocrat, Sir Robert Cecil.[54] Smuts, as early as the summer of 1918, had penned a volume entitled "The League of

Nations: A Practical Suggestion." Many of the proposals he listed here were subsequently incorporated into the Covenant. Throughout his life, he gave the organization unwavering support. Robert Cecil, a Minister in the British government, was a tireless crusader for the League. He had even quit a ministerial position to head the League of Nations Union in support of the League, and played an important role in winning Britain's ratification for the Treaty and the Covenant.[55]

The League needed publicity to bolster its reputation and hence its effectiveness as a mediating body. Luckily, through the presence of strong personalities, it was able to attain its aims. Included among the notables were Leon Burgeois, the fiery radical senator from France; the above mentioned Fridjof Nansen; the Czech, Edward Benes; the Greek lawyer, Nicholas Politis; and the Swedish socialist, Branting.[56] In its heyday, the League served to catapult many diplomats into fame. They included Aristide Briand from France, and Gustave Stresemann in Germany, and Austen Chamberlain from Britain, all of whom achieved their reputations through performances at the League's Assembly.[57]

The Secretariat, the body of the League most immediately concerned with the day-to-day operations, did not have anyone with the charisma of these individuals. The ranking officer, Eric Drummond, was not an effective publicist. Tall and lean with "a small head, a long neck with a prominent Adam's apple, a long nose and pale gray eyes, Drummond, an heir to a Scottish earldom, with his wiry appearance resembled a 'Scottish terrier.' "[58] Until his appointment as Secretary-General, he had been in the British Foreign Office for nineteen years, serving successively as private secretary to Edward Grey, Herbert Asquith, and then Arthur Balfour. Though a "perfect secretary" with a genius for organization and the "rare gift for conciliating divergent positions" in controversies, he was a shy man and apparently "frightened of speech-making."[59] So whenever occasions arose which required public appearances, Drummond entrusted the task to Nitobe.[60]

Ishii Kikujiro, Japanese representative on the League's Council, had asked Drummond why he always sent Nitobe out on these publicity drives. Drummond replied that "Nitobe is the most effective speaker that we have."[61] The hundreds of speeches that Nitobe had made over his long and diverse career now served him well. He had developed the knack of tuning in to the receptivity of his listeners and had polished his delivery style to become a popular lecturer. Whenever he spoke, he captured his audience with well crafted speeches that abounded with wit and humor. In the early years, he made forays into various parts of Europe to crusade for the League. The best known of these early efforts has been printed in a pamphlet, "What the League Has Done and Is Doing." The original text of this publication came from a lecture delivered at the University of Brussels on September 13th and 14th, 1919.[62]

But Nitobe was valuable to Drummond not only as a speaker. As the only Japanese of rank in the Secretariat, he served as a conduit for the Secretary-General to pass information to and from the Japanese government. His constant interactions with Foreign Ministry people, such as Ishii, moreover, provided him with inside information that was often useful to the Secretariat. Whenever visitors from Japan arrived in Geneva, Nitobe or his deputy, Harada Ken, served as hosts. The most distinguished Japanese guest that he entertained, and whom Drummond found "a friend to the League," was the Royal Prince Kitashirakawa who came in July 1922.[63]

Japan's role in the League from the very first had been ambiguous. Only after much debate, had she decided to join the league.[64] Though she supported the League, her foreign policy did not rely much upon the League's mechanisms. Indeed, Thomas Burkman points out, Japanese diplomats such as Ishii were more favorable to regional accords, as worked out in the Locarno agreements, than the mediation of the League.[65] Throughout the 1920s, Japan avoided using Geneva as a forum for her foreign affairs problems, but she avidly participated on the technical commissions, in areas such as Health or Labor.[66] A notable example of Japan's lack of reliance upon the League is how she dealt with the United States on the Immigration issue.[67] Though there were some rumours in the Secretariat that the Japanese might bring the issue to the League for arbitration, the Japanese skirted the League altogether. While Nitobe served in Geneva, the only major issue that Japan participated was in making a belated proposal regarding the Geneva Protocol.[68]

Japan could not be active in the League for two main reasons. One was political; the other, geographical. The first was the League's preoccupation with European-centered problems which, for Japan as a Far East regional power, was of indirect concern at best; and the second problem, not unrelated to the first, was the great physical distance of Japan from Geneva.[69] These barriers, which effectively isolated Japan in the League's deliberations, were of major concern to Drummond and Nitobe alike. At the Director's Meeting on October 22, 1924, Nitobe announced that he would visit Japan on a short trip to promote the League. He called on the Directors to inform him of any matter that they would like him to discuss with members of the Japanese government.

Since he had assumed office five years before, he had returned home. He wanted to touch Japanese soil again and see the changes in Tokyo after the Great Earthquake the year before. Probably most of all he wanted to see his family; there had been a new addition whom he had never seen, his granddaughter, Takeko, who was born in 1920. There were also personal chores to attend to, such as the reconstruction of his Kamakura summerhouse which the earthquake had completely destroyed.[70]

He sailed from Marseilles on November 2nd on board the S. S. *Hakusan* and arrived in Japan thirty-six days later.[71] He took the Indian Ocean route. Despite his relatives and many friends in the United States, he purposely avoided going there. Earlier that year, the U.S. Congress had passed the General Immigration Act which so angered him that he swore never to step foot in the country until the act was revoked.[72] Eight years later, he would break this vow.

Nitobe began to stump for the League even before he arrived in Japan. On board ship, Nitobe gave a lecture to Japanese passengers; and on a stop-over in Shanghai, he gave several speeches to three different organizations. Arriving in Kobe on December 8th, he wasted no time: two speeches were delivered, one at the League of Union Branch in Kobe, and later that day to a general audience of about 950 in Osaka. His visit home was filled to the brim with a grueling work. Katherine Willard Eddy, a missionary and English teacher working with the YMCA in Tokyo, who lived in the Nitobe's Koishikawa home while the Nitobe's were in Geneva. She recollected Nitobe's visit with great clarity:

In the morning when he left for conferences all the helpers in the house ... assembled in the hall, one holding his cane, another his coat, another his hat, etc., and then when he was fully ready they stood under the porte cochere, bowing low as he entered his car and was driven away. When he returned at night, no matter what the time, again they were there to greet him, both doors wide open and all the lights turned on, and fatigued though he was he always had some pleasant bit of the days [*sic*] doings to pass on to them. They and we realized day by day that we were living under the same roof with a great man....[73]

Aside from about a week's break during the New Years, when he spent with his family and attended to personal affairs, Nitobe was busy with public appearances until he left Japan on February 15th. He "spoke 85 times and the audiences total[ed], at the lowest estimate, more than 50,000." He spent forty-six days lecturing and another twenty-five days giving interviews to the press. His listeners were varied and included members from all strata of society. Members of the Royal Family, including the Prince Regent Hirohito and Prince Chichibu, invited him to speak at the Emperor's residence on the January 17th and 19th respectively; and he addressed the Privy Council and four ministers of government on January 18th.[74]

He also spoke to *Seiyukai* Dietmen, to influential bankers and business-men, engineers and educators, industrialists and religious leaders, pharmacists and merchants, university and college students, women's and foreigners groups, and many other organizations. Most of his speeches were delivered in or around Tokyo, though he made one long speaking tour to central and western Japan from January 10th till the 30th. It included Nagoya, Kyoto, Osaka, Nara, Wakayama, Kobe, Okayama, Fukuoka, Nagasaki, Kumamoto, Yawata, and Hiroshima. All who came heard him preach and praise the ideals of the League.

Nitobe, who soon after his appointment to the League had written in 1920 to Foreign Minister Uchida to gain support for the League in Japan, found the government fully in support of the League. Shidehara Kijuro, the Foreign Minister told him that "neither he — nor his predecessor — has ever had any difficulty in obtaining in Parliament what he asked for the expenses of the League."[75] But Nitobe found that Japanese generally were ignorant of the League, except for some youthful supporters. Though he did not encounter much active opposition, some, particularly those in military and educational circles, held grave reservations about the League's utility. In his report to Drummond, Nitobe identified and summarized into ten points the skepticism that he found many to harbour:

1. Is not the League a super-State — "a house on a roof", as we say? Does it not intrude into the sovereign rights of an independent State? [*sic*]
2. Can war really be avoided, when the history of every nation has shown it to be so frequent and apparently so inevitable?
3. Can man ever be so tamed as to outlive his instinct of pugnacity?
4. For the maintenance of world peace, is the League radical enough in its conception and democratic enough in its constitution, and universal enough in its composition?
5. Is it true that the League is secretly manned by the Jews, whose ultimate purpose is the disruption of all organized society?
6. Are the nations of the world, including the Members of the League, really inclined to resort to peaceful means, or is not so-called "Peace" a pretence for a veiled preparation for war? What is the meaning of the Singapore Base?
7. Is not the League an instrument of the Great Powers for the prosecution of their own selfish ends?
8. Is it not an organization convenient and profitable only to Europe? What benefit does it confer upon Asia and upon Japan in particular?
9. Is the League worth the money our country pays for its support?
10. As long as America stays outside its pale, can the League be of much use to Japan?[76]

Nitobe expended much effort to dispel these doubts. To each, he countered and parried. Though not originally a diplomat, he had, in representing the League's interest in Japan, to become one. His arguments were uneven and not well developed. Regarding the first five objections, he did not spend much time; to the first he pointed to the five-year history of the League to show the charge "unfounded." To the second and third, he dismissed as too "academic." To the fourth, which he considered to come from the political left, instead of directing himself to the question, he took it as an opportunity to comment on the communists in Japan. He saw them as Russian puppets, who were too "occupied with general propaganda as to afford little time to make assault on the league." The fifth point he categorically rejected as without foundation, though he expressed surprise that anti-Semitism "should even find entrance into Japan."[77]

Items six to ten were more difficult for him. On the question of whether nations were sincere in their resorting to peaceful means to solve conflict, he noted that the league was not a compulsory organization, that each member was "free to prepare itself for an emergency." On the British fortification at Singapore, he thought that it "may be a political maneuver on the part of the Conservative Government to pander to the demands of the Pacific dominions." On item seven, he pointed that it is idle to debate the dominant influence of the Great Powers. Such things are facts. Rather, it is more important to ask whether they "have become more so since the establishment of the League?"[78]

On the question of the benefits of the League to Japan, a concern that both Eric Drummond and Nitobe worried about, he pointed to Japan's position on the Council as a permanent member. He elaborated on this point:

> The ordinary man must be told that this position [on the council] is not only highly honorable, but very valuable in ordinary times and priceless in extraordinary times. As far as the yearly allocation is concerned, it must be considered an insurance policy against War, and as such it must not be expected to yield immediate profit. Moreover, Japan will find in a few years that the wisest course for her to pursue in her diplomacy is to bring it in line with the world's public opinion as mirrored in the League.[79]

On the last question of the League's effectiveness without America, one that even the Prince Regent put to him, Nitobe could "only express the hope that the United States may come in, and the belief that she will." He also pointed to encouraging signs in this direction, which included the United States' participation in various committees, and the many Americans who were seriously engaged in studying the League. Vis-a-vis America, "the noblest, and the wisest thing for Japan to do," he concluded, "is to conduct herself within the League so as to prove herself above suspicion, and thus even pave the way for America's entry."[80] Little did he know that these issues that he found so vexing would again engage him fully nine years later after his return to Japan.

Most encouraging to him on his visit was the growth of the Japan League of Nations Union which had some 2,300 members in nineteen branches throughout the country.[81] It was extreme active while he visited, and some ten new branches were inaugurated. Among its activities was a monthly magazine, sponsoring frequent lectures by prominent men, classes on the League, and the issuing of pamphlets.[82]

Nitobe left Kobe to return home on February 15, 1925 on the S. S. *Kamo Maru*. He again took the Indian Ocean route stopovers at Shanghai and Hong Kong, where he delivered addresses to mixed groups of Japanese, Chinese and Americans. He arrived back in Geneva in late March and gave a summary report of his Japan visit at the Directors Meeting on April 8th. A month later, he formally initiated a branch office for the League's Information Section in Tokyo. This was approved by the Sixth Assembly in the autumn of 1925.[83]

## Life in Geneva: the Glorious Years

Geneva was "a third-rate European city of little international importance" when the League moved there in October 1920. It was a tourist attraction. Located on the extreme western shoreline of Lake Leman, the city boasted a magnificent natural setting second to none in Europe. Its blue-green lake, the snow-white peak of Mount Blanc in the distance, the little grey and green houses dotted over the hilly landscape, the gushing torrents of the Rhône, the needle-like spire of the medieval Saint Pierre cathedral, and the rose-colored hue of a cool summer evening, all added to a fairy-tale-like atmosphere, which excited the imagination of the diplomats seeking a place to build a visionary future world of peace and harmony.[84]

The choice of Switzerland to locate the League was politically astute. Since its confederation in 1848, the Swiss have kept a low posture in European political affairs and maintained a strict neutrality in both the Franco-Prussian war and the recent Great war. Geneva, which was honored to host the world organization, historically had a reputation as a haven for political exiles; liberals, social revolutionaries, and anarchists had sought refuge there. Despite its harsh and intolerant Calvinist traditions, it had its periods of liberalism. There, Jean Jacques Rousseau had written his famous tract, the *Social Contract*; later in the nineteenth century, writers such as Byron, Shelley, and George Sand were attracted to Geneva to live and work. The city retained its tranquility until the League, with its army of diplomats, bureaucrats, technical experts, stenographers and clerks all with their families, descended upon it late in 1920.[85]

In August 1920, Drummond purchased the recently renovated Hotel National in downtown Geneva in August 1920 for five and a half million francs to house the Secretariat. "[B]aths, wash-basins, and hot-water pipes were torn out. The bedroom furniture was removed" as the various offices of the international civil servants were set up.[86]

Nitobe, one of the four highest-ranking men in the League, spent six years at his office here, commuting back and forth daily in a chauffeur-driven car provided by the League. His salary, 75,000 francs per annum (about $15,000 U.S.) plus expenses, was more than sufficient for him to pursue the conspicuous lifestyle of a high-level diplomat.[87] He and Mary rented a house in suburban Bellevue, some five miles north of the city. It was a large and spacious home with a huge immaculately kept lawn that fronted the shore of the lake. It commanded a superb view of the majestic Mount Blanc in the distance.

Ayuzawa Iwao, who represented Japan at the ILO, and who was a frequent visitor with his wife to the home, recollected with special clarity a weekend when he saw "Madame Curie, Henri Bergson, Gilbert Murray, and Albert Einstein, genially conversing while seated around white-painted tables on the lawn." Afterwards, Ayuzawa continues, the venerable Einstein, a musical as well as mathematical genius, entertained the Nitobes' guests with a violin performance.[88] Ayuzawa's wife, Fukuko, likened the Nitobes' home to the famous eighteenth-century salon of the Madame de Staël, at whose gatherings the literary and cultural elite of Europe attended. It had stood in the village next to the Nitobes' home.[89]

Guests were a regular part of the Nitobes' social life. Whenever friends and acquaintances arrived in town to see him, Nitobe invited them to his home for a luncheon or dinner. William Faunce, president of Brown University and a long-time friend of the family, visited Geneva in the first week of September 1922 to observe the second assembly's proceedings. Nitobe reserved him a room at the Hotel Bellevue and invited him for dinner at their home before he left Geneva.[90] Faunce, who had not seen them since 1912 when he visited Japan, wrote to his wife that "[they are] the same sweet unselfish spirits as when I saw them in Tokio."[91] The guests that evening numbered some fourteen, many from the Health section of the League. Faunce was impressed by their varied backgrounds. Men and women of all nationalities made it hard for "general conversation across the table." He himself sat beside "a brilliant Polish woman" whose conversation "he found most instructive." Her husband was a "distinguished Austrian royalist" loyal to the Hapsburg.[92]

Faunce shared his impressions of Nitobe's character in the same letter. He was, the Brown University President said, "an urbane, witty cosmopolitan, tender-hearted, Christian" who was the most "beautiful soul" he had met. "He will have a front seat in Heaven."[93] This impression was shared by many friends and acquaintances. James Shotwell, professor of International Relations at Columbia University, who got to know Nitobe at the League and whose friendship continued until the latter's death, refers, in his autobiography, to Nitobe as a "one of the finest gentleman of any nationality I have ever met."[94] When he retired, Albert Dufour-Feronce, a German who was appointed Under-Secretary General as Nitobe's replacement, expressed concern that people would "compare him with the 'saint' Nitobe."[95]

His physical appearance contributed to his sage-like image; he had aged considerably while in Geneva. The once full and dark black hair was now grey, and he was balding a bit in the back; his smartly-trimmed moustache was completely white. But his face, which during his *ichiko* years projected an image of a proud and even haughty patrician, had mellowed. His eyes, which had troubled him all his adult life, had now weakened to a point where he even feared blindness.[96]

To Blanche Weber Shaffer, who was then a student at the University of Geneva, Nitobe was a model to emulate. In him, she saw a mature gentleman full of knowledge, a "modern Erasmus," who also possessed a deeper wisdom that held compassion for people. She recalled fondly his love for little children, whom he called "chubbikins," and his sensitivity to people's needs. "Dr. Nitobe," she wrote later, "is one of the people who has had the deepest influence on my life.... [He] has been to me the unusual combination of a great teacher, a wise and understanding friend and a fairy godfather."[97]

Many other similar testimonials remain. They reveal Nitobe's profound impact upon people in Geneva. In addition, he was one of the most popular internationalists in Geneva. F. L. Whelen, who worked for many years at the League, wrote:

> In the League's early days, at a Christmas party, [where] many members of the Secretariat were present, the guests were asked to write down in order 1, 2, 3 three names ... they regarded as the most popular people in Geneva. My recollection is that all put the same name, Inazo Nitobe, No. 1. Nansen and Cecil were the most frequent No. 2 and ... a variety [of others] No. 3.[98]

But Nitobe's gracious charm in social intercourse and his pleasant disposition in the day-to-day grind of the League's activities did not come without effort. He worked hard to win and maintain his reputation. And though he reveled in the honors and adulation, he apparently had another motive. He considered this reputation not only a personal triumph but also a victory for Japan.[99] As a Japanese internationalist, he represented Japan in the eyes of Westerners. He felt that his behavior in international circles must be impeccable. "Do not do anything to shame Japan" was his motto, and he repeatedly stressed it to his Japanese underlings. At times, this concern with "proper behavior for Japan's sake" seemed to go to extreme, and, it seems today, paranoid lengths. Kamiya Mieko, Maeda Tamon's daughter, recalled a conversation between Nitobe and her mother after they had arrived in Geneva in 1923. Paying a courtesy call on Nitobe, Mrs. Maeda received the following stern warning from Nitobe:

> How many people did you say came? Four? Why it's exactly as Maeda *kun* told a newspaper reporter: 'It's like a zoo.' This is serious business. Four people and with children also! This place is not like Japan, where one can just raise children without doing anything else. On the contrary, you are representing the

Japanese government here. Socializing with the various representatives from different countries is a back-breaking chore. Each word that you utter, each act that you perform, reflects the level of civilization in Japan. I hope that you will reflect carefully and live a lifestyle that would not bring any shame upon Japan.[100]

In their own lifestyles, the Nitobes had to make various adjustments to the Geneva society. At their social functions, along with the delicious food prepared by their chiefs, the Nitobes served red and white wine. In Japan, they had refrained from alcohol, but in Geneva they adjusted their customs accordingly. To his daughter, Kotoko, who was concerned about the wine at their table, Nitobe retorted, "think of it as medicine; is not morally wrong to drink, as long as one does not get drunk."[101]

Since French was one of the two official languages of the League, and the dominant local language in the city, Nitobe and Mary took lessons from a private instructor.[102] Although Nitobe appears to have used it when necessary, he was not comfortable in it, and did not use it in public. When French visitors from the International Bureau came to visit the Secretariat, he asked, at a Directors meeting, for "some fluent speaker" to help him guide the visitors around. Pierre Comert, head of the Information Section, volunteered.[103]

Though Nitobe's behavior was gentlemanly and proper in international society, he was a different person with his fellow Japanese. He was more relaxed and was not as careful of the niceties of courtesy and etiquette that he so carefully observed when in the company of Westerners. Kawanishi Tazuko, recalls his voracious appetite when dining among Japanese. She once served sukiyaki at a gathering of Japanese, and Nitobe "shocked her by eating six or seven bowels of rice with the sukiyaki." Seeing her surprise, she continued, "Nitobe chuckled and showed her a bottle of digestives."[104] He loved eating with other Japanese at the only Japanese restaurant in Geneva where he ate to his heart's content as he entertained his younger companions with humorous stories of his earlier days.

Nitobe submitted his resignation from his post at the League on December 6th, 1926, though he continued his duties until the end of the month. In January of the following year, he left Geneva with his family.

### Notes

1. The League of Nations Society in Canada, *A Handbook on the League of Nations* (Ottawa: The League of Nations Society in Canada, n.d.), p. 101.
2. Denys P. Myers, *Handbook of the League of Nations*, p. 3. On the drafting of the Covenant, see Frank P. Walters, *A History of the League of Nations*, (1952; rpt. London: Oxford University Press, 1967), pp. 30-39; John Bassett, *The League of Nations* (New York: Longmans, Green and Co., 1928), pp. 1-4; Elmer Bendiner, *A Time for Angels* (New York: Alfred A. Knopf, 1975), pp. 78-103; George Slocombe, *A Mirror to Geneva: Its Growth, Grandeur and Decay* (1938; rpt. Freeport, New York: Books for Libraries Press, 1970), pp. 32-36.
3. On Japan's role in the deliberations in Paris, see Masatoshi Matsushita (New York: Columbia University Press, 1929), pp. 15-35; also Thomas Burkman, "Japan, the League of Nations, and the New World Order," *Diss.* University of Michigan 1975, pp. 227-76.
4. For Japan's strategy at the Peace Conference and a background into the Shantung issue and the Western Pacific islands in a wider context of great power rivalry, see Richard Storry, *Japan and the Decline of the West in Asia, 1894-1943* (London: MacMillan Press, Ltd., 1979), pp. 111-14. Published works and reference materials relating to the League of Nations and collective security abound. See George W. Baer, *International Organizations, 1918-1945: A Guide to Research and Research Materials* (Wilmington, Delaware: Scholarly Resources Inc., 1981) for an excellent bibliography of primary and secondary sources on all aspects of the League of Nations. I am indebted to Professor George Egerton for pointing out to me this guidebook, which proved invaluable in writing this chapter.
5. For an account of the publishing activities of the League in its heyday, see Secretariat of the League of Nations, *Ten Years of World-Co-operation* (London: Hazell, Watson and Viney, Ltd., 1930). Also Myers, *Handbook*. Though it is standard opinion today that "the League has failed" in its peace-keeping tasks, when one considers the range of activities that the League engaged in, many of which are forerunners of those that exist today, the difficulties of condemning the League in a blanket statement becomes immediately apparent. For an objective judgment on the League's work, see Gerhard Niemeyer, "The Balance-Sheet of the League Experiment" in *International Organization*, 6 (1952), 537-58.
6. For a detailed analysis of the weaknesses of the League, with a particular focus on the office of Secretary-General, see James Barros, *Office Without Power: Secretary-General Sir Eric Drummond, 1919-1933* (New York: Oxford University Press, 1979); also his *Betrayal from Within: Joseph Avenol, Secretary*

*General of the League of Nations, 1933-1940* (New Haven: Yale University Press, 1969).

7   E. H. Carr, *International Relations Between the Two World Wars* (1937; rpt. London: MacMillan and Co., Ltd., 1965), pp. 98-130; Walters, p. 295.

8   The most detailed account of the League listed above (note 2) is Frank Walters, a former high official in the Secretariat; for an opposite and highly critical view see Elmer Bendiner, *A Time For Angels*.

9   For an quantitative analysis of the coverage of news of the League in the Tokyo *Asahi*, see Burkman, pp. 298-99.

10  *Rirekisho* I, entry for 4 March 1919; Tsurumi Yusuke, *Goto Shimpei* (Tokyo: Keiso Shobo, 1965), IV, 3.

11  See "Roosevelt of Far East Here," *San Francisco Chronicle*, 22 Mar. 1919, p. 17. A clipping of this article is reproduced in *Kinen* I, p. 147. Nitobe in this article is referred to as the "Burbank" of Japan.

12  Details of the trip with Goto are from Tsurumi, pp. 7-100.

13  Ibid., pp. 7-46. Goto's party when they left Tokyo consisted of Nitobe, Kasama Akio, Tajima Michiji, Washio Shogoro and Goto's son, Ichizo, who enrolled at Columbia University in New York. Mary Nitobe apparently joined them on the West Coast. In Chicago, the party was joined by Kawakami Kaoru (Karl), a foreign correspondent for the *Tokyo Nichi Nichi* who accompanied the party to New York.

14  Ibid., pp. 50-66. Nitobe anecdote of Robert Cecil is found in his *Ijin gunzo*, reprinted in *Zenshu*, V, 367-69.

15  Tsurumi, *Goto Shimpei*, p. 72.

16  Sato, p. 123.

17  Nitobe's appointment is briefly mentioned in Barros, *Office Without Power*, p. 68.

18  Lewis Auchincloss, Letter to Eric Drummond, 21 June 1919, Edward M. House Papers, Sterling Memorial Library, Yale University, New Haven, Conn., and quoted in Barros, *Office Without Power*, p. 68.

19  Tsurumi, *Goto Shimpei*, pp. 82-88.

20  Ibid., p. 88. Tsurumi points out that one condition that Goto put to Chinda was that Nitobe also be appointed to the House of Peers along with appointment to the League. Peerage, however, came to Nitobe after his retirement from the League.

21  Nitobe Inazo, Letter to Anna Chase, 12 August 1919, in FHLNP.

22  Konoe Fumimaro "Nitobe sensei" in NHTS, p. 173. For Konoe's work with Saionji at the Peace Conference, see Oka Yoshitake's excellent biography, *Konoe Fumimaro: A Political Biography* (Tokyo: Tokyo University Press, 1983).

23  The other two major bodies were the Assembly and the Council. The powers of each is defined in the Covenant. See Myers, *Handbook of the League of Nations*, pp. 24-52, for a concise organizational summary of the League; see also Walters, pp. 40-61.

24  During the planning stages of the League, some representatives wanted the

position of Secretary-General to be politically eminent. Robert Cecil proposed the title "Chancellor," which suggests greater powers, but in subsequent debate, a less influential position was created. See Barros, *Office Without Power*, pp. 1–19.

25 Walters, pp. 76–77; see also, Frank G. Boudreau, "International Civil Service" in *Pioneers In World Order*, ed. Harriet Eager Davis (New York: Columbia University Press, 1944), pp. 76–86.

26 For the selection of the Secretariat's high-level personnel and the problems associated with it, see Barros, *Office Without Power*, pp. 60-8; The League of Nations Society in Canada, *A Handbook on The League of Nations*, pp. 120–21, gives a list of the ranking members of the Secretariat in 1924.

27 Boudreau, p. 80.

28 Slocombe, p. 70; Boudreau points out other factors which helped to make a successful Secretariat, see p. 81–83.

29 League of Nations Documents and Publications, "Minutes of the Directors Meetings," 27 April 1921. On microfilm from Research Publications, Inc., New Haven, Conn., reel 1 (Henceforth Directors Meeting Minutes).

30 Bendiner, p. 134. Both Fosdick and Monnet did not remain at their post for long; after America's rejection of the League, Fosdick resigned. Monnet departed in 1923, and his position was filled by Joseph Avenol. Italy, as a middle power, was represented on the Secretariat from January 1920 by Bernardo Attolico, who held the other Under-Secretary General's rank.

31 Frank Walters, "The Late Dr. Nitobe" in NHTS, pp. 432–33.

32 Sugimura Yotaro, "Remmei jidai no sensei," p. 429.

33 Walters, "The Late Dr. Nitobe," p. 435.

34 Irene Stafford, "Dr. Nitobe," in NHTS, p. 461.

35 William Faunce, President of Brown who visited Nitobe in September 1922, commented about Nitobe's views on the postwar reconstruction work in a letter to his wife: "I have talked with him [Nitobe] again about Europe and get no light, save that the need is spiritual, not political." See William Faunce, Letter to Sadie Faunce, 23 August 1922, Faunce Papers, The John Hay Library, Brown University, Providence, Rhode Island (henceforth FPRU).

36 Myers, *Handbook*, p. 379.

37 Directors Meeting Minutes, 20 Aug. 1919.

38 Ibid, 7 July 1920.

39 The International Bureaux's budget allocation in 1925 amounted to 18,000 Swiss francs. See Confidential Circulars, "Memorandum by Financial Director," 13 May 1925. Appended to Directors Meeting Minutes, reel 2.

40 Directors Meeting Minutes, 3 March 1922; "International Organisations," *Monthly Summary of the League of Nations*, 2 (1922), 50 (hereafter cited as *Monthly Summary*).

41 Secretariat of the League of Nations, *Ten Years of World Co-operation*, p. 442.

42 Directors Meeting Minutes, 3 March 1922; *Monthly Summary*, 2, (1922), 50,

97.
43 For a summary of the work of the Committee for Intellectual Cooperation, see Secretariat of the League of Nations, *Ten Years*, pp. 313-29; Walters, *History*, pp. 191-94.
44 Directors Meeting Minutes, 31 Dec. 1920.
45 *Monthly Summary*, 2, (1922), 96, 118.
46 Directors Meeting Minutes, 1 June 1922; 14 June 1922.
47 Ronald Steele, *A Biography of Albert Einstein* (New York: Penguin Books, 1975), p. 308; for a summary view of the Committee's accomplishments and failures, see Walters, p. 193.
48 For some of the difficulties facing the Committee in the initial years, see Secretariat of League of Nations, *Ten Years*, pp. 314-17.
49 Ibid, pp. 318-29.
50 Directors Meeting Minutes, 21 December 1922; 8 May 1924; 18 March 1925; 8 April 1925. Harada joined Nitobe early in 1920 and remained a close deputy throughout the latter's stay in Geneva. On Harada's appointment, see Nitobe Inazo, Letter to Foreign Minister Uchida, 20 February 1919, Goto Shimpei Papers, Goto Shimpei Memorial Hall, Mizusawa City, Iwate Prefecture. Reprinted in *Kinen* II, p. 168.
51 Directors Meeting Minutes, 10 August 1921;12 August 1925.
52 For Nitobe's relationship to the Quaker International Center, see Betram Pickard, "Inazo Nitobe" in NIKK, pp. 332-34; for Nitobe's relationship with the International Women's League, see Mercedes Randall, *Improper Bostonian: Emily Greene Balch* (New York: Twayne Publishers, Inc., 1965), pp. 286.
53 John Morton Blum, *Woodrow Wilson and the Politics of Morality* (Boston: Little, Brown and Company, 1956), pp. 181-99.
54 Slocombe, pp. 78-95.
55 George W. Egerton, *Great Britain and the Creation of the League of Nations: Strategy, Politics, and International Organization: 1914-1919* (Chapel Hill, N. C.: North Carolina University Press, 1978).
56 Slocombe, p. 74.
57 Slocombe, pp. 82-83.
58 Slocombe, pp. 5-6.
59 Slocombe, p. 70; Barros, *Office Without Power*, p. 25.
60 Bendiner points out (page 134) that Nitobe and Anzilotti "never worked as closely with Drummond as did Fosdick and Monnet in those early months." However, a reading of the Directors Minutes from 13 August 1919 onwards reveals that until his retirement, Nitobe was privy to all confidential information and reports, and frequently made suggestions on items outside his own sphere of activities, which lay in cultural and educational activities.
61 Ishii Kikujiro, "Nitobe Inazo hakase o omou" in NHTS, pp. 419-20.
62 Reprinted in *Zenshu*, XV, 371-400. See above pp. 4-25.
63 Directors Meeting Minutes, 1 October 1919, 2 June 1920, 2 April 1922, 28 March 1923, 5 April 1923, 16 May 1923, 31 October 1923, 5 June 1924,

210  PART TWO (COMMENTARY) BACKGROUNDS AND CRITICAL ESSAYS

20 June 1924, 8 October 1924, 22 October 1924, 18 March 1925, 8 April 1925, 20 May 1925.
64  For a discussion of the benefits to Japan of a League membership, see Matsushita, pp. 155–69.
65  See Burkman, "Japan, the League" p. 289.
66  For Japan's participation at the League on the issues of health and other related matters, see "Mission of Dr. Rajchman in the Far East," report to the Secretary-General, Confidential Circular #1, appended to Directors Meeting Minutes, reel 2. See Matsushita (pp. 121–54) for an account of Japan's work on the various League commissions.
67  Directors Meeting Minutes, 5 June 1924, 20 June 1924.
68  Reported in "Mission of Dr. Rajchman."
69  Another barrier which Matsushita points out (p. 158) is the linguistic and cultural one.
70  Nitobe Kotoko, "Taidan: chichi Inazo o kataru" in *Kinen* I, p. 87.
71  The details mentioned here on Nitobe's trip to Japan come from a report dated 4 April 1925 entitled "The League of Nations Movement in Japan" which Nitobe submitted in to Secretary-General Eric Drummond. This unpublished report at the League of Nations Archives in Geneva (Box R1573). I am grateful to Professor Thomas Burkman for providing me with a copy of this precious document.
72  Nitobe Inazo, Letter to Nicholas Murray Butler, 25 May 1931, Butler Library, Columbia University, New York.
73  Katherine Willard Eddy, Letter to Passmore Elkinton, n.d., in FHLNP.
74  Nitobe, "League of Nations Movement." Appended to this report is a "Programme of Lectures" that include the date, the place, the character of the audience, and the estimated number of listeners.
75  Nitobe, "League of Nations Movement," p. 1; for a printed version of Nitobe's letter to Uchida, see *Kinen* I, p. 168. Japan's share of the League's budget, as a middle power, was 60 units in 1928, or $291,000. This was equal to Italy's share, and next to Great Britain, France and Germany. See Matsushita, p. 157.
76  Nitobe, "League of Nations Movement," pp. 2–3.
77  Nitobe, "League of Nations Movement," pp. 3–4.
78  Nitobe, "League of Nations Movement," p. 4.
79  Nitobe, "League of Nations Movement," p. 5.
80  Nitobe, "League of Nations Movement," p. 6.
81  Nitobe, "League of Nations Movement," p. 6.
82  Nitobe, "League of Nations Movement," p. 6.
83  Directors Meeting Minutes, 18 March 1925, 8 April 1925; Thomas Burkman, "The Geneva Spirit" in John F. Howes (ed.), *Nitobe Inazō: Japan's Bridge Across the Pacific* (Boulder & Oxford: Westview Press, 1995), p. 195. See note 51 of Burkman's paper for a good account of the relationship between the Japan League of Nations Association and the League's Tokyo informa-

tion office.
84 For an excellent description of Geneva, see Slocombe's Chapter Four, "The City of Calvin," pp. 37–45.
85 Belgium had fought to have the League established at Brussels, but Wilson, whose decision apparently carried the most weight, after originally voting against Geneva, changed his mind to have the headquarters there. See Bendener, p. 121, 136; also Slocombe, p. 37.
86 Slocombe, p. 63.
87 Confidential Circulars, "Memorandum by Financial Director," 13 May 1925. Appended to Directors Meeting Minutes, reel 2.
88 Ayuzawa Iwao, "Nitobe sensei no kokusai teki koken" in NIKK, pp. 329–30.
89 Ayuzawa Fukuko, "Arigataki Nitobe sensei" in NHTS, pp. 466–70.
90 Nitobe Inazo, Letter to William Faunce, 15 May 1922, in FPBU.
91 William Faunce, Letter to Sadie Faunce, 23 August 1922, in FPBU.
92 William Faunce, Letter to Sadie Faunce, 25 August 1922, in FPBU.
93 William Faunce, Letter to Sadie Faunce, 23 August 1922, in FPBU.
94 Shotwell, The *Autobiography of James Shotwell* (New York: Bobbs and Merrill, 1960), pp. 133, 282.
95 Sugimura, p. 430.
96 Nitobe Inazo, Letter to Kawano Kisa, 7 January 1920, reprinted in *Kinen* II, p. 86. In this letter to his sister, Nitobe describes his physical appearance and his failing eyesight.
97 Blanche Weber Shaffer, Letter to Passmore Elkinton, 18 January 1942, in FHLNP.
98 F. L. Whelen, Letter to Passmore Elkinton, 5 January 1940, in FHLNP.
99 Harada Ken, "Junebu nite" in NHTS, p. 457.
100 Kamiya Mieko, *Henreki*, in *Chosakushu*, 9 (Tokyo: Misuzu Shobo, 1980), p. 19.
101 Nitobe Kotoko, "Taidan," in *Kinen* I, p. 93; also Yasutomi Shozo, "Nitobe sensei no omoide" in NHTS, p. 447. Yasutomi sees the Nitobe's use of alcohol as "a spiritual sacrifice."
102 Kamiya, *Henreki*, pp. 21–22.
103 Directors Meeting Minutes, 28 July 1923.
104 Kawanishi Tazuko, "Omoide" in NHTS, p. 463.

# VIII. Conclusion

## Teruhiko Nagao

Inazo Nitobe wrote a short book *Bushido: The Soul of Japan* in California in 1899, where he was recuperating from a mental illness which had compelled him to retire from all work in Japan. The book was published early in 1900, and a revised edition was published in 1905. The latter edition, published by Putnam's Sons in New York, made the book a world-wide best-seller. It is well-known that Theodore Roosevelt, President of U.S., was sufficiently impressed to buy and distribute many copies of it to his friends.

The book can easily be seen as an expression of nationalism. Some thirty years after the Meiji Restoration in 1868 when Japan opened itself to foreign influences, a nationalistic fervour was born among the generation brought up in the rapidly modernizing and westernizing Japan of the 1870s and 1880s. Nitobe's book was preceded by Kanzo Uchimura's *How I Became a Christian: The Diary of a Japanese Convert* (Chicago, 1895), and followed by Tenshin Okakura's *The Ideals of the East* (London, 1903), *The Awakening of Japan* (New York, 1904), and *The Book of Tea* (1906), all written in English.

No less strong among these writers, however, was the tendency toward internationalism. This is not surprising, because their nationalism was not so much a matter of self-assertion as an attempt to map Japanese culture within an international perspective. They received their higher education almost entirely from Western teachers, mainly from America, and, in that process, absorbed much of Western culture into their outlook. Their response may more properly be called a record of the encounter between East and West which happened in Japan in the latter half of the nineteenth century — happened quite dramatically, as the two had not met before and were so different from each other.

This applies particularly to Nitobe. He was a great admirer of Western culture, especially British. As mentioned above, he was taught mostly by American teachers, studied in Johns Hopkins University, and married an American lady. But in those days, much of American culture was far closer to its British inheritance than now. Most certainly he was the first admirer, and probably the first reader, of Thomas Carlyle, in Japan. He studied in Germany, too, but his prime access to Western culture was always through English. It is highly probable that he was the first reader of Karl Marx's *Das Kapital* in Japan, and it appears that he read the book in the English translation by Samuel Moore and Edward Aveling.[1] Nitobe's specialities were by turns agriculture, economics, law and colonial policy, but they were always accompanied by his continuing engagement with literature. His English writings are permeated with Shakespearean allusions. He was also responsive to contemporary literature. Rudyard Kipling was his exact contemporary, and we find Nitobe, when writing *Bushido* in 1899, already quoting from Kipling's poem "Recessional" written in 1897.

Nitobe was fascinated by the culture of the British Empire in its full maturity. We can even say that Nitobe's *Bushido* is in a way a study of the parallels between Japanese 'samurai' and the British gentlemanly code that had its origins in European chivalry. Nitobe expresses this stance at the outset of his book; he says, 'It is a pleasure to me to reflect upon this subject in the language of Burke, who uttered the well-known touching eulogy over the neglected bier of its European prototype.' And this is wound up with a rather humorous reference to 'the boyish desire of the small Britisher, Tom Brown,[2] "to leave behind him the name of a fellow who never bullied a little boy or turned his back on a big one."'

Everywhere in the book we feel the author's relaxed sense of the pleasure of writing. Probably, while he was gradually recovering from his illness in California, Nitobe looked back upon his own life up to that point, and found some satisfaction in his constant efforts to become 'a bridge across the Pacific' — an ambition he set himself when a young student. He worked diligently, read many books, and absorbed the advanced culture of Western countries. He met wonderful people in America, especially Quakers in Philadelphia, and married an American Quaker lady. Such was the past he looked back upon.

Probably he wanted to summarize this encounter with a different culture. In writing this book, he had no ambition; he didn't expect that it would become a bestseller. He wrote it mostly for his own enjoyment, just like a diary or a confession.

As a record of an encounter between different cultures (in Kipling's words, the meeting of 'East and West'), the book is a fascinating work in a quite unique genre. It had a prophetic aspect, too, for, from our point of view, the book seems to have prefigured Nitobe's vigorous activity as an internationalist in his later life. He was a man of fine action rather than of fine writing. His achievements as under-secretary-general in the newly established headquarters of the League of Nations (1920-1926) and his desperate efforts (at once heroic and pathetic) to stem the dangerous growth of Japanese militarism (1931-1933) certainly deserve a book-length assessment.

Running through all those activities we find the same principle, the same belief set down in this early work. In his later talks Nitobe liked to quote Kipling's 'Oh, East is East, and West is West, and never the twain shall meet.' But his purpose was always to direct his audience's attention to the lines which come after that: 'But there is neither East nor West... /When two strong men stand face to face....' Difference and similarity, similarity and difference — that is Nitobe's theme in the book. The whole book seems to transmit to us a message that different cultures and different languages are given us in order to be enjoyed, not to cause strife among peoples; that we do not wish those differences wiped away from the world, for we can always find underlying such differences similarities denoting common humanity. Nitobe's activities in Geneva were supported by this belief, and the belief has not lost its relevance in the present-day world, rather we are more in need of it.

Here, it is important to note Nitobe's strict use of the words nationalism and internationalism. In his definition, nationalism and patriotism can be used as synonyms for each other, but they are sharply distinguished from chauvinism and jingoism. The essential feature of the former is to love one's own country, while that of the latter is to hate the rivals of one's own country. The difference may look slight at first, but the shift in emphasis makes a great difference. They are totally different from each other, sheer opposites. And the nationalism or patriotism so defined is one and the same thing as internationalism. Internationalism is again distinguished from cosmopolitanism. Cosmopolitanism tries to wipe away all the differences of countries. It negates all kinds of national and nationalistic feelings. Nitobe supports internationalism, not cosmopolitanism. And internationalism presupposes the existence of nationalism and patriotism. The man who loves his own country will inevitably love the world with its variety of nationalities. And the man who loves the world will inevitably love his own country as the nearest and dearest part of it.

This strictness of terminology reminds us of the method used by Carlyle's precursor, Samuel Taylor Coleridge. Very often our discussion loses its point because of the vagueness of language. In order to overcome this, Coleridge proposed what he termed desynonymization; that is to say, distinguishing and separating two words which have been used indiscriminately as synonyms.[3] The most famous is the distinction between fancy and imagination. Other examples are talent/genius, allegorical/symbolical, delirium/mania, fanaticism/enthusiasm, delusion/illusion, invent/discover, division/distinction, reputation/fame, which all contributed to clarifying his discussion. Nitobe is doing a similar thing in distinguishing between the terms of nationalism/chauvinism and internationalism/cosmopolitanism.

Nobody will deny that there is a formidable vagueness of meaning around words like nationalism and patriotism. It is largely this vagueness that damaged Nitobe's reputation in Japan. Nitobe was a nationalist or patriot, but it was in the sense defined and clarified by himself. However, the generations that came after his death took it wrongly. In 1935, a translation of *Bushido* was published by Koukun-seibikai — apparently an educational body with a strongly patriotic (or rather chauvinistic, in Nitobe's terminology) commitment.[4] Besides the translation of *Bushido*, the book contains pictures of the Emperor visiting various places ('gyoukou' as such an imperial progress was called), admonitory essays by people of high position, and a historical essay on "Bushido and Hojo Tokimune"[5] by Privy Councillor Viscount Kikujiro Ishii. The translator was a certain Harusato Kondo, a member of the board of that educational body. But how much he was read in the Western culture can be guessed by a sample from the opening paragraph of his translation, which, when translated back again into English, runs somewhat like this: 'It is a pleasure to me to reflect upon this subject in the language of Burke, who *composed a poem* (*kanashii ippen no shi wo tsukutte*) in which he uttered the well-known touching eulogy over the neglected bier of its European prototype.' (*Italics added.*) Burke's *Reflections on the Revolution in France* a lyric poem!

It appears that the word 'bushido' became particularly popular after Nitobe's death. In 1941 when the chauvinistic atmosphere totally engulfed the nation, a book entitled *The Essence of Bushido* edited by the Bushido Society appeared.[6] It is a collection of militaristic essays sandwiched by "Military Discipline (senjin-kun)" and "Emperor's Words to Soldiers (gunjin chokuyu)." Nitobe's *Bushido* is nowhere to be found, but in the preface a reference is made to Nitobe: 'When Japan defeated Russia in battle after battle of the Russo-Japanese War, other countries wondered what a nation Japan was. At that time our great Dr Inazo Nitobe wrote *Bushido* in English and gave the answer to their question. Indeed, the bushido has been a driving force of our nation's prosperity and we are in more need of it at this moment when we have launched into the great enterprise of building an Asian empire.' (*translated from the original Japanese.*)

In both cases, it is clear that Nitobe's name and his book's title were exploited for militaristic purposes. In other words, Nitobe's nationalism or patriotism was distorted and dragged into the camp of chauvinism or jingoism, complete opposites in Nitobe's terminology. After the war when the whole nation began to look back with disgust to the militaristic fever of the past, Nitobe's reputation suffered for the second time. His nationalism was again confused and identified with chauvinism, and criticized accordingly. The misunderstanding of Nitobe started in this way with the vague use of the word. Though the publication of *The Collected Works of Inazo Nitobe* in the latter half of the 20th century did much to dispel this misunderstanding, it still lingers, as is seen in the newspaper article by Jiro Iinuma (1991)[7] or in Yuzo Ota, *Inazo Nitobe as a Bridge Across the Pacific* (1986)[8] which casts doubts on Nitobe's pacifism and internationalism.

The same misunderstanding sometimes labelled him even as an imperialist. How can it be, when the man as spokesman for the League of Nations writes:

> The Treaty of Versailles tolled the knell of Imperialism. Some may say Imperialism is by no means dead. I grieve to say that it

still looks very alive. But though Imperialism is not yet buried, the Covenant [of the League of Nations] has dealt it a fatal blow. Henceforth an Imperialist will not be tolerated in the polite Society of Nations. Backward races will no longer be exploited as victims of Imperialism.[9]

Much care is needed when we discuss nationalism in Nitobe. In his terminology, it was a concept diametrically opposed to chauvinism or jingoism. Internationalism and nationalism go together and are one and the same thing. At least such was his ideal. To what extent he was true to his ideal in his actual career should be approached and assessed by various historical and political considerations, which will be complicated ones, to be sure. But whatever the verdict, one thing is clear. If Nitobe appears to have veered from his ideal in some spheres of his activities, the blame should be rather laid on the time which made impossible such a happy coexistence of nationalism and internationalism. In my view, Nitobe was faithful to his ideal to the last. He tried to stick to his mission as a builder of bridges and as such he fell a victim in the disruption of those bridges caused by the rampant nationalistic (or we should say chauvinistic) atmosphere in the age of the international struggles leading to the Second World War.

Notes

1 The Nitobe Memorial Library of Hokkaido University shows that Nitobe owned a copy of Karl Marx, *Capital; a critical analysis of capitalist production* (Translated from the third German edition, by Samuel Moore and Edward Aveling and ed. by Frederick Engels. New York: Humboldt Publishing Co., 1886).
2 The hero of Thomas Hughes' best-selling novel *Tom Brown's Schooldays* (1857).
3 Samuel Taylor Coleridge, *Biographia Literaria*, ed. by James Engell and W. Jackson Bate (London: Routledge & Kegan Paul, 1983), vol. 1: 82-85.
4 *Bushido in Japanese* by Dr Inazo Nitobe, trans. by Harusato Kondo, Director of Kokun-seibikai, with "Bushido and Hojo Tokimune" by Privy Councillor, Viscount Kikujiro Ishii. Keibundo-shoten, 1935.
5 Hojo Tokimune (1251-1284) is the 8th regent to Kamakura shogunate (military dictator of Japan), under whom the country fought off two Mongol invasions, the only serious foreign threats to the Japanese islands before modern times.
6 *The Essence of Bushido (Bushido no shinzui)*, ed. by Bushido Society (Bushido-gakkai), Teikoku-shoseki-kyokai, 1941.

7 Jiro Iinuma, "Was Inazo Nitobe a Liberalist?" *Mainichi Newspaper* (evening number), 26 Aug. 1981.
8 See above p. 150, note 16.
9 "What the League of Nations Has Done and Is Doing." See above p. 20.

# A Nitobe Chronology

**Morioka Period 1862∼1871 (ages 0∼9)**
    1862    Born in Morioka, Sept. 1, Inanosuke Nitobe, third son to Jujiro Nitobe, retainer to the Nambu Lord.
    1867    Father Jujiro dies.
                                        [Meiji Restoration 1868]
    1871    Grandfather Tsutou dies. Changes his personal and family names to Inazo Ota. Sent to Tokyo.

**Tokyo Period 1871∼1877 (ages 9∼15)**
    1872    Enters a private English school.
    1875    Admitted to the Tokyo School of Foreign Languages.
    1877    Withdraws from above and matriculates in Sapporo Agricultural Collge.

**Sapporo Period (I) 1877∼1883 (ages 15∼21)**
    1877    Signs his name to "Covenant of Believers in Jesus."
    1880    Mother Seki dies. First encounter with Carlyle's *Sartor Resartus*.
    1881    Graduates from Sapporo Agricultural College, and becomes an official in the Government House of Hokkaido.
    1883    Goes up to Tokyo and matriculates in Tokyo University in order to study "economics and English literature." Expresses his desire to become "a bridge across the Pacific."

**American Period 1884∼1887 (ages 22∼25)**
    1884    Withdraws from Tokyo University, Aug., and leaves for America, Sept. Matriculates in The Johns Hopkins University, Oct.
    1885    Joins the Society of Friends in Philadelphia.
    1886    Meets Mary Powell Elkinton.

**German Period 1887∼1890 (ages 25∼28)**
    1887    Studies in the University of Bonn.
    1888    Studies in the University of Berlin.
    1889    Studies in the University of Halle. Restored to the original family name Nitobe.

1890   Goes to America, Oct., on his way to Japan.

**Sapporo Period (II) 1891~1897 (ages 28~35)**
1891   Married to Mary Powell Elkinton in Philadelphia, Jan. 1. Returns to Japan as professor of Sapporo Agricultural College, his Alma Mater.
1892   Their son Thomas born, only to die after a week.
1895   Opens the Ragged School.

[Sino-Japanese War 1894-95]
1897   Retires from Sapporo Agricultural College for illness, Oct.

**Recuperation Period 1897~1900 (ages 35~38)**
1898   Goes to California to take a change of air for his health.
1899   Writes *Bushido: The Soul of Japan*.
1890   *Bushido: The Soul of Japan* published, early in Jan.

**Taiwan Government House Period 1900~1906 (ages 38~44)**
1901   Begins to work for the Taiwan Government House.
1903   Holds in addition a professorship of law in Kyoto University.

[Russo-Japanese War 1904-05]

**Ichiko School Headmaster Period 1906~1913 (ages 44~51)**
1906   Headmaster of Ichiko, a preparatory school for Tokyo Imperial University.
1909   Also works as editorial adviser to a magazine "Jitsugyo no Nihon (=Japanese Enterprise)." Holds in addition a professorship of law in Tokyo Imperial University.

**University Professor and President Period 1913~1920 (ages 51 ~57)**
1913   Retires from headmastership of Ichiko, and becomes a professor of law in Tokyo Imperial University.

[First World War 1914-18]
1918   Appointed president of a newly founded Tokyo Woman's University.

**Geneva Period 1920~1926 (ages 57~64)**
1920   Under-Secretary-General of the newly established League of Nations.
1922   Contributes to the establishment of International Committee for Intellectual Cooperation, the forerunner of the present-day UNESCO, and becomes intimate with Henri Bergson, Gilbert Murray, Madame Curie, and Albert

Einstein.
1926 Retires from the League of Nations, his successor being a Yotaro Sugimura. Becomes member of the House of Peers.

Last Years: 1927~1933 (ages 64~71)
1927 Returns to Japan, Mar. 16.

[Great Depression 1929]

1929 Becomes the chairman of the Japan branch of the Institute of Pacific Relations (IPR). Attends the conference of IPR in Kyoto.

[Manchurian Incident 1931]

1931 Attends the conference of IPR in Shanghai.

[Shanghai Incident 1932]

1932 Criticizes the Japanese military clique in a private talk, reported in the local newspaper ("Matsuyama Incident"), and forced to apologize before the veterans group.
Leaves for America, Apr. 14.

[May 15 Incident 1932]

1933 Returns to Japan, Mar. 25.

[Japanese withdrawal from League of Nations Mar. 27, 1933]

Departs for Canada, Aug. 2, to attend the conference of IPR in Banff. Dies in the Royal Jubilee Hospital in Victoria, Oct. 15.

[Feb. 26 Incident 1936]
[Nanking Massacre 1937]
[Pacific War 1941–45]